PUBLIC

PUBLIC offerings

ORGANIZED BY PAUL SCHIMMEL

COORDINATED BY CIARA ENNIS

EDITED BY HOWARD SINGERMAN

ESSAYS BY
YILMAZ DZIEWIOR
MIDORI MATSUI
LANE RELYEA
PAUL SCHIMMEL
KATY SIEGEL
HOWARD SINGERMAN
JON THOMPSON

THE MUSEUM OF CONTEMPORARY ART, LOS ANGELES

Thames & Hudson

public offerings

FIRST PUBLISHED IN THE UNITED STATES OF AMERICA IN PAPERBACK IN 2001 BY
THAMES & HUDSON INC., 500 FIFTH AVENUE, NEW YORK, NEW YORK 10110
FIRST PUBLISHED IN THE UNITED KINGDOM IN 2001 BY THAMES & HUDSON LTD,
181A HIGH HOLBORN, LONDON WC1V 7QX

LIBRARY OF CONGRESS CATALOG CARD NUMBER 00-109465

BRITISH LIBRARY CATALOGUING-IN-PUBLICATION DATA
A CATALOGUE RECORD FOR THIS BOOK IS AVAILABLE FROM THE BRITISH LIBRARY

ISBN: 0-500-28284-6
PRINTED AND BOUND IN GERMANY

GUEST EDITOR HOWARD SINGERMAN
MANAGING EDITOR SUSAN MARTIN
SENIOR EDITOR LISA MARK
EDITOR JANE HYUN
EDITORIAL ASSISTANT ELIZABETH HAMILTON

CURATORIAL PROJECT DIRECTOR CIARA ENNIS

ART DIRECTION JONATHAN BARNBROOK
DESIGNERS JONATHAN BARNBROOK
JASON BEARD
MARCUS MCCALLION
PRINTER DR. CANTZ'SCHE DRUCKEREI,
OSTFILDERN, GERMANY

THIS PUBLICATION ACCOMPANIES THE EXHIBITION "PUBLIC OFFERINGS," ORGANIZED BY PAUL SCHIMMEL AND PRESENTED AT THE MUSEUM OF CONTEMPORARY ART, LOS ANGELES, 1 APRIL—29 JULY 2001.

"PUBLIC OFFERINGS" IS MADE POSSIBLE IN PART BY THE SYDNEY IRMAS EXHIBITION ENDOWMENT, MARIA HUMMER AND ROBERT TUTTLE, AUDREY M. IRMAS, THE ANDY WARHOL FOUNDATION FOR THE VISUAL ARTS, THE JAPAN-UNITED STATES FRIENDSHIP COMMISSION, THE JAPAN FOUNDATION, THE BRITISH COUNCIL, BRENDA R. POTTER AND MICHAEL C. SANDLER, PASADENA ART ALLIANCE, AND NINAH AND MICHAEL LYNNE.

PROMOTIONAL SUPPORT HAS BEEN PROVIDED BY KLON-FM 88.1.

Director's Foreword

Monographic exhibitions and broad, thematic surveys of recent works—these are the staples of most contemporary art museums. Certainly, MOCA has distinguished itself in these fields. From the retrospective of James Turrell, which opened at MOCA in 1985, to the 1999 retrospective of Barbara Kruger, MOCA has consistently organized major exhibitions of the most significant artists of our time. Similarly, MOCA's thematic surveys, exhibitions such as "A Forest of Signs: Art in the Crisis of Representation" (1989), and "Helter Skelter: L.A. Art in the 1990s" (1992), have consistently defined significant issues and moments in recent art.

Perhaps more distinctive to MOCA, however, have been a number of large historical surveys. This series of projects began with "Automobile and Culture" (1984), and has included such major exhibitions as "Reconsidering the Object of Art: 1965–1975" (1995); "Out of Actions: Between Performance and the Object, 1949-1979" (1998); and "At the End of the Century: One Hundred Years of Architecture" (2000). No contemporary art museum has consistently approached the history of art with such ambition.

"Public Offerings" offers yet another model for MOCA, and for contemporary art museums. This exhibition puts the tools of historical investigation and analysis at the service of a contemporary survey. The international group of artists assembled in this exhibition include many of the leading figures to emerge over the past decade. In short order they have become among the best-known artists of our time and, collectively, their work addresses many of today's most pertinent artistic issues. "Public Offerings" is concerned fundamentally with the question of origins. The exhibition seeks to trace the roots of artistic identity in the 90s, describing the mechanisms and structures by which identities were established, and searching out the defining works by which a generation of artists discovered their personal and public identities.

"Public Offerings" was conceived and developed by MOCA Chief Curator Paul Schimmel. The exhibition at once typifies his consistent engagement with the work of emerging artists, as well as his commitment to historical scholarship. Indeed, he admits to a longstanding concern for the early moments of artistic careers and movements, a fascination evidenced by such exhibitions as "Hand-Painted Pop: American Art in Transition, 1955-62" (1992). That concern receives its fullest elaboration to date in "Public Offerings."

An exhibition of this magnitude is made possible by the generosity of a number of individuals and institutions. I would like to acknowledge the generosity of The Sydney Irmas Exhibition Endowment, Maria Hummer and Robert Tuttle, Audrey M. Irmas, The Andy Warhol Foundation for the Visual Arts, The Japan-United States Friendship Commission, The Japan Foundation, the British Council, Brenda R. Potter and Michael C. Sandler, Pasadena Art Alliance, and Ninah and Michael Lynne. I also thank the numerous lenders who have generously parted with important works from their collections to support this groundbreaking exhibition.

Finally, the twenty-four artists whose works are included here participated actively in the conception and realization of this exhibition. Their dialogues with Paul Schimmel provided the foundation for this project, and their support has been crucial. "Public Offerings" is about those artists and their art, and to them we owe our deepest thanks.

Jeremy Strick
Director
The Museum of Contemporary Art
Los Angeles

Acknowledgements

The artists in "Public Offerings" have entrusted MOCA with something irreplaceable: their early work. Moreover, they have allowed me to be the first to historically contextualize it. For each of these artists, who incidentally can still be described as young, there is only one "breakthrough" body of work, and only one first opportunity to have that work viewed through the lens of history.

I have asked these visionary and pioneering artists to stretch their relationships to their work, stepping back to allow us this first stab at resituating it within the broader social, intellectual, and artistic climate in which it was created. I am deeply grateful for their faith in allowing, and in some cases encouraging, the organization of an exhibition that brings a disparate group of artists from Europe, the United States, and Asia into a context none of them could have imagined at the time they were making these works.

This hybrid contemporary-historical exhibition provides a level playing field that brings together the formative works of a generation of artists emerging in the late 80s and early 90s that was only vaguely aware of what was going on simultaneously in other parts of the artworld. For these artists, who have all shown extensively in both solo and group exhibitions, "Public Offerings" represents a unique look at their work as part of the art history of a decade that has only just passed. I am grateful for and appreciate the grave responsibility of historicizing their artistic development before they have even reached mid-career.

MOCA's history of working successfully with new artists and new works, in conjunction with my own commitment to wrestling with the history of contemporary art, has informed the artists' decisions to allow—and in a few cases acquiesce to—their involvement in "Public Offerings." Like the work itself, their participation demonstrates a certain act of faith—one for which I am deeply appreciative.

MOCA is an exceptional institution allowing and encouraging artists and curators to create both new works and new models for curatorship. For this atmosphere, and the institution's willingness to take risks despite the possibility of failure, I am grateful to MOCA's former Director Richard Koshalek, under whose guidance this exhibition was first initiated.

The lion's share of the show's organization has been accomplished during the two years that Jeremy Strick has been director of MOCA and I am deeply appreciative of the enormous amount of support and encouragement he has offered to this ambitious project. From the moment that Jeremy joined the staff, he made everyone including myself aware of his commitment to "Public Offerings" as an essential part of MOCA's programming matrix.

Other members of the administrative staff that have been central in the organization of the exhibition include Kathleen Bartels, outgoing Assistant Director, for the administrative and communications support she has brought to the exhibition; Director of Development Paul Johnson who, in a short period of time, has marshaled support for the exhibition and has worked tirelessly in developing support; and Chief Financial Officer Jack Wiant, who has been, as always, a reasoned, thoughtful, and supportive partner in developing an appropriate and accurate financial plan. In this effort, both he and I were ably and unrelentingly assisted by Exhibitions Coordinator Stacia Payne, who has been extraordinarily diligent in coordinating the complex financial and administrative aspects of this exhibition.

The exhibitions department has been instrumental in both the conceptualization and execution of the installation and I am deeply grateful to Brian Gray, Exhibitions Production Manager; Jang Park, Chief Exhibition Technician; and Zazu Faure, Exhibitions Production Coordinator, for their professionalism and commitment to excellence. Media Arts Technical Manager David Bradshaw has also been essential in organizing technical support for new media in the exhibition. Each member of the exhibitions department brings a commitment to fulfilling the artists' visions to best present their work, for which I am grateful.

Chief Registrar Robert Hollister and his staff have worked diligently in the handling of loans, insurance, packing, shipping, and crating of the sometimes demanding and complex works included in the exhibition.

I am grateful to Kim Kanatani, outgoing Director of Education, and Caroline Blackburn, Adult Programs Coordinator, for facilitating a greater understanding and appreciation of the ideas and works of art included in this exhibition. Through art talks, lectures, and special projects, the Education Department brings a significant contribution to the public's appreciation of MOCA's programs. As well, Katherine Lee, Media Relations Coordinator, has worked tirelessly and almost single-handedly in informing the public and press in a thoughtful manner about our programs.

From the exhibition's inception, the accompanying publication was always seen as an opportunity to both reflect upon and illustrate the works in the exhibition. But the catalogue and its essayists were, in some ways, given the more significant responsibility of examining the social, cultural, and educational climate in which these works were made to describe how these artists developed—and to do so on an international level.

Howard Singerman, who has a long history with The Museum of Contemporary Art, was invited to collaborate early on given his long-standing commitment to analyzing the impact of art schools on twentieth-century art. He was called upon not just to contribute an essay but more importantly to participate in the basic conception of the exhibition by developing a publication that could stand alone as a document that grappled with the complex relationship between art schools and the development of artists in the 90s. I am deeply grateful to him for his extraordinary commitment and involvement in the catalogue, as well as his superb scholarly contribution. It is a testament to his invaluable role as editor of "Public Offerings" that he managed to elicit the same dedication and rigor from the essayists.

I want to acknowledge each of the essayists for their contributions to the catalogue—Yilmaz Dziewior for Berlin, Midori Matsui for Tokyo, Lane Relyea for Los Angeles, Katy Siegel for New York, and Jon Thompson for London.

In addition to the ground-breaking studies these art historians, artists, critics, and professors have developed for "Public Offerings," the catalogue has been significantly enriched by a series of individually commissioned texts on each of the artists and the works included in the exhibition. Indeed, these entries provide a specific and detailed view of the works themselves as a direct counterpart to the more generalized and theoretical contributions of the essays. In addition to entries written by the aforementioned essayists, I am grateful for those from Leslie Dick, Ciara Ennis, Miwon Kwon, Thomas Lawson, Matthew Ritchie, and MOCA curators Russell Ferguson and Ann Goldstein.

I am especially grateful to Ann Goldstein, not only for her contribution to the catalogue, but for introducing me to the work of Diana Thater and Jorge Pardo, who were among the artists in her "Pure Beauty" exhibition, seen here at MOCA in 1994.

I would like to thank Susan Martin, who brought exceptional skill and energy to the editing and compilation of the catalogue. As an independent consultant, she took the reins from Stephanie Emerson, former Senior Editor at MOCA, who contributed greatly to the early development of the catalogue. Thanks also go out to John Alan Farmer for his sagacious editorial consultation. I am grateful as well for the participation of Thames and Hudson as our co-publisher.

The catalogue could never have come to its full realization without the dedication of Jane Hyun, Editor; Elizabeth Hamilton, Editorial Assistant; and Lisa Mark, MOCA's new Senior Editor who, having only recently joined the staff, made a significant contribution in the final weeks of putting this catalogue to bed. And finally, I would like to thank our visionary designer Jonathan Barnbrook for his exceptional work on the catalogue's layout and conception. He has imparted every aspect of the design with his adventurous creativity, devising a physical structure that reflects the two complementary aspects of the exhibition—the critical/theoretical side and the artist/producer side—while at the same time demonstrating tremendous grace under pressure.

I have benefited greatly from the assistance of Diane Aldrich during the beginning stages of this exhibition, and Natalie Ochoa, Assistant to the Chief Curator, who has handled myriad details surrounding the organization of "Public Offerings."

One person at MOCA has made a particularly significant contribution to the realization of this exhibition: Ciara Ennis, Project Coordinator and Exhibition Director for "Public Offerings." Indeed, this exhibition would have been inconceivable without the enthusiastic dedication that began when she, having heard about the exhibition while still a student at the Royal College of Art in London, applied for an internship with us. Over the last three years, she has completely and totally immersed herself in the organization of "Public Offerings," including working with all of the artists, essayists, and staff members in the realization of this complex and large-scale survey.

Many colleagues have provided invaluable help in the research and development of this exhibition. For this I would like to thank Marina Abramovic; Taro Amano; Eric Black; Kate Blake; Sacha Craddock; Jan Debbaut; Paul Cornwall-Jones; Chris Dercon; Gil Friesen, for his unwavering and enthusiastic support of "Public Offerings;" Alexander Godschalk; Jaap Guldemond; Yuko Hasegawa, Director, Contemporary Art Museum, Kanazawa; Frank Hettig; Mathilde Heyns; Ute Klissenbauer; Stephan Koehler; Kasper König; Tom Lawson; staff of The Mondrian Institute, Amsterdam, especially Annet Gelink, Mariska van den Berg, and Melle Daamen; Lars Nittve; Barbara Noell; Karel Schampers; Stephan Schmidt-Wulffen; Karsten Schubert; Nicholas Serota; Theo Tegelaers; Christopher Tannert; Dominic van den Boogerd; Tanywa Wallroth; and Franz Erhard Walther. Each of these people generously gave their time, knowledge, and commitment to assist me in the conceptualization and realization of "Public Offerings."

Certain institutions have been extraordinarily generous in making significant loans from their collections. I would like to thank Maxwell Anderson at the Whitney Museum of American Art; Howard Fox from the Los Angeles County Museum of Art; Hudson at Feature, Inc.; Thomas Krens at the Guggenheim Museum; Patrick McCaughay from the Yale Center for British Art; Eileen and Peter Norton of the Norton Family Foundation; Eriko Osaka, Chief Curator, Contemporary Art Center, Art Tower Mito; Hidenori Ota from Ota Fine Arts; Andrea Rose, Director of Visual Arts, The British Council, for her very generous support of this project from the very early stages; David Ross, Director, San Francisco Museum of Modern Art; Charles Saatchi, Jenny Blyth, and Nigel Hurst from The Saatchi Collection, London; and Kirk Varnedoe at The Museum of Modern Art, New York.

The following galleries were instrumental in facilitating and making individual loans: Brian Butler from 1301 PE, who has been an enormous help during the entire exhibition process; Gabriel Catone and Thea Westreich at Art Advisory Services, New York; Kirsten Biller, Tim Blum, and Jeff Poe at Blum & Poe; Kirsty Bell and Gavin Brown from Gavin Brown's enterprise; Luis Campaña from Gallery Campaña; Sadie Coles HQ; Bruno Brunnet and Nicole Hackert from Contemporary Fine Arts; Jeffrey Deitch of Deitch Projects; Robin Vousden and Susanna Greeves from Anthony d'Offay; Barbara Gladstone and Jessica Frost at Barbara Gladstone Gallery; Marian Goodman; Ursula Hauser, and Manuela and Iwan Wirth at Hauser und Wirth; my dear friend Max Hetzler; Anton Kern Gallery; Martin Klosterfelde and Nikola Dietrich at Klosterfelde; Lisson Gallery; Roland Augustine, Lawrence Luhring, and Katy Schubert at Luhring Augustine; Matthew Marks and Jeffrey Peabody at Matthew Marks; Victoria Miro, Glenn Scott Wright, and Andrew Silewicz at Victoria Miro; Helly Nahmad; Alexander Schröder and Thilo Wermke from NEU Gallery; Tim Neuger and Burkhard Riemschneider at neugerriemschneider; Maureen Sarro at Friedrich Petzel; Max Protetch; Shaun Caley at Regen Projects; Anthony Reynolds; Jay Jopling at White Cube; and David Zwirner.

I would also like to thank the following artists and private collectors for loans to the exhibition. Many of these works are fragile, highly valued, and of great personal importance to these artists and collectors and I am deeply grateful for their generosity in making these works—many of which have not been seen since they were first acquired—available to a larger public. These people are Renalto Alpegiani, Marcus Benziger, Ruth and Jake Bloom, Eileen Cohen, Clarissa Dalrymple, Bernd Lohaus and Any de Decker, Thomas Demand, Harald Falkenberg, Gil Friesen, Tony Ganz, Michael Joaquin Grey, Claudio Guenzani, Susan and Michael Hort, Marjorie Jacobson, Rachel and Jean-Pierre Lehmann, Clayton Press and Gregory Linn, Kent and Vickie Logan, Michael Lynne, Daniel Melnick, Tracy and Gary Mezzatesta, Chris Ofili, Michael Ovitz, Laura Owens, Lari Pittman, Jason Rhoades, Andrew Silewicz, Norman and Norah Stone, Bunny and Jay Wasserman, Jon Weaver, Thea Westreich, Rachel Whiteread, Lorrin and Deane Wong, and Cerith Wyn-Evans.

I would also like to add my personal thanks to those of Jeremy Strick in order to convey my gratitude to the funders who have provided significant resources for this exhibition: The Sydney Irmas Exhibition Endowment, Maria Hummer and Robert Tuttle, Audrey M. Irmas, The Andy Warhol Foundation for the Visual Arts, The Japan-United States Friendship Commission:, The Japan Foundation, the British Council, Brenda R. Potter and Michael C. Sandler, Pasadena Art Alliance, and Ninah and Michael Lynne. Their gifts have made "Public Offerings" a reality.

In organizing the exhibition I have benefited enormously from the enthusiastic support offered by members of the Board of Trustees who saw its importance to MOCA. Certain individuals deserve particular thanks, including Susan Bay-Nimoy, Ruth Bloom, Clifford J. Einstein, Gil Friesen, Bea Gersh, Lenny Greenberg, Dallas Price, Bob Tuttle, and Dean Valentine.

However, one Trustee in particular, Chair of the Board Audrey Irmas, has once again played a pivotal role with her encouragement and enthusiastic philanthropic support. This has been the case for several exhibitions I have had the opportunity to organize for The Museum of Contemporary Art and it is with deepest gratitude that I dedicate this to Audrey—for this is as much her "Public Offerings" as it is mine.

Paul Schimmel
Chief Curator
The Museum of Contemporary Art
Los Angeles

Public Offerings

The formative work of any artist holds a place of privilege. Although this work may not have the authority, grandeur, or confidence of an artist's later mature period, it embodies in its simplicity a sense of yearning, questioning, and searching that can only be defined as inspired. It points to that moment when an artist begins to eliminate some of the distractions of what he or she has learned and to cultivate others on the way to discovering who he or she will become. For young artists, art school is both a public rena where they can engage in a dialogue about their work with teachers, visiting artists, and other students, and a private one in which they are insulated from the pressures of public exhibition. "Public Offerings" features breakthrough works produced while the artists were still in school or not long after they graduated. In each case, these works proved to have an extraordinary impact on the subsequent creative development of these artists as well as on their critical and commercial reception.

BY PAUL SCHIMMEL

¶ The work of art as it marks a transformation has been one of the central themes of my curatorial endeavors. As their titles suggest, the exhibitions "The Interpretive Link: Abstract Surrealism into Abstract Expressionism, Works on Paper, 1938–1948" (1987) and "Hand-Painted Pop: American Art in Transition, 1955–62," curated with Donna De Salvo (1992), focused on works of art that seemed to me to be situated in a space between historical movements whose boundaries had been taken for granted—between Surrealism and Abstract Expressionism in the former, and Abstract Expressionism and Pop Art in the latter. "Public Offerings" is not a historical reconsideration, and cannot claim the distance of those earlier exhibitions, but it too addresses the work between two places, the work of art in transit. Whereas "The Interpretive Link" and "Hand-Painted Pop" looked at works that fit between and link two great eras (as I put it in "Hand-Painted Pop"), "Public Offerings" focuses on the oeuvres of twenty-five artists of the generation that emerged during the late 80s and early 90s. This group of artists—which has come to be regarded as among the most significant of its generation—emerged from the space between two other borders we take for granted today: the art school and the artworld. "Public Offerings" examines the breakthrough works that these artists produced at this crucial stage in their development.

¶ By any standard, the late 80s was a heady period for the contemporary artworld. The generation of artists who emerged during the decade was younger and more visible than any other generation in recent history. New York's status as the center of the artworld since the 40s had eroded with the emergence of other internationally recognized art scenes such as those in Cologne and, later in the decade, Berlin, London, Los Angeles, and Tokyo, among others. And, although no one anticipated it at the time, the art market, which had continued in its expansion since the late 70s, was on the verge of slowing down, meaning that young artists starting their careers would have to be more resourceful than ever.

¶ By the mid-80s young artists attracted by the growth of opportunities for personal and professional success in the artworld as recorded in the pages of art magazines and the popular press had begun to pour into art schools in unprecedented numbers. This phenomenon not only occurred in internationally recognized institutions—such as the Staatliche Kunstakademie in Dusseldorf; Yale University in New Haven, Connecticut; and California Institute of the Arts (CalArts) in Valencia, California—but in an ever-widening orbit of art schools in cities around the world, including art divisions within colleges and universities. As the demand for coveted places within these institutions increased, art schools, which had once seemed peripheral, became increasingly central to nurturing the emergent new generation.

¶ During the 80s, the institutional character of the schools themselves was changing. In the United States, England, and elsewhere, the neo-conservative political and economic policies that might be abbreviated as "Reaganism" or "Thatcherism" played a significant role in this process. As governmental support for educational institutions, including art schools, decreased, these institutions became more reliant on private funding and earned income. And as dramatic as the impact was upon educational institutions in the United States, where there had been a long history of private and public partnership, an even more dramatic and deeper impact was felt in Europe and Asia, where there had not been such an extensive history. Art schools and departments were forced to rethink hiring policy for both part-time and tenured faculty, the provision of scholarships, and even the financial implications of their basic educational mandates. Many schools out of necessity evolved into institutions that, in some respects, began to more closely resemble commercial enterprises. As their budgets were slashed, even university departments began, like the free-standing art schools, to rely more heavily on artists to teach on a part-time basis rather than to hire teachers for tenure-track positions. When recession hit the artworld in 1989, a number of artists whose careers had taken off during the 80s sought the shelter and relative economic security of academe.

¶ As scholarship and student loan opportunities for students dried up, going to school perpetually funded by government support was no longer a viable option and the schools themselves, increasingly streamlined, were anxious to push students through. For these reasons, and because of the opportunities the magazines and markets seemed to promise (at least before the downturn), young artists tended to complete their educations more quickly than those of previous generations and also tended to be more motivated to create opportunities for themselves within the commercial arena. If, in the past, schools had functioned as laboratories in which artists could slowly develop their work in a prolonged period of gestation, the new fast-track approach sped up the introduction of young artists to the public art-world of museums, galleries, and auction houses and interaction with collectors, curators, and critics.

¶ These institutional shifts also had an impact on how young artists perceived themselves as artists. The radical, nonconformist, anticommercial ideals that had been integral to many progressive artists of the late 60s and 70s began to give way to a new paradigm that had emerged in the 80s. This paradigm increasingly accepted commercial success as a necessity not to be shirked rather than as a goal that would undermine the purity of conviction inspirational to the work itself. But even though the new generation had learned from the overheated artworld of the 80s the ins and outs of how to forge a successful career, their aesthetic was nevertheless more rooted in the art of a less commercially oriented era: the late 60s and 70s. In this respect, the new generation was influenced less by its teachers than by its teachers' teachers, many of whom would remain influential throughout the 80s and 90s—John Baldessari at CalArts and later at Art Center College of Design and the University of California at Los Angeles, Mel Bochner at Yale, Jon Thompson and Michael Craig-Martin at Goldsmiths, and others. The generation of students represented in "Public Offerings" acknowledged the impact of Minimalism, Conceptualism, and process-oriented and performance-based work as central, and recognized as particularly important predecessors artists such as Eva Hesse, Donald Judd, Bruce Nauman, Robert Ryman, Richard Serra, Robert Smithson, and Mierle Laderman Ukeles, as well as artists associated with such movements as Pattern and Decoration. The language, structure, and form these and other artists of the late 60s and early 70s offered became the foundation on which the new generation laid its own concerns. The new generation typically injected a highly personal and often social content, synthesizing the private gestures of its 60s and 70s predecessors and the public gestures of those from the 80s.

¶ The artists included in "Public Offerings" are distinguished in part by their youth. Born during the 60s, most were in their early to mid-twenties when they produced the works included in the exhibition—works that have come to be considered among the most progressive and significant of the period. Perhaps their youthfulness can be seen as part of a broader cultural pattern. Across the twentieth century, in almost all fields of creative endeavor, younger and younger generations of professionally educated individuals have been responsible for many of the most radical advancements of human knowledge. Not just in the realm of culture, but in fields like nuclear physics, molecular biology, advanced mathematics, and technology (as the emergence of dot-com culture exemplifies), an increasingly more sophisticated and confident youth culture reigns. And, of course, youth culture as a demographic is also the target audience of media and advertising, as well as a favorite subject. Thus, it is not surprising that within the visual arts, at least since the post-World War II era, each generation of artists has found its voice in the work of younger artists. While many of the Abstract Expressionists, for instance, were well into their forties before they found their own visual language, many of the Pop artists wrestling with the dominance of the New York School began to receive international recognition in their thirties. This trend continued throughout the 70s and 80s. The examples of Frank Stella and Richard Serra—both of whom received at a young age the kind of acclaim that at the time seemed to be reserved only for old masters—have become less the exception and more the norm.

¶ In addition to its youth, the new generation is also distinguished by its international character. Never before has a generation of artists moved more seamlessly from school to artist-run gallery to the traveling circuit of international residencies, teaching appointments, biennials, and other goverment-sponsored exhibitions. The fact that artists increasingly produced work for these specific contexts meant that studio practice, which had formerly been centered in the artist's city of residence rather than in the world at large, became internationalized. This shift was made possible by the expansion of air travel, the invention of new media technologies that facilitated the rapid transmission and dissemination of information globally, as well as the emergence of new regional centers. New artistic communities in numerous cities came to international prominence, as exhibitions exploring the 90s art scenes in Los Angeles, the Young British Artist phenomenon, Tokyo Pop, and the new generation of German artists have revealed. The communities in London and Los Angeles are particularly relevant to "Public Offerings" in that they were substantially shaped by the presence of exceptional art schools. And however local they might be as scenes, they are also, simultaneously, very fast bridges to the international. (In this regard, it is worth noting that although important artists were emerging from other centers in Africa, Asia, and Latin America, art schools in these countries generally have not assumed the same functions as in cities like London and Los Angeles; indeed, many internationally recognized artists from these countries completed their schooling and forged their careers not in their places of origin, but in the West.)

¶ Another factor that distinguishes many of the artists of the new generation is their relationship to the art market. During the late 80s, the inflation of an art market fueled by unprecedented levels of speculation ended even more dramatically than it started. The new generation was unleashed into a commercial void that extended well into the mid-90s. Yet, the contraction of the art market in a sense liberated these artists by giving them the freedom of believing that they had nothing to lose, which in turn opened up spaces of potentiality. Out of necessity, they cultivated a self-reliant, entrepreneurial spirit that helped them create an infrastructure that would support their ambitions. With the collapse of a number of younger galleries founded during the 80s, many of which had supported emerging artists, these artists developed new outlets for their work—the commercial equivalent of the alternative spaces of the 70s. They exhibited in houses, apartments, garages, industrial sites, and other spaces self-managed or managed by gallerists of their own generation, often with modest resources. What from our current view in the booming late 90s appears to be a commercially sophisticated generation of artists marketing themselves with uncanny success was in fact the result of economic necessity.

¶ Ultimately, "Public Offerings" is a historical exhibition about the making of the artist in the 90s. It is a process in which museums, galleries, auction houses, magazines and journals, and art schools all play a part; in which aesthetic concerns intermingle with economic realities and desires; and in which the personal melds with the social and the historical. The exhibition examines this process through the lens of the art school which, in the context of the 90s, became in many respects the crucible in which these factors fused together to create the contemporary artist. All of the artists included in the exhibition were indelibly shaped by their experiences in art schools (albeit sometimes only in reaction), institutions that functioned as conduits between the domains of private and public. In their simplicity, clarity, directness, and fragility, the breakthrough works by these artists present a dramatic counterpoint to the more glamorized, theatrical, and sensational works that we have come to associate with 90s art. As works that take private endeavors into the public arena they are, in fact, public offerings.

Janine Antoni is renowned for her aggressively physical sculptural process. Using her body in conjunction with a variety of banal materials—such as lard, chocolate, soap, and hair dye—Antoni performs actions that evoke femininity and domesticity. The art-historical references evident in her work further serve to contextualize her feminist practice within a larger field of artistic production. Nowhere is this more evident than in Gnaw *(1992), an early work that became a blueprint for much of her later practice.*

¶ Gnaw *comprises two 600-pound cubes—one of chocolate, the other of lard—and a three-paneled, mirrored cosmetic display case. Using her mouth as a tool, Antoni nibbled the corners of both cubes, leaving visible teeth marks on the chocolate and facial impressions on the softer lard. The chocolate fragments, blended with spit, were recycled into immaculate heart-shaped candy trays, while the lard residue was combined with wax and bright red pigment to create 130 tubes of lipstick.*

The four distinct elements that make up Gnaw *can be read as relics of a private ritual that trace the artist's intimate engagement with all aspects of the work. Her actions evoke associations with infantile aggression and repressed libidinal desire, while the determined erosion of each cube can be seen as a reaction to the pristine production values and male-dominated practice of Minimalism.*

¶ The radically transformed by-products of the chocolate and lard cubes highlight their intended significance.

The relationship between the heart-shaped trays and lipstick, aside from containing vast amounts of fat, points to the manipulation of women's desires by these ubiquitous signifiers (made more apparent by the association of chocolate with its psychoactive ingredient, phenylethylamine). The chewing and spitting out of the nauseating lard underscores these feminist concerns by simultaneously alluding to the binging/purging behavior associated with bulimia as well as the anxiety of conforming to narrow standards of female beauty. In its original configuration at Sandra Gering Gallery, New York, this subtext became more evident as the cube of lard imploded and hemorrhaged on its marble plinth, lending an undeniably abject quality to the work.

JANINE ANTONI

¶ The emphasis on performance and use of the artist's own body as both material and subject is clearly inspired by feminist art practices that emerged during the 60s and 70s, but not exclusively so.

The physical discomfort Antoni experienced while chewing the cubes—ulcers, blisters, and nausea—is equally informed by the performance/endurance work of Chris Burden and Paul McCarthy, both of whom emphasized process over product and tested the limits of endurance to the point of mental and physical exhaustion. Antoni's masochistic tendencies have much in common with her contemporary, Matthew Barney. Both artists privilege process as epicenter and indulge in psycho-sexual rituals to question the expectations and stereotypical nature of prescribed gender roles.

While Gnaw reflects the active exploration of identity politics in the art and culture of the early 90s, Antoni's work also embodies multiple art-historical references that encourage a re-reading of these earlier movements and their impact on current artistic practice.

Ultimately, Gnaw remains open-ended, demanding that viewers re-imagine the process by which it was made and, in so doing, come to their own unique understanding of the work.

Ciara Ennis

Gnaw, *1992*

 Gnaw, ***1992***

92
LIPSLICK
LIPSLICK

Matthew Barney's first show exploded the body, providing the viewer (or voyeur) multiple points of entry.

The work presents a mise-en-scène of the "anal sadistic" position, a visual demonstration of a psychological state. Meaning swings, suspended, as the athletic apparatus of that specifically American sport, football, becomes a figuration of immaterial and inaccessible psychic functions. Yet the intensity of Barney's body work reverses this operation, until the psycho-dynamic structures invoked in the work function as keys to the body itself. Art objects are generally assumed to convey or at least contain ideas; here, Barney manipulates theory to produce a body, a corporeality, undoing the usual order. In this work, the object is no longer subordinated to its job of revealing an idea.

¶ Jacques Lacan's "Mirror Stage" illuminates the relation of viewer to the body imaged in the mirror, an idealized body that appears to have attained a mastery the viewer lacks. In the discrepancy between the (bodily) experience of the infant ("sunk," as Lacan says, "in his motor incapacity and nursling dependence"[1]) and the reflected body image (a figure which only appears outlined, competent, complete) lies the primordial instigation of subjectivity: Lacan suggests we exist in the incommensurable space of fantasy and identification elaborated (for example) between the television-sports viewer and the television-sports star, between a childish Matthew Barney and his hero Jim Otto, legendary center for the Oakland Raiders.

American football is the quintessential television sport, subject to the exigencies of television advertisement, and presented with an immediacy and intimacy that perpetrates and invites bodily and psychic identification with the players. (Lacan's essay is titled "Le stade du miroir," the French word "stade" meaning stadium as well as stage.)

MATTHEW BARNEY

¶ Matthew Barney takes psychoanalytic theory and operates it like an art-producing machine, analogous to muscle-producing machinery—the bench, the curl bar—encountered in the gym.

Resistance is a key concept—in psychoanalysis, and in football—where one runs up against blocks and occasionally makes a temporary, always illusory, breakthrough. The "Mirror Stage" examines a moment when the infant, before language, has the mental capacity to (mis-)recognize itself in the mirror, yet lacks the gross motor skill to hold itself upright. It is held to the mirror by its mother, or stuck in an apparatus of support: a sling, a harness, a "trotte-bébé." Barney makes his way across the space of the gallery, naked, harnessed, inverted, dangling, displaying the rock-climbing equipment (hooks, ice-screws) that hangs from his body like jewelery, enabling his ordeal. The architecture of the gallery itself becomes an exploded maternal body, a ceiling from which the muscular, yet infantilized body hangs suspended.

¶ Jim Otto's surname is itself a palindrome, or mirror image; the double zero on his football jersey opens up a field of speculation. If sexual difference can be reduced to the zero-one binary, if the binary is fundamental to language, does Otto's insignia represent an embryonic state, before gender is determined, before sex can be assigned? In the hybrid interpenetration of hi-tech materials, psychoanalytic maps, and biological formations, Barney's work conflates the tropes and structures of art and sport, inviting us to go back, before difference, before language, to that place where the body was all our being, our orientation, our architecture.

Through a doubled figure (00), a double movement articulates the zone of the mirror, a zone of infantile desire and thwarted mastery. Barney presents both the abject infant and the armored hero, the spectator and the actor, in a performance of subjectivity that puts every hierarchy at risk: gender, meaning, and being.

Note

1. Lacan, "The mirror stage as formative of the function of the I as revealed in psychoanalytic experience" (1949), in Écrits: A Selection (New York: W.W. Norton & Co., 1977), 1-7.

Leslie Dick

REPRESSIA, *1991. Detail and installation at Stuart Regen Gallery, Los Angeles, 1991*

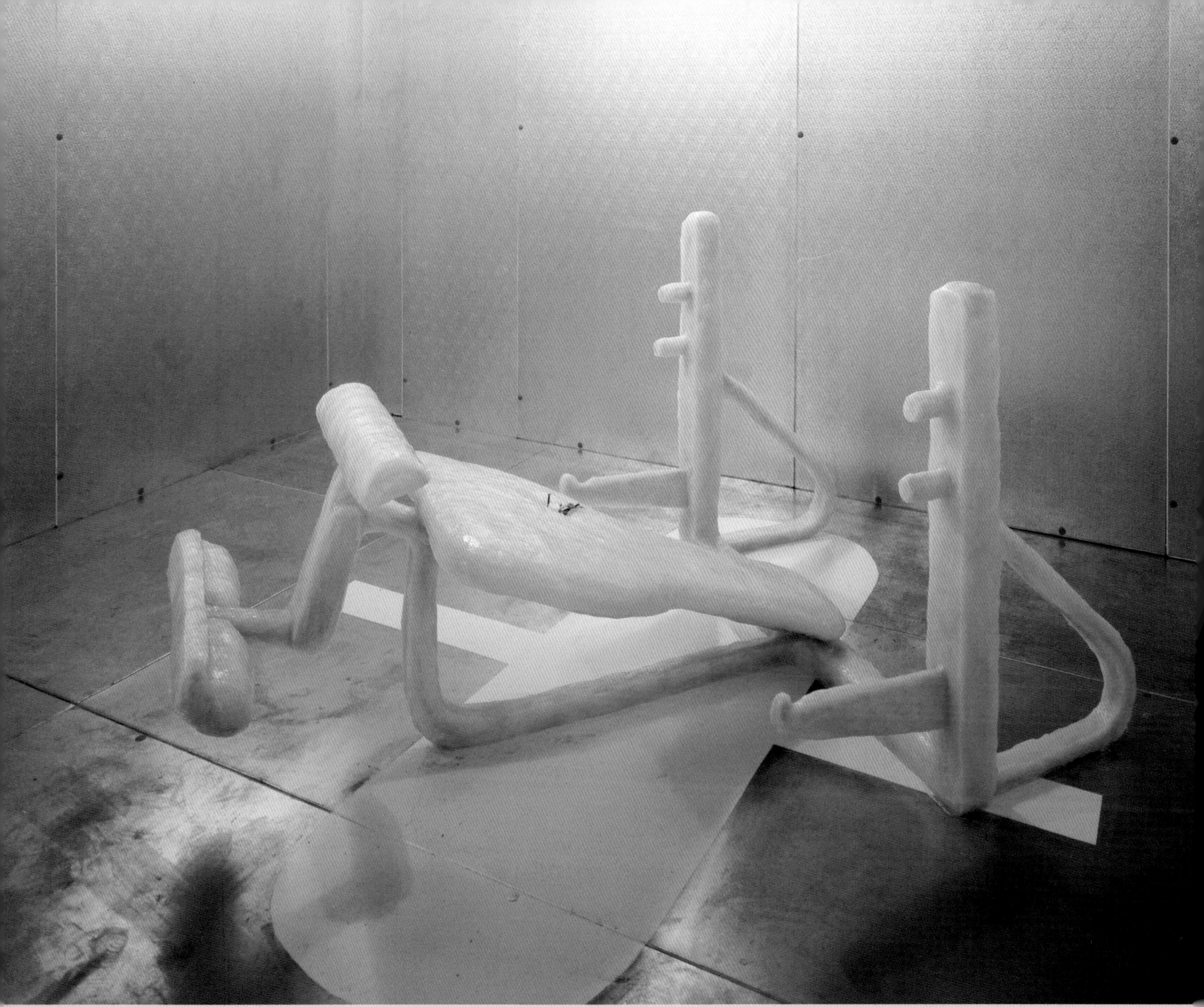

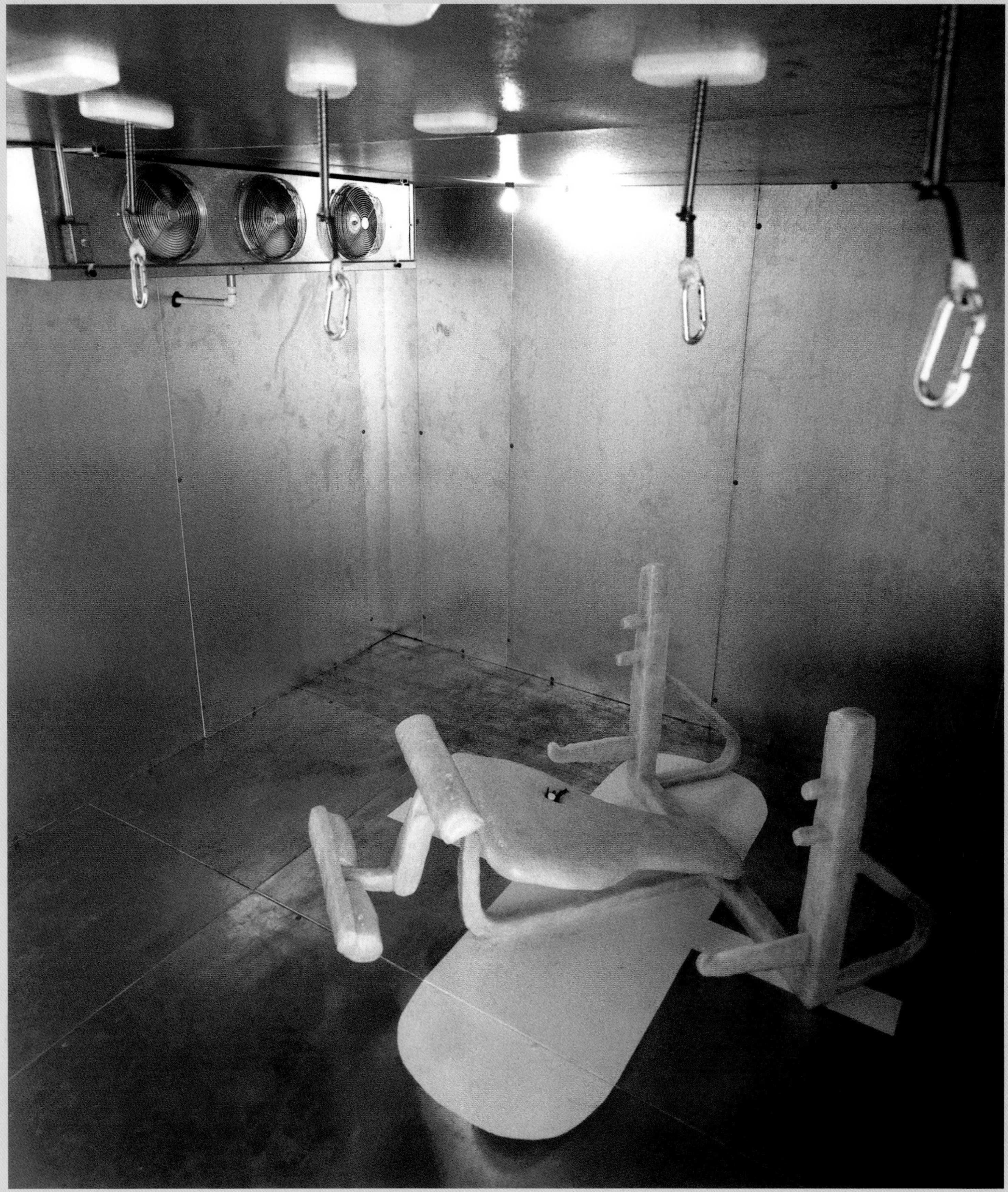

Transexualis, 1991. Detail and installation at Stuart Regen Gallery, Los Angeles, 1991

Stills from the videoaction **DELAY OF GAME**, *1991*

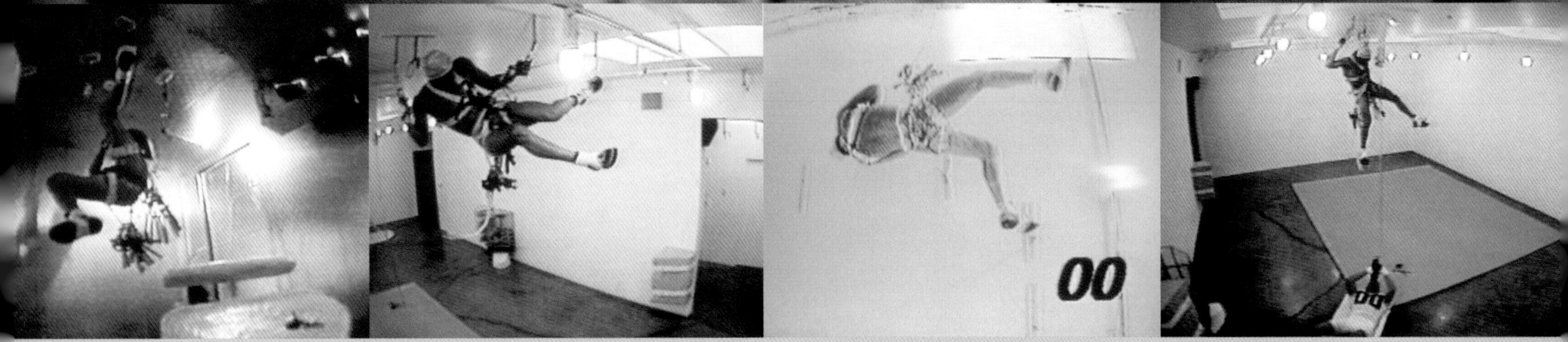

Stills from the videoaction MILE HIGH Threshold: FLIGHT with the ANAL SADISTIC WARRIOR, *1991*

Thomas Demand's exquisitely produced and compelling photographic tableaux seduce the viewer despite their apparently banal subject matter, including unexceptional interiors and architectural façades.

Although devoid of people, the images seem to resonate with an intense presence, suggesting a sudden or violent departure. At the same time, there is an undeniably clinical and sanitized aesthetic to these photographs that belies any possibility of human intervention. This incongruity subtly erodes confidence in the validity of the image, provoking a thorough scrutiny of each and every detail.

Upon closer inspection, Demand's color photographs of "real places" are found to be fakes. They instead depict immaculately produced, three-dimensional cardboard and paper models made after photographs of significant cultural and political events culled from newspapers and other mass-media outlets.

¶ Although Demand exhibits photographs, his primary concern is the sculptural process. His labor-intensive practice entails the fabrication of full-scale environments. The model's progress is continually checked through the camera's lens, which is set up in a permanent position during construction. Strangely troubling, these images of mundane settings and their prosaic titles provoke a sense of unease and doubt—a strategy deliberately employed by Demand to delay recognition of the original referent's narrative. Once discovered, there is no going back. The subtext of the photograph, which in turn is a rendition of an historical event, becomes inseparable from the image. In the case of Flur (Corridor) *(1995), this feeling is justified. On first glance, the depiction of a fluorescent-lighted hallway with unremarkable yellow doors is deceptively bland, but perceptions undergo a radical shift when one* ***realizes that the corridor leads to the apartment of serial killer Jeffrey Dahmer.***

THOMAS DEMAND

¶ *Implied psychological or physical violence permeates many of Demand's works and is often masked behind a kind of fastidious order. This can be seen in* Archiv (Archive) *(1995), in which shallow square boxes of equal size and color are seen arranged in a grid-like structure on shelves. The diagonal of a ladder ruptures the uniformity of the frame and signals a disturbance.*

The subtle impression of irregularity triggers the understanding that something is amiss: none of the boxes are labeled and the contents of one have been removed. Puzzlement turns to dismay when the viewer realizes that the image pictured is a reconstruction of the archives of Leni Riefenstahl, whose film Triumph of the Will *(1934) became one of history's greatest propaganda victories.*

¶ Sprungturm (Diving Platform) *(1994), another work reflecting upon Germany's malevolent past, is both iconic and monumental in stature. The isolated structure of the diving board recalls the spectacle and display of the 1936 Munich Olympics, played out by classically proportioned Aryan youths to embody the omnipotence of the Third Reich. Power and the desire for world domination of a very different kind is the subtext of* Ecke (Corner) *(1996), which features a typical dormitory room with books and papers strewn across a desk in total disarray. The lack of organization suggests a sloppy and chaotic mind, but* Ecke *is actually a recreation of Bill Gates's room at Harvard where Microsoft was initially conceived.*

¶ *These highly intelligent works function like "cleaned up memories"—sterilized and removed from context, yet vaguely familiar. While their impassive and artificial nature raise important issues about systems of representation and the validity of photographic truth, their power lies in the disjunction between the object depicted and its connection to the history and hidden meaning inherent in the original. In this way they resemble crime scenes where the viewer, much like a detective or psychoanalyst, is a given a set of clues and is asked to decipher the narrative in reverse.*

Ciara Ennis

30 **Flur (Corridor),** ***1995***

Sprungturm (Diving Platform), *1994*

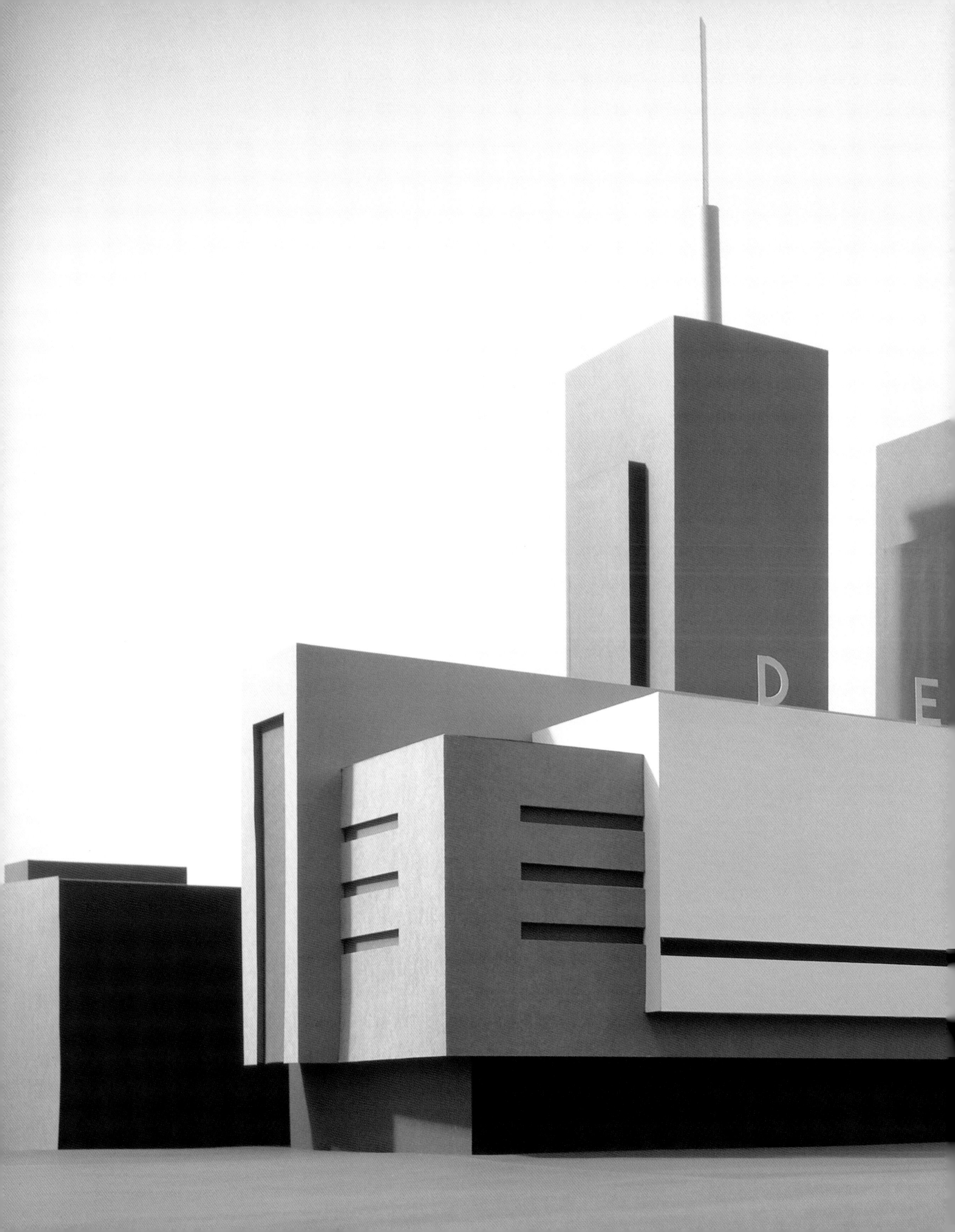

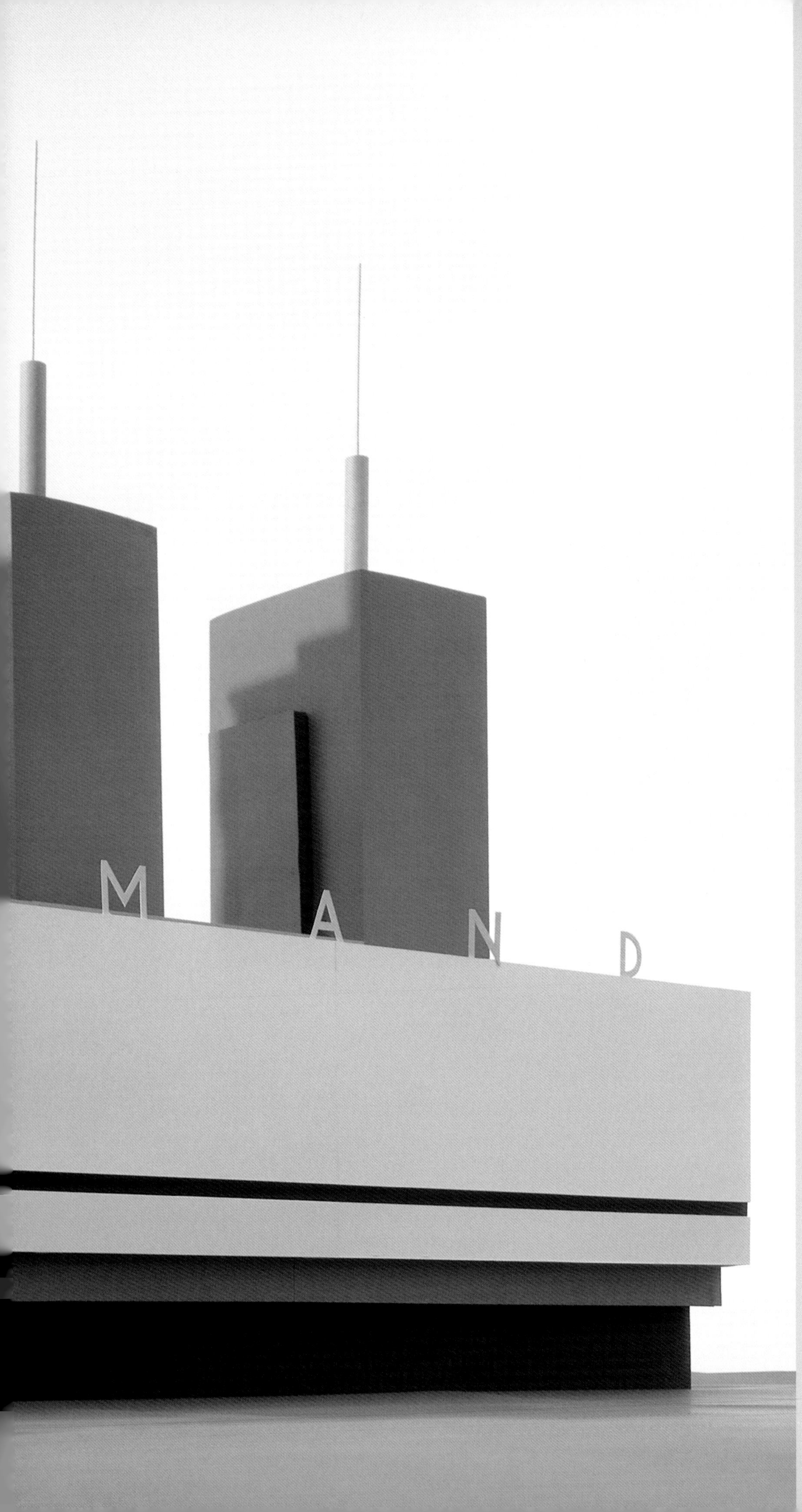

Fabrik (Mit Namen), ***1994***

One way to understand Renée Green's Import/Export Funk Office (1992–93)—to navigate through its books and magazines, video monitors and boom boxes—is with a quote from theorist Barbara Johnson. In an anthology that Green included on the Funk Office's shelves as it appeared in New York in 1992, Johnson writes: "Questions of difference and identity are always a function of a specific interlocutionary situation—and the answers, matters of strategy rather than truth." Identity is formed and proffered in response to a question posed by a particular situation, and all the possible answers, too, come with questions: "Compared to what? As of when? In what context? For what purpose? With what interests and presuppositions?" Race—indeed, any specific response to the request that one embody a particular identity—is a bargain, a weighted, uncertain, and often viciously unequal exchange of values and positions. This economy might begin to suggest what Green's Office deals in, what gets imported and exported.

¶ Green has a partner in the Import/Export Funk Office. Her interlocutor is the German music critic Diedrich Diederichsen and, in videotaped interviews, it is she who poses questions to him. Diederichsen, one of the founders of the German music magazine Spex, is her "participant informant" on German youth culture and its mix of music and politics, particularly on the role of hip-hop as imported culture and increasingly as a homemade product. The Office, then, deals in translations; included in it is a dictionary of hip-hop terms—from "bad" to "word"—for nonnative speakers, although who the native is in Green's ethnography isn't obvious. Her examination of Diederichsen's library, of his habits and habitus, turns a very familiar table: historically, the African has been the native object of Europe's ethnographic investigations. At the same time, the culture Green asks Diederichsen to stand for—founded in contemporary African-American experience—is in some sense hers, one that she might represent for him.

RENÉE GREEN

¶ *The logic of the* Import/Export Funk Office *isn't circular; rather, the work, especially in its earlier versions, is structured as a rectangle. Green and Diederichsen's positions in the present*

are mirrored and squared by Theodor Adorno and Angela Davis, who studied philosophy with Adorno in Frankfurt during the mid-60s. Represented in photographs and audiotapes, in books drawn from Diederichsen's and Green's libraries and from black music's textual past, Adorno and Davis situate the Funk Office*'s beginnings in the 60s, in and among the fraught relationships between the theorizations of an older European left and the practices of a newer American one, and between white youth culture and black nationalism. The dialogue Adorno and Davis stand for in the* Office*, the one that Green and Diederichsen continue in the present around the name "hip-hop," concerns the ownership and liberatory power of cultural practice and the means and modes of revolutionary action. It concerns as well the buying and selling of culture and the importing and exporting of the sounds and images of revolution.*

¶ *As antipodes, Adorno and Davis reiterate the structural positions Diederichsen and Green occupy: masculine/feminine, white/black, European/American. Yet the texts and images and sounds filling the field that the four demarcate—shopworn books on the office shelves, cassettes in the walkmans and VCRs—seem to promise ways of rereading and rethinking, even spaces for acting beyond those polar positions.*

Howard Singerman

COLLECTANEA
R
LEXICON
FUNK
STATION

***Import/Export Funk Office**, 1992–93. Installation at Galerie Christian Nagel, Cologne, 1992*

Import/Export Funk Office, *1992–93. Installation at Galerie Christian Nagel, Cologne, 1992*

DATA
SOURCE BOOK
THE SHOOK-UP GENERATION
NEWS CLIPS
RE. GERMANY

Michael Joaquín Grey had his first show at Petersburg Gallery in New York in 1990.

It was a confusing time in the New York artworld. After the financial crash of 1987, "pluralism," a nonsense category that had been around since the 70s simply meaning "everything," had finally supplanted painting as the default form. At this moment of maximum monetary and intellectual flux, Grey's show was a critical and financial success. Admiration focused on a group of linked pieces that seemed to perform two quite distinct tricks simultaneously, producing a creditable compass reading for a turbulent artscape.

¶ Firstly, approaching art from a scientific background with a degree in genetics, Grey addressed elemental processes of sculpture on a far more utilitarian basis than his antecedents. Although Grey's first body of work was formally tied to artists like Robert Smithson, Walter De Maria, and Bruce Nauman, the works in the Petersburg show had the authority one attaches to functional objects—the result of real inquiries into the fundamental nature of things—quite distinct from the speculative respect we attach to elegant hypotheses. At the moment of its emergence his work was already closing the circle with the laboratory. By claiming materials and methods that ranged from exotica like silicon airgel fresh from the labs at Berkeley to more conventional materials like sculpy and steel, Grey assumed extraordinary formal latitude.

Michael Joaquín Grey

¶ Grey's use of slightly exotic, self-determining materials to fabricate work and his subsequent integration of them into sculptural forms were to have an enormous influence on his closest colleague, Matthew Barney, who supplied a third element: the withheld glamour and celebrity of a reproducible body. But the work also spoke to larger issues, specifically the construction of a new kind of artistic operating environment. Only by claiming authority over all levels of production, no matter how complex, could the promise of pluralism be fully incorporated into an individual artist's practice. This was a liberating moment that still affects the artworld.

¶ The second salient feature in Grey's work was the inclusion of a narrative, a primitive cosmology embedded in sculptural form. Between Erosion Blocks: Units of Growth/Decay (1990); Low Density Silicon Airgel (Solid Smoke) (1990); and Cast River (1988), Grey mapped an elemental landscape of earth, air, and water. Two other works, My Sputnik and Electron M. (Microscope) (both 1990), successfully cast themselves as autobiographical poles in his exploration of the micro-macro world. Grey saw these narrative links as essential to the larger utility of the work, distinguishing them from the stand-alone formalism of his predecessors and bringing a metaphysical longitude to the stainless intelligence of the sculptures.

Artists as diverse as Liam Gillick, Katy Schimert, and Rirkrit Tiravanija were learning the same lesson, along with its corollary rule; in art, as in science, total freedom has a price. For Grey, whose work continues to broaden in scope, that price was the movement of his work beyond the narrow confines of the artworld, resulting in his most pluralistic project yet: a biomechanical toy and modeling system called ZOOB.

Matthew Ritchie

My Sputnik *(1990)*,
Electron M. (Microscope) *(1990)*,
L-River *(1989), and*
Erosion Blocks: Units of Growth/Decay *(1990)*
Installation in Petersburg Gallery, New York, 1990

Electron M. (Microscope), ***1990***

My Sputnik, *1990*

48 **Erosion Blocks: Units of Growth/Decay,** ***1990***

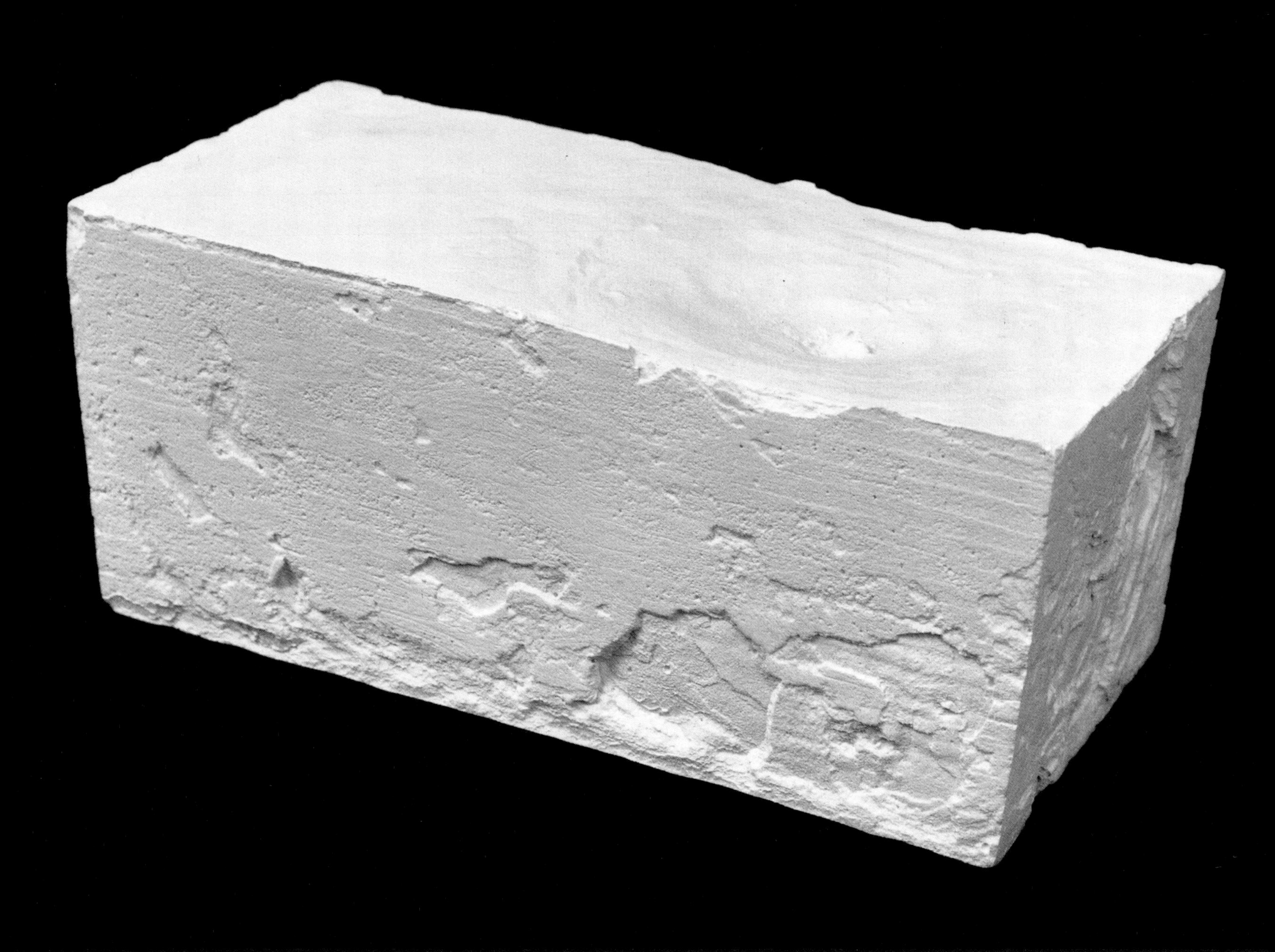

There is always something powerful about the titles of Damien Hirst's early works.

Like the chanting of a poetizing magus, Hirst's carefully contrived use of words seems to carry the pieces far beyond a simple or easily described identity or state of affairs, extending their potential meaning into areas of experience heavily loaded with ambivalent psychological effect.

Sometimes too he seems to seek out a kind of ontological no-man's land where analysis breaks down—a location beyond the reach of rational thought.

¶ Hirst's two-part installation piece In & Out of Love (1991) is typical in this respect. Shown at Woodstock Street in 1991, it takes the emotional trials of the human heart as its subject, and turns these trials into metaphors. They become an array of clearly articulated oppositional forces affecting our most intimate experiences as social beings: living and dying, desire and indifference, affection and repulsion, freshness and fatigue, hunger and satiety.

DAMIEN HIRST

¶ However there is also a much larger, more abstract purpose at work in the piece. It bridges the gap between natural languages and cultural discourse; between the real, the consequential, and the scientific (cause and effect, in other words); and between the image systems of the aesthetic, the more fluid domain of human sentiment and poetry. To this end Hirst has placed the person of the artist at the very center of the work—a ghosted presence—smoking and drinking and socializing with his own kind.

The absent figure functions as the cross-over point where a number of quite distinct allegorical formations and sign systems come together as a consolidated aesthetic experience. The artist here is characterized as a once live, now mortified and pinned down "collectible," much like the exotic Malaysian butterflies compelled to live out their life cycles as energizing aesthetic presences in In & Out of Love. He too lives a life characterized by the rituals of display and conspicuous self-consumption and is, by implication, also bound by his own behavioral obsessions and contradictions.

¶ Although he is seldom referred to as a critical or polemical artist, there is nevertheless a highly reflexive dimension to much of Hirst's work. This showed itself first in the Medicine Cabinets and later came into sharp focus in the earliest of the vitrine pieces: works like A Thousand Years (1990) and Still Pursuing Impossible Desires and The Asthmatic Escaped (both 1992). His method hinges upon the turning of allegory into meta-allegory by neutralizing the kind of narrative line one usually associates with soap operas, B-movies, and horror films. Our engagement then, in the first instance, is with the bruising reiteration of banal meanings. But this is quickly replaced by an abiding fascination with the way in which meaning constitutes and renews itself. In the case of In & Out of Love the allegory takes flight from the suburban exotic and greenhouse kitsch and ends in a meditation on the impossibly fixed meanings in the language game that is our experience of the world of things.

Jon Thompson

In & Out of Love (White Paintings & Live Butterflies), ***1991***
Installation at Woodstock Street, London, 1991

In & Out of Love ***(detail)*****, *1991***

In & Out of Love 1991 *Installation at Woodstock Street, London, 1991*

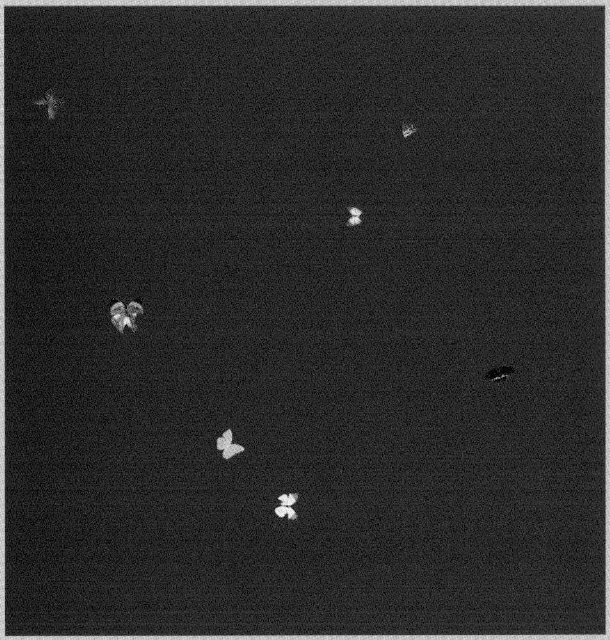

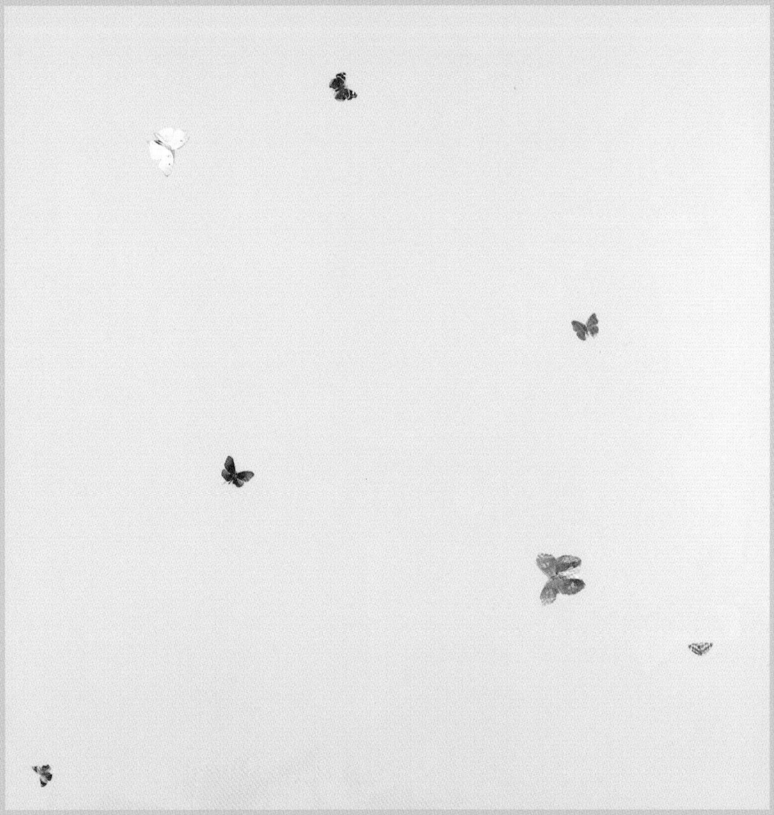

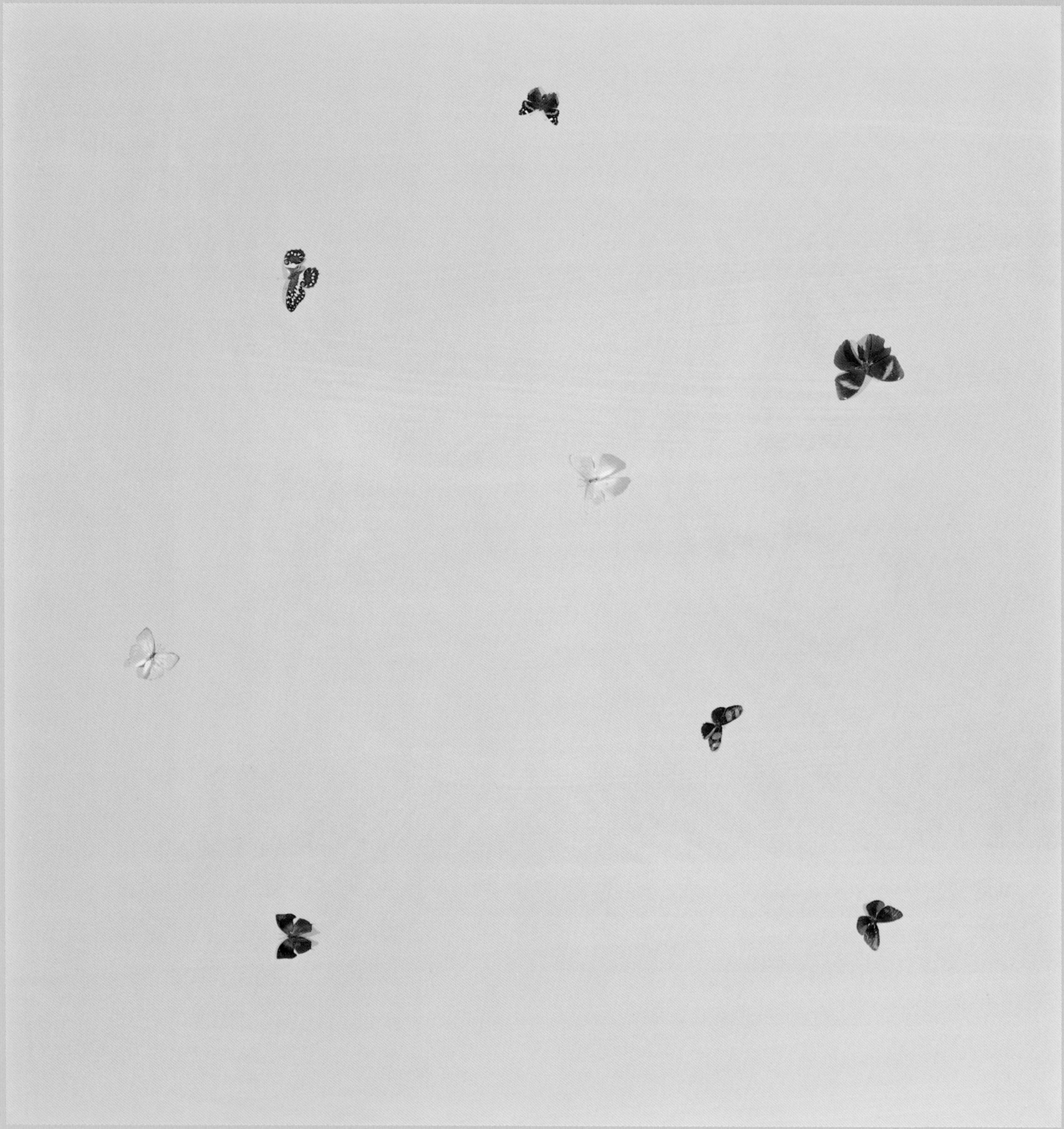

In & Out of Love *(details)*, 1991

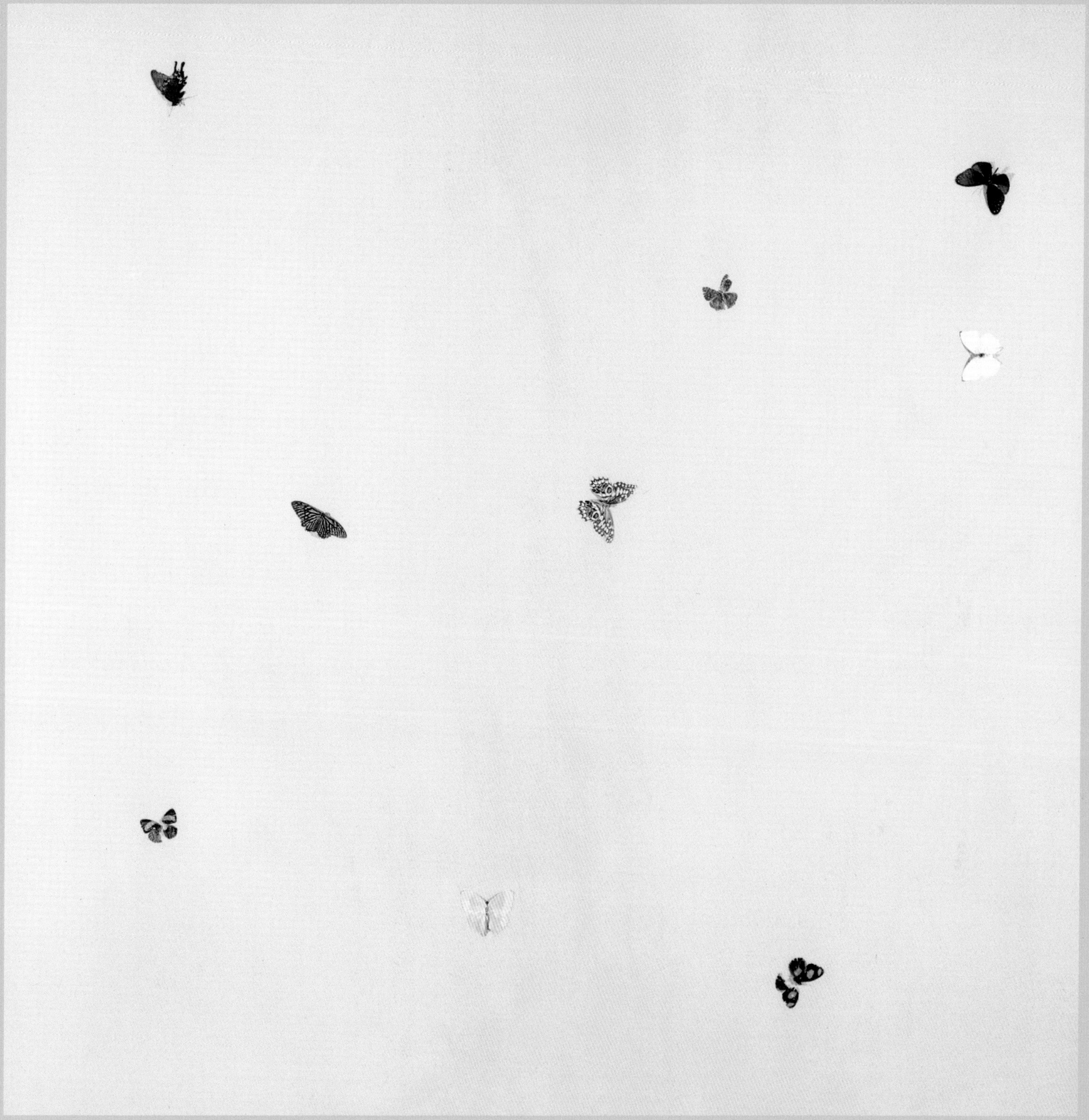

 In & Out of Love *(details)*, 1991

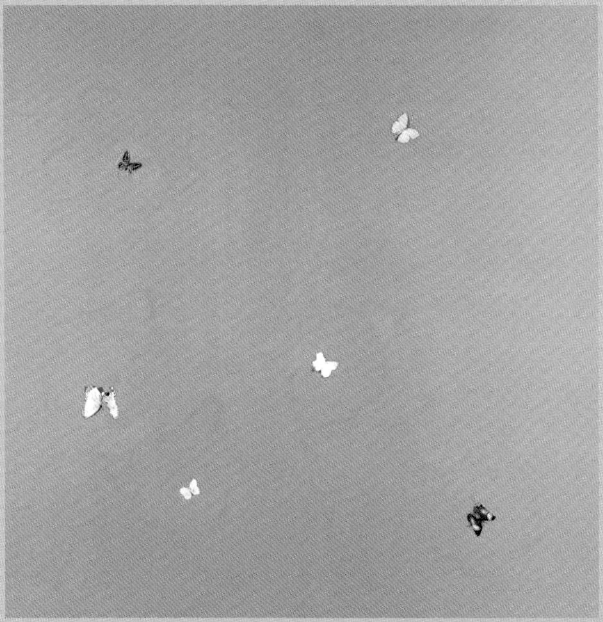

During the late 80s Gary Hume made a lengthy series of single-color paintings—more than thirty canvases in all. Apart from high-gloss surfaces, their only distinguishing feature was a low-relief image, life-sized, of hospital-style doors.

Most of them shared the title Magnolia Door, *individualized through the addition of a Roman numeral. These works marked a radical break from the paintings that had preceded them. They signaled a decisive move away from Hume's earlier preoccupation with more traditional, formal aspects of "modernist" abstract painting towards a more conceptual, analytical space in which aesthetic considerations were tempered by philosophical, critical, and social considerations. The key to this more complex conceptual territory lies in the generic title* Magnolia.

¶ The "door" paintings are made with household paint color-coded as "magnolia" on most commercial color charts. The generic title not only labels the works but also the material from which they are made.

In this regard, it seems to function as a certain kind of tautological closure. Hume would appear to be quite literally "shutting the door" on any extension of meaning beyond the mere facts of the work. Further consideration, however, suggests its function is altogether more complex. As a device for closure it is far too neat to be taken at face value, too bleakly opaque not to provoke a more probing address. There is a strong whiff of paradox about it, too.

GARY HUME

The same device that works to curtail extended meaning at the general level also serves to hold aesthetic closure—the relational rhetoric usually associated with the notion of good painting—at bay. We are face to face with a painter who, in the very act of painting, seems intent upon denying painting its historic identity and aesthetic ground.

¶ In the British context too, the color-word "magnolia" is the very opposite of aesthetic "signing," referencing instead both the institutional and the domestic as social and class constructs. The paintings diagrammatize, in an almost subliminal form, flush doors with kick plates and matching porthole windows of the kind commonly found in public institutions, from hospitals and schools to social-security offices and the recreational facilities of prisons. These references are heavily reinforced by their color. Domestically speaking the color magnolia was, both mythically (I'm thinking here of sitcom culture) and actually, the color that the aspiring working class painted their sitting rooms at a particular moment in the changing social landscape of Britain after World War II.

And here we hit upon one of the most curious and provocative aspects of Hume's Magnolia Door series—the invocation of memory. The tautological naming of the image has an almost Proustian aspect to it. It is not, strictly speaking, a contemporary reference, but looks back to Hume's childhood and the prevalent taste of his parents' generation. What at first sight seems to excise human sentiment ends up as a stunningly oblique way of speaking of human feelings as they are consecrated by memory.

Jon Thompson

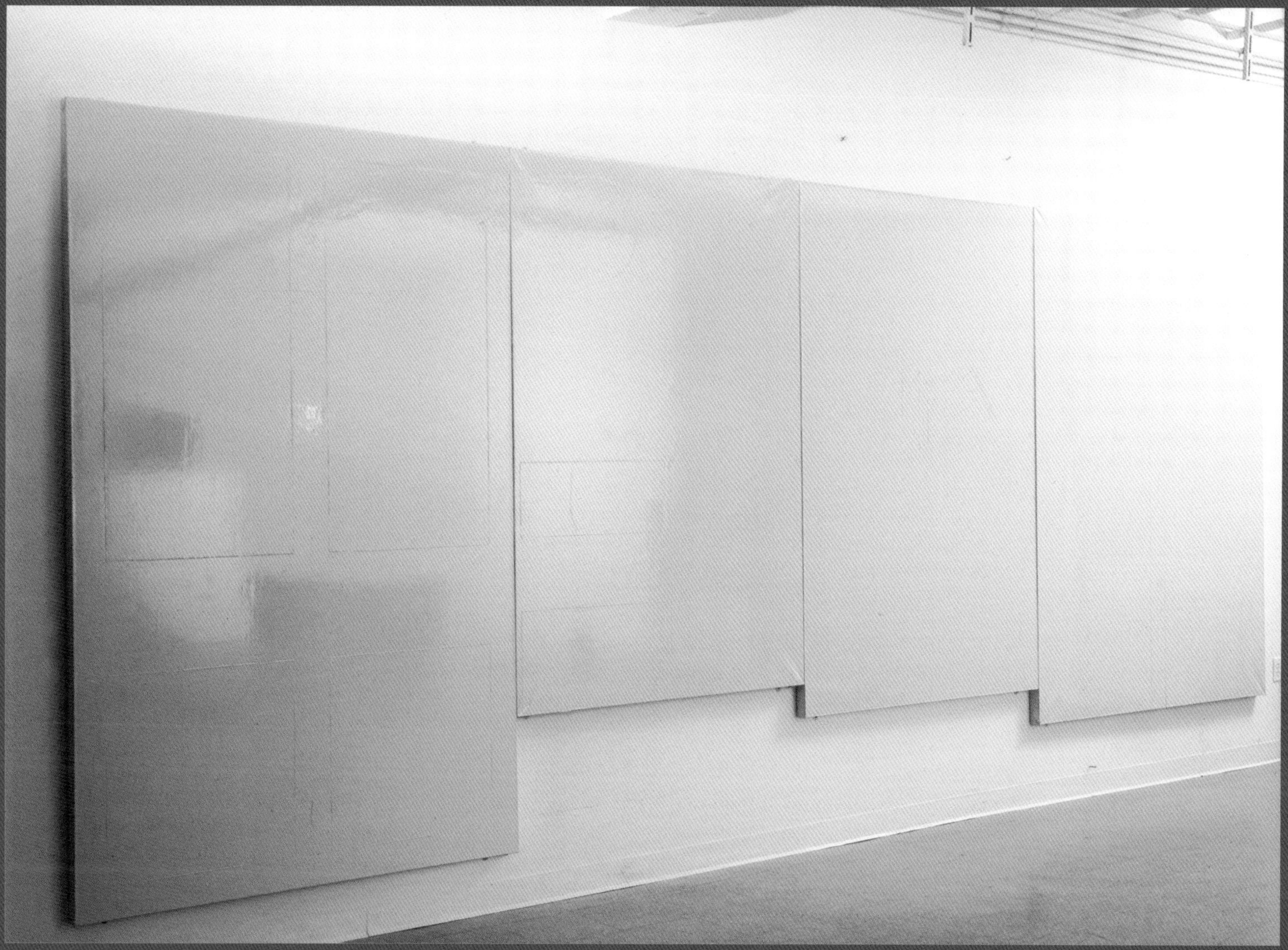

60 **Four Subtle Doors I**, *1989/90*

Magnolia Door XI, *1989*

62 Magnolia Door XXIV, ***1989/90***

Magnolia Door XXVI, ***1989/90***

Despite their enormous size and material complexity, an absence worries Toba Khedoori's drawings. The broad paper fields she prepares edge-to-edge with thin applications of wax are mostly left derelict, unengaged by her relatively tiny imagery.

The resulting sense of quiet is what most commentators have remarked on, but it's a quiet that shouldn't be confused with peacefulness. The work's reticence feels too enforced, more the product of imposed constraints and structural limitations than some sort of elegant modesty.

There are, for instance, no horizon lines to provide a pictorial world for Khedoori's depictions of worldly things, to convert her wax grounds into ground, planes upon which her buildings or railroad cars might stand or travel. There's neither a drama to participate in, nor even a stage where it can unfold. And there's also no sky, no air; her iconography doesn't float buoyantly but instead looks embalmed, literally stuck in a gummy, waxen oblivion.

This sense of placelessness is further heightened by the work's ill-defined framing edges, making the fields themselves seem as if they have no beginning, middle, or end. Khedoori's work lacks not just actors and events but the very conditions for their appearance. And at the same time there's an excess of representational labor and hardware, of technique and rudimentary pictorial convention and sheer space, all of which are displayed as if in suspended animation, like frozen hieroglyphs disconnected from narrative's grammar and syntax.

TOBA KHEDOORI

¶ But it's in Khedoori's very approach to the task of representation that the poignant emptiness in her work most forcefully takes shape. She begins on the floor, pushing and spreading heated wax over a large surface; there's little form or color here to deploy or adjust, just thick, malleable material being applied to another material through broad bodily gestures.

But then Khedoori's process drastically switches gears to a kind of tight-wristed, hard-edge drawing most reminiscent of architectural studies; the floor is replaced by a completely different register, something more like a drafting table and the grid of graph paper and T-square. The finished work ends up stricken by the split between these two phases—between inarticulate physicality and overly articulate detail, between viscous, formless matter and the abstract ideation characteristic of model-making and architectural plans. And also made conspicuous is all that's been omitted in that split—namely, the inhospitableness both registers share toward depicting a social world.

Whether hunched over the floor or over the table, Khedoori's process circumvents the traditional painter's stance before a window-like pictorial space; she seems never to assume an upright posture and visual orientation appropriate to looking and reaching over and across as if toward others and their endeavors. The results are monumentally scaled pictures of fossilized bits of social infrastructure haunted by the impossibility of their ever being inhabited and acted upon. And it's this impossibility that becomes the elegiac subject matter of Khedoori's art.

Lane Relyea

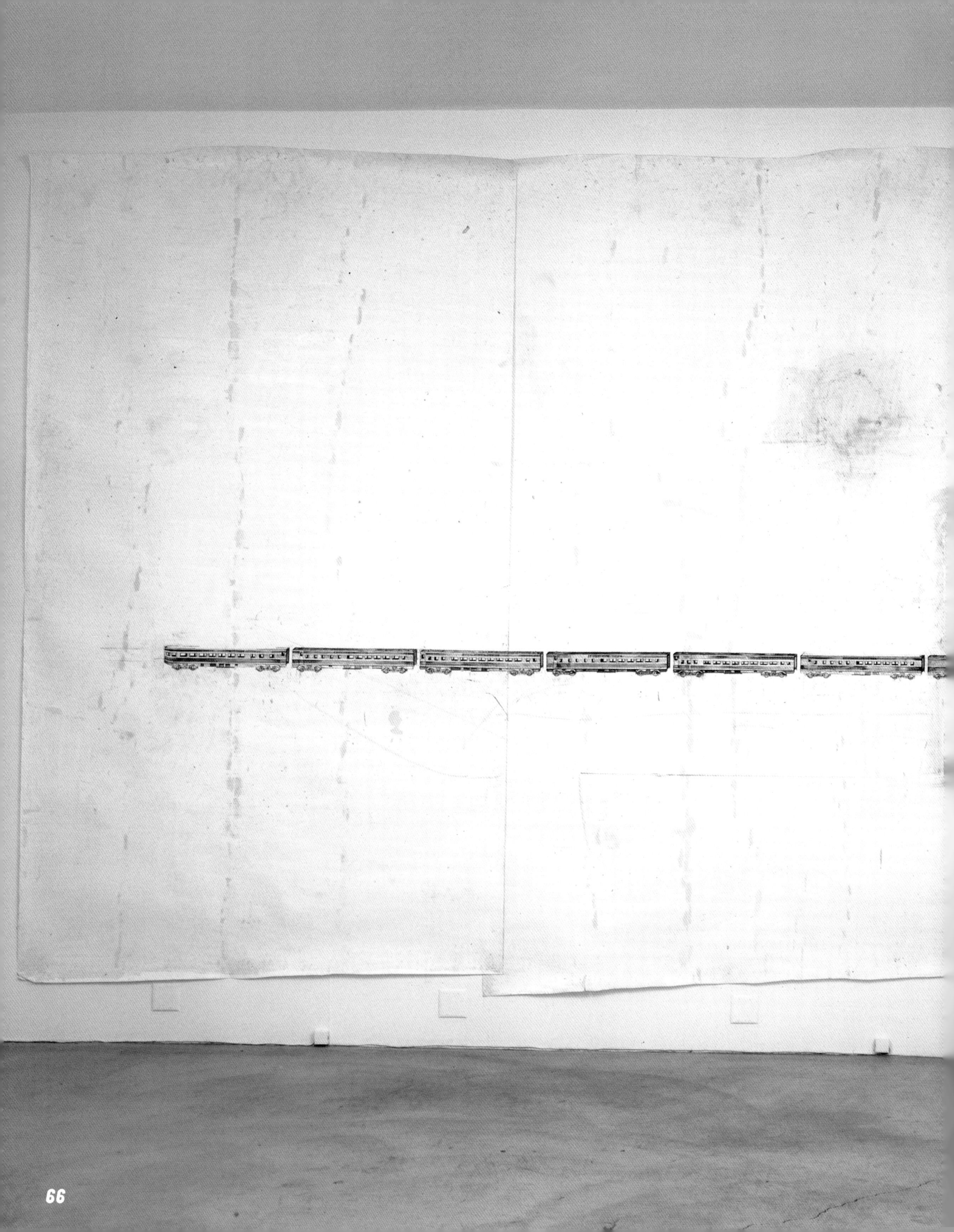

Untitled (Train), ***1993***

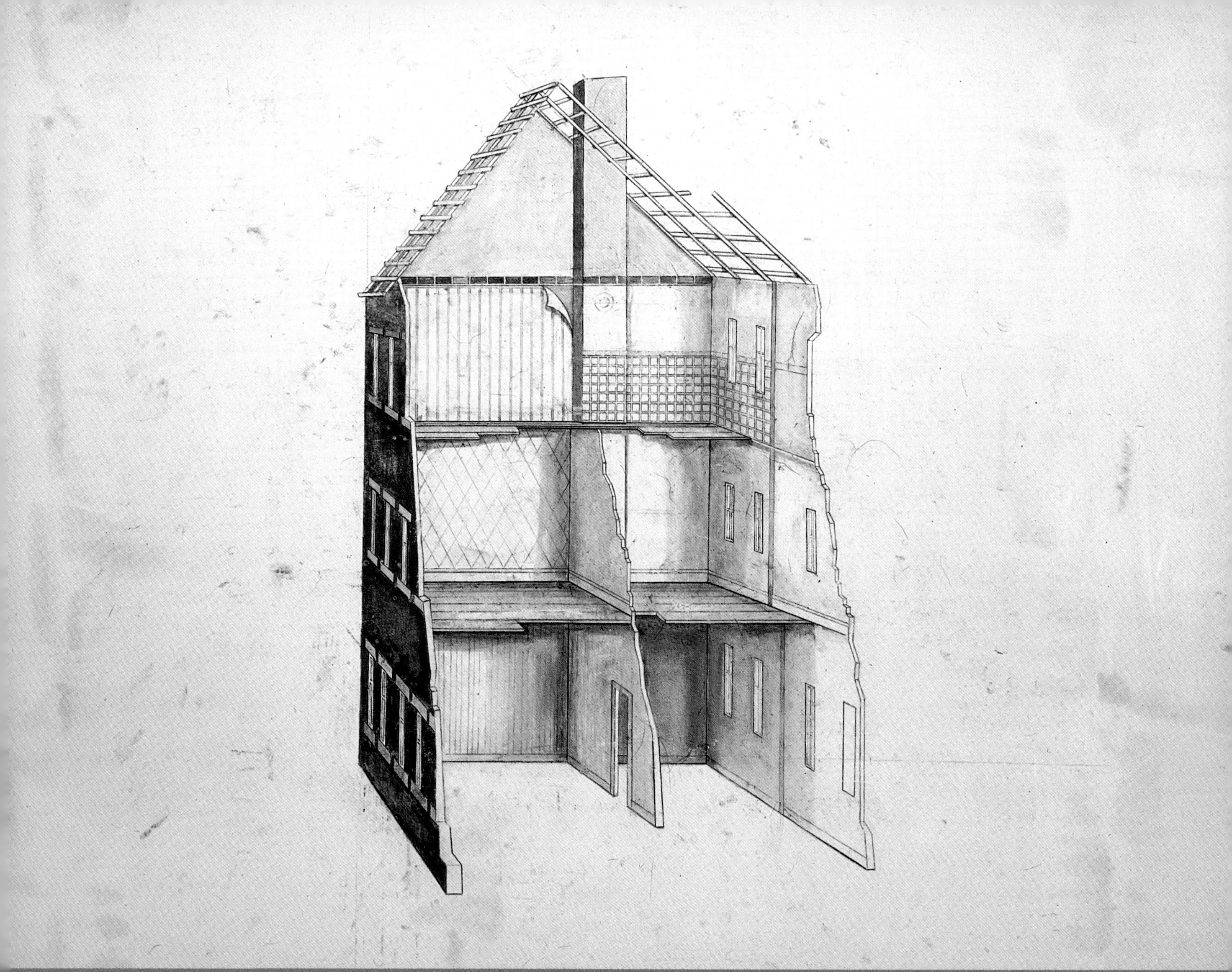

 Untitled (Windows), *1994*

Sharon Lockhart made the short film Khalil, Shaun, A Woman Under the Influence *(1993) and a photographic series derived from it,* Shaun *(1993), for her graduation show at Art Center College of Design in Pasadena.* Auditions, *another series of photographs, were made six months later. Although the works are independent of each other, they combine to demonstrate the degree to which Lockhart's work has been driven by an engagement with cinema.*

¶ Khalil, Shaun, A Woman Under the Influence *is a film in three sections that mixes together various filmic tropes, including documentary, Hollywood special effects, and conventional narrative. The first two sections focus respectively on Khalil and Shaun, young boys who appear to be suffering from a serious and rapidly advancing disease resulting in horrible skin lesions. These sections take their point of departure from footage of make-up tests conducted by Dick Smith for William Friedkin's* The Exorcist *(1973). The effect is straightforwardly horrific in the first section with Khalil, although it could also be variously interpreted as a test, as part of an ongoing narrative, as documentary, or as a medical record.*

The second, with Shaun, is more problematic for the viewer because Shaun breaks character, talking to Lockhart off-camera, laughing, and generally fooling around. One might expect that the third and final section would resolve the ambiguities of the first two, but instead it consists of a remake of a scene from John Cassavetes's film A Woman Under the Influence *(1974).*

The scene in question does explicate a number of narrative issues, but the narrative in question is that of Cassavetes's film, not Lockhart's. For Lockhart, narrative is treated almost like a piece of set design, a background against which the actors are set. The "real" relationship between them plays alongside and against the "fictional" relationship dictated by the plot of the source material.

¶ The series of photographs Shaun relates to the make-up tests. As in the film itself, viewer expectation for some kind of coherent narrative sequence is confounded. The apparent stages of the disease follow no arc, whether of decline or of cure. Despite their close relationship to the film, we are forced to look at the photographs outside of filmic convention. Also paralleling the film, viewers are left unsure of the extent to which the photographs show the young actor in or out of his role. As Timothy Martin has written, "The role is merely a kind of trapping device or leaky container from which little expenditures or leakages of personhood may spill. Lockhart, like Cassavetes, desires these little leakages because they are accidental and defy her control." [1]

¶ Lockhart returned to the idea of the screen test for Auditions. The series of five photographs show children acting out a scene from François Truffaut's L'Argent de poche (Small Change, 1976). The scene in Truffaut's film shows a first kiss, and Lockhart has chosen to depict the moment just before the kiss itself. The evident self-consciousness of the young actors sets up an alienation effect in the viewer comparable to that produced by Shaun's breaking character in the earlier film. In this work the five photographs in their sequence do at first suggest something of an implied narrative, although that effect is undercut by our awareness that we are seeing the same scene repeated over and over.

¶ In both Khalil, Shaun, A Woman Under the Influence and Auditions Lockhart uses older films as source material from which her own work then deviates. Her resistance to any easy resolution is already established. She remains uninterested in didactic statements or in reaching a decisive conclusion. Today, she continues to pursue a rigorously serialized structure in combination with a lushly cinematic style. Her work emerges in an ever-evolving series of hybrid forms, all of them suffused by her ongoing engagement with, and disruption of, various kinds of narrative.

Note

1. Timothy Martin, "Documentary Theater," in Sharon Lockhart: Teatro Amazonas (Rotterdam: Museum Boijmans Van Beuningen, 1999), 17.

Audition One:
Simone and Max, *1994*

Audition Two:
Darija and Daniel, *1994*

Audition Three:
Amalia and Kirk, *1994*

Audition Four:
Kathleen and Max, *1994*

Audition Five:
Sirushi and Victor, *1994*

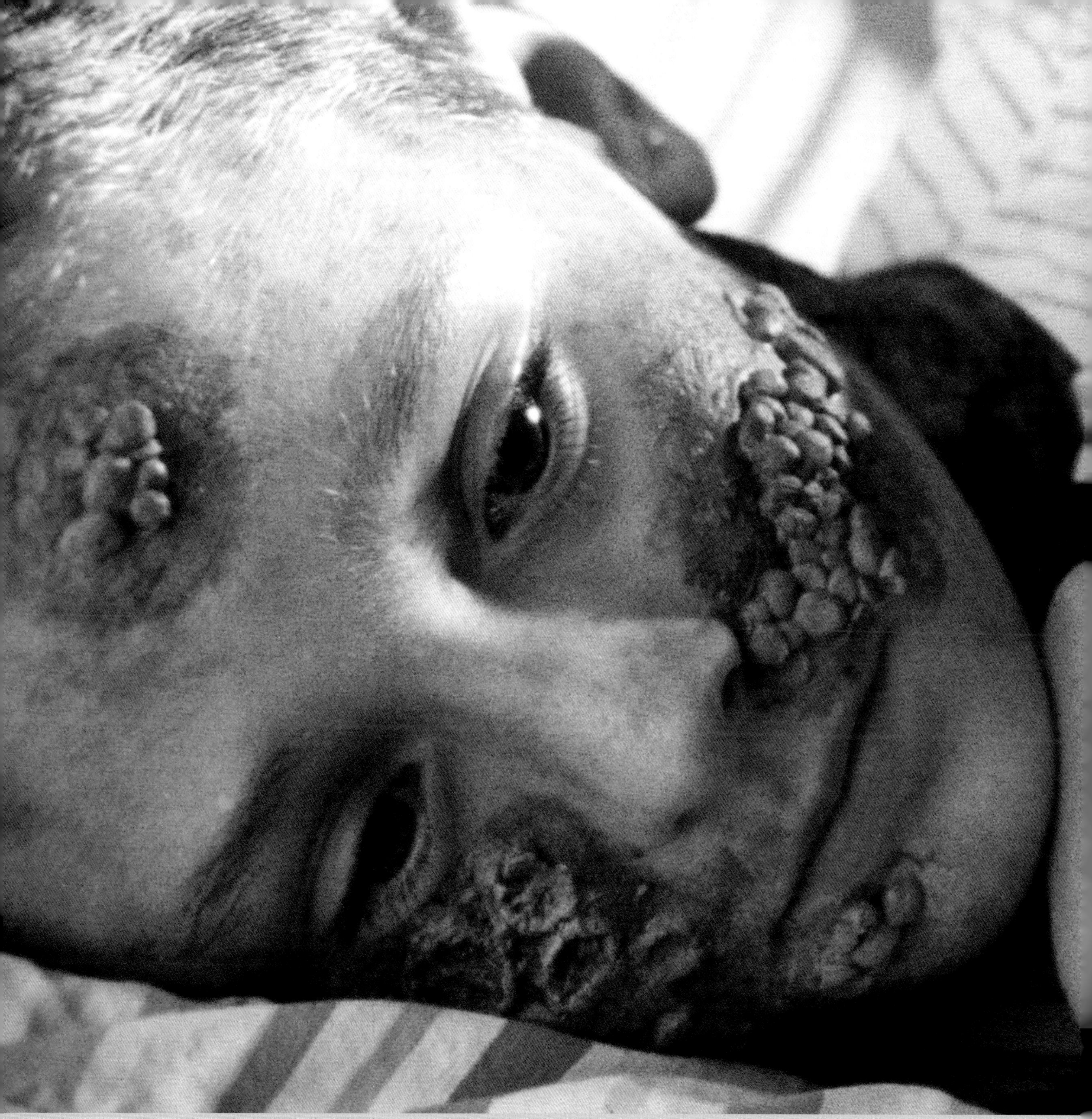

 Still from Khalil, Shaun, A Woman Under the Influence, *1993*

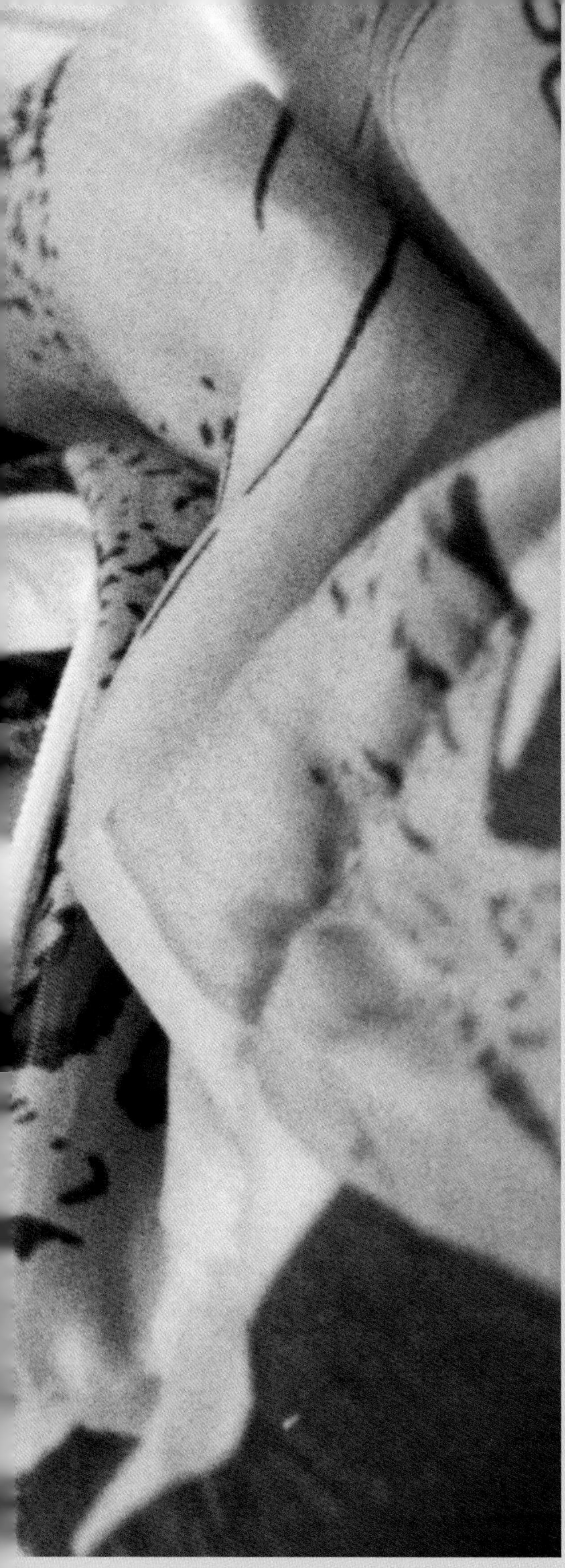

Quintessentially British, Sarah Lucas exploits the brash and sensationalist tactics of the tabloid press to explore issues of gender and representation within working-class culture. By translating vernacular slang into visual form, Lucas lays bare the underlying brutal and misogynist nature of this language. Originally exhibited together in 1992, Two Fried Eggs and a Kebab and The Old Couple (both 1992) articulate these concerns in a provocative and playful manner. Although willfully crude in their construction and use of materials, both works subtly subvert this rawness by referencing Dada, Surrealism, and Pop. In Two Fried Eggs and a Kebab, Lucas evokes the female form using a second-hand table, a couple of fried eggs, and pita bread stuffed with meat.

This act of reducing women to debased and humiliated sex objects is made more apparent by the framed photo at the "head" of the composition—re-contexualizing Magritte's infamous painting, Rape (1934). The reduction of the body to junkyard parts is also evident in The Old Couple. In this case, both sexes are stripped down to their vulgar symbolic representations—a candle and set of false teeth—to sit on two wooden thrift-store chairs.

These surrealistic props behave in oddly conflicting ways. Both the candle and false teeth are mournfully suggestive of bodily decay and a sense of loss, but also function as sardonic signifiers of potency: the candle acting as erect phallus, and the false teeth evoking the threat of castration.

SARAH LUCAS

¶ *Lucas uses her own image as a tool to perform a masculine identity as a means of self-empowerment. Refusing to conform to the narrow conventions of female beauty, she plays with an androgynous image that allows her to assume a relatively fluid, but always powerful sexual identity. In* Divine *(1991), Lucas appears tough, butch, and sexy. She slouches with legs splayed open, aggressively goading the viewer.*

This subversion of stereotypical male and female roles projects conflicting images that are both threatening and seductive. A similar device is employed in Eating a Banana *(1990) in which Lucas, ambiguously dressed in a tough leather jacket, suggestively eats a banana while staring provocatively at the camera. Re-positioning the woman as aggressor by alluding to castration, the image is both violent and sexual. Lucas's* The Receptacle of Lurid Things *(1991)—a life-sized cast of the artist's middle finger monumentalized on a tall pedestal—performs an abusive gesture, becoming a celebration of female strength and also of crude aggression. This "laddish" attitude is also evident in* 1-123-123-12-12 *(1992). Here Lucas references British skinhead culture by customizing a pair of old Doc Marten boots with razor blades inserted into the toe caps. In these works, Lucas postures as "one of the boys," invoking a masculine and working-class identity not so much as a form of judgement, but as a way to reclaim that attitude for herself, allowing for a more credible and truthful feminized agency.*

¶ *The visible anger that drives these formative works is as much class-based as it is fueled by an investigation of gender and sexuality. By co-opting the class-specific language of tabloids, Lucas succeeds in communicating to the largest possible audience, while simultaneously revealing its sexist and fundamentally reactionary structure. This directness and uncompromising aggression is convincingly offset by the deployment of an absurdist and typically British humor that avoids an overly didactic and critical position. The thematic, conceptual, and formal approaches contained within this early body of work has formed the basis of her current practice.*

Ciara Ennis

 Divine, *1991*

Mussolini Morning, *1991*

 The Old Couple, *1992. Installation at Kingly Street, London, 1992*

Two Fried Eggs and a Kebab, *1992*

Figleaf in the Ointment, *1991*

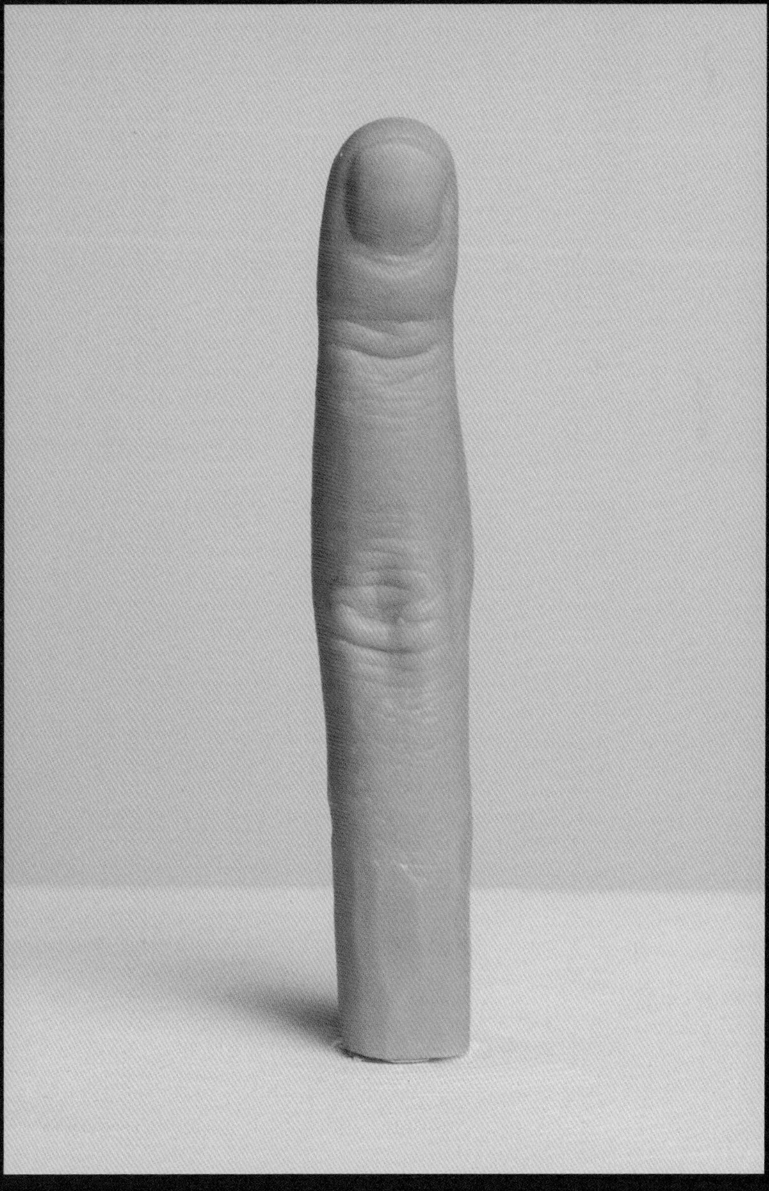

The Receptacle of Lurid Things, *1991*

1-123-123-12-12, *1992*

Steve McQueen made Bear (1993) at a time when he was dividing his working life between London and New York and the question of location—culturally, politically, and professionally—was an almost constant preoccupation.

Although McQueen was initially a very accomplished young painter, during the late 80s he became more and more preoccupied with the medium of film. Indeed by 1990 he had abandoned painting altogether and taken to the movie-camera, pursuing a long-term ambition to direct films. The new generation of black filmmakers, people like Isaac Julien and Spike Lee, seemed to him to enjoy a broader field of representational possibilities and offer a richer model for future work.

Never entirely comfortable with the exclusivity of the artworld, McQueen also nurtured very real doubts about its appropriateness as a site from which to reflect on the broad range of issues bearing down on his life-experience, with its roots in the West Indian Diaspora. For this reason too, the ambition to make movies never really left him.

STEVE McQUEEN

¶ However, by satisfying his need to treat narrative—albeit in a highly circumscribed form—making *Bear* allowed McQueen to put his movie-making ambitions on the back burner for a time. McQueen's early works were shot in black and white and always at close range, with the possible exception of *Five Easy Pieces* (1995); linguistically speaking, *Bear* remains the most cinematic of them. As the film director John Carpenter famously pointed out, the close interpersonal encounter—the fight scene, the boxing or wrestling match—is in many respects the perfect cinematic subject. It places the reactive human presence at the imaginal center of things and provides the camera with the opportunity to feast on the physical body in motion and dwell on the semaphore of facial expression. It also places the viewing subject in a manifestly privileged position.

Bear exploits all of these factors. It takes the body as its subject, but in a rather unexpected way. McQueen's is a passionate, preeminently sensual, muscular, specifically male body, rather than the self-conscious, theory-laden, mostly degendered body familiar in contemporary critical discourse. The wrestlers are replete, thinking and feeling social beings locked into a negotiation of imminent relationship that runs the whole gamut of emotions from passivity to anger to aggression, from affection to anxiety to fear.

There is, then, an openness and a grandeur about McQueen's naked wrestlers that permits them to function in a psycho-social affirmation of the human condition in general, and this is greatly enhanced by his preferred strategy of presentation. *Bear* is shown in a closed black box with the projected image taking up the whole of one wall. In this closed space the viewer experiences an intense state of sexualized coenethesia; senses in his or her own body the physical trials and inner feelings of the protagonists; and comes to empathize with the shifting mirage of intimacy and the gathering force of physical exultation.

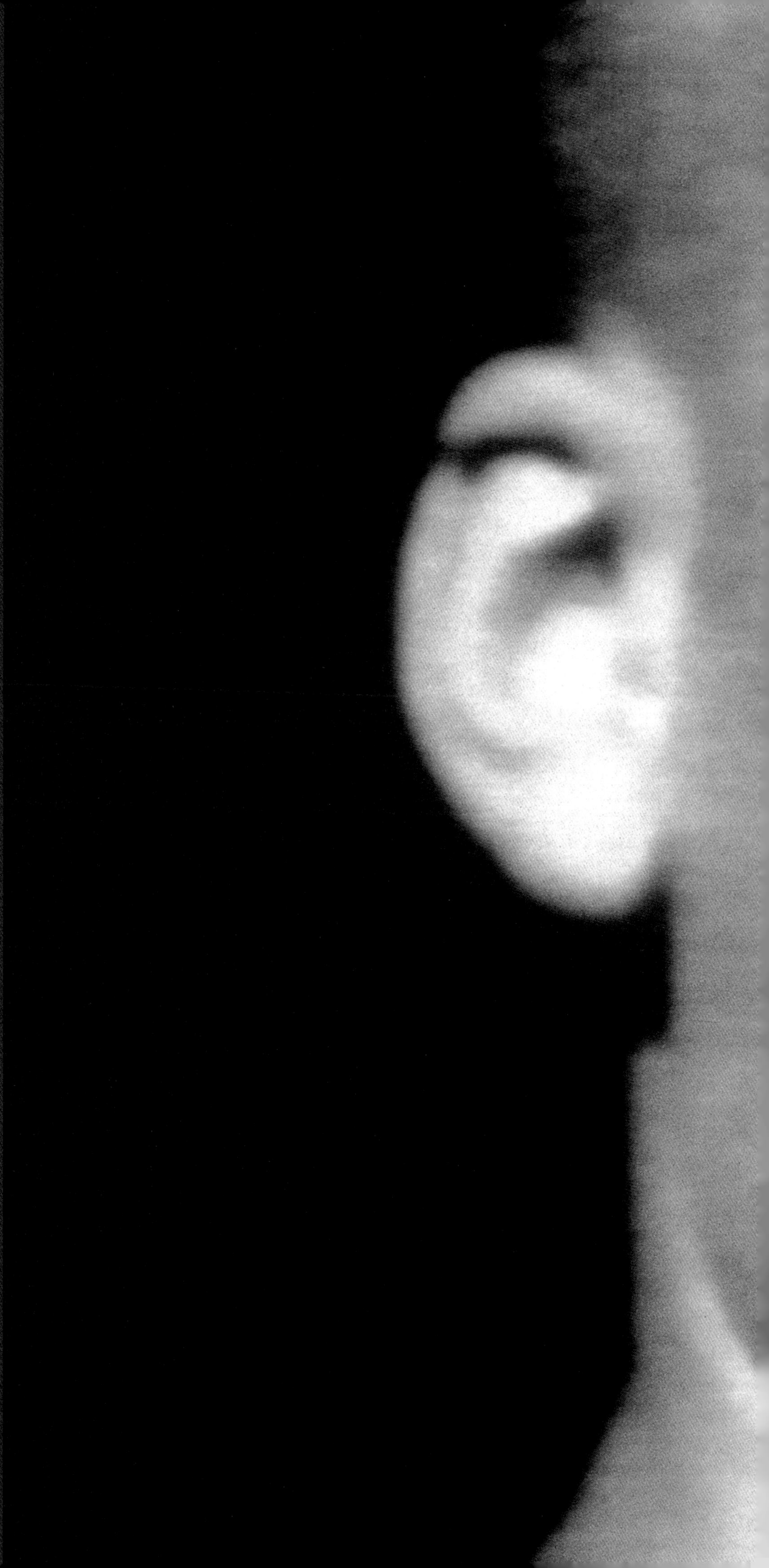

88 *Still from* Bear, *1993*

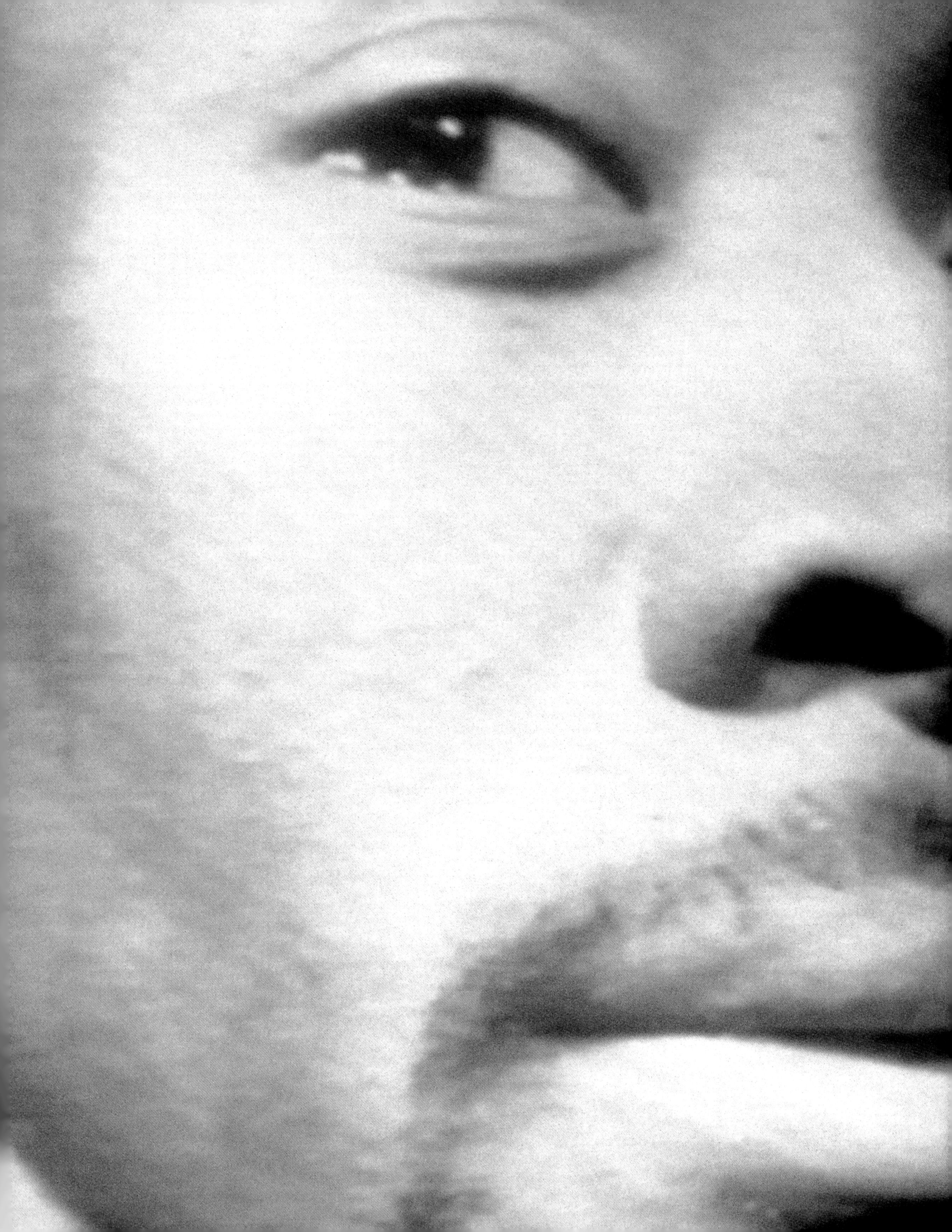

Takashi Murakami emerged in 1991 as a central figure of New Pop, an art movement that used images of Japanese subculture to criticize complicity between Japanese consumerism and imperialism. Beyond mere iconoclasm, Murakami was concerned with the formation of a new discursive space and field of production for young artists. Originally trained in *nihonga*—an eclectic painting genre combining traditional Japanese painting techniques, post-impressionist reductions of images, and Cubist compositional experiments—Murakami was skeptical about the derivative nature of Japanese contemporary art, opposing its authority by championing the cultural relevance of Japanese *manga* and *anime* for the post-60s generation. For Murakami *anime* and *manga* also represented a unique genre created from eclectic and idiosyncratic imitations of American pop culture, a paradox that provided him with a model for his own art.

¶ Murakami's relation to *nihonga* is more complex. While defying its hegemony as a national art patronized by the imperial family, Murakami wanted to emulate its popular influence. This ambivalence was apparent in his 1991 installations *Sansei no hantai nanoda* and *Randosel Project*. The clownish act of bestowing patriarchal authority to a character appropriated from a slapstick Japanese comic, and the "cute" representation of militarism, respectively, undermined the power systems in which *nihonga* was embedded. His mastery of *nihonga*'s meticulously flat coloring and geometrical composition endowed Murakami's Pop readymades with plastic beauty.

TAKASHI MURAKAMI

¶ First presented in a 1992 group show entitled "Anomaly," Sea Breeze embodies Murakami's breakthrough. A gigantic round steel wheel adorned with eight 16,000-watt klieg lights—the kind used to illuminate baseball stadiums at night—the work is housed in a trailer whose walls are painted fluorescent yellow-green on one side and brilliant red on the other. When the shutters on the trailer are raised and the powerful beacons lit, Sea Breeze transforms the encounter between viewer and artwork from a visual experience into a physical one—emitting such intense light and heat that it is impossible to approach or look directly at it. Slowly revealing itself as the shutter rises, Sea Breeze is an enigmatic presence that both seduces and repels—its inhibiting qualities constituting a prominent condition of its charm.

¶ The overwhelmingly decorative accomplishment of Sea Breeze frustrates any conjecture about its references or didactic interpretation. A three-dimensional sculpture evoking a planar composition of color and geometrical patterns, Sea Breeze anticipates Superflat, an aesthetic movement of Murakami's own invention. Superflat brings together threads as diverse as the playful lines, ornamental coloring, and exaggerated proportions cultivated by anime and seventeenth- and eighteenth-century Japanese painting and sculpture in order to assert the uniqueness of Japanese vernacular sensibilities transformed through contact with American Pop.

Midori Matsui

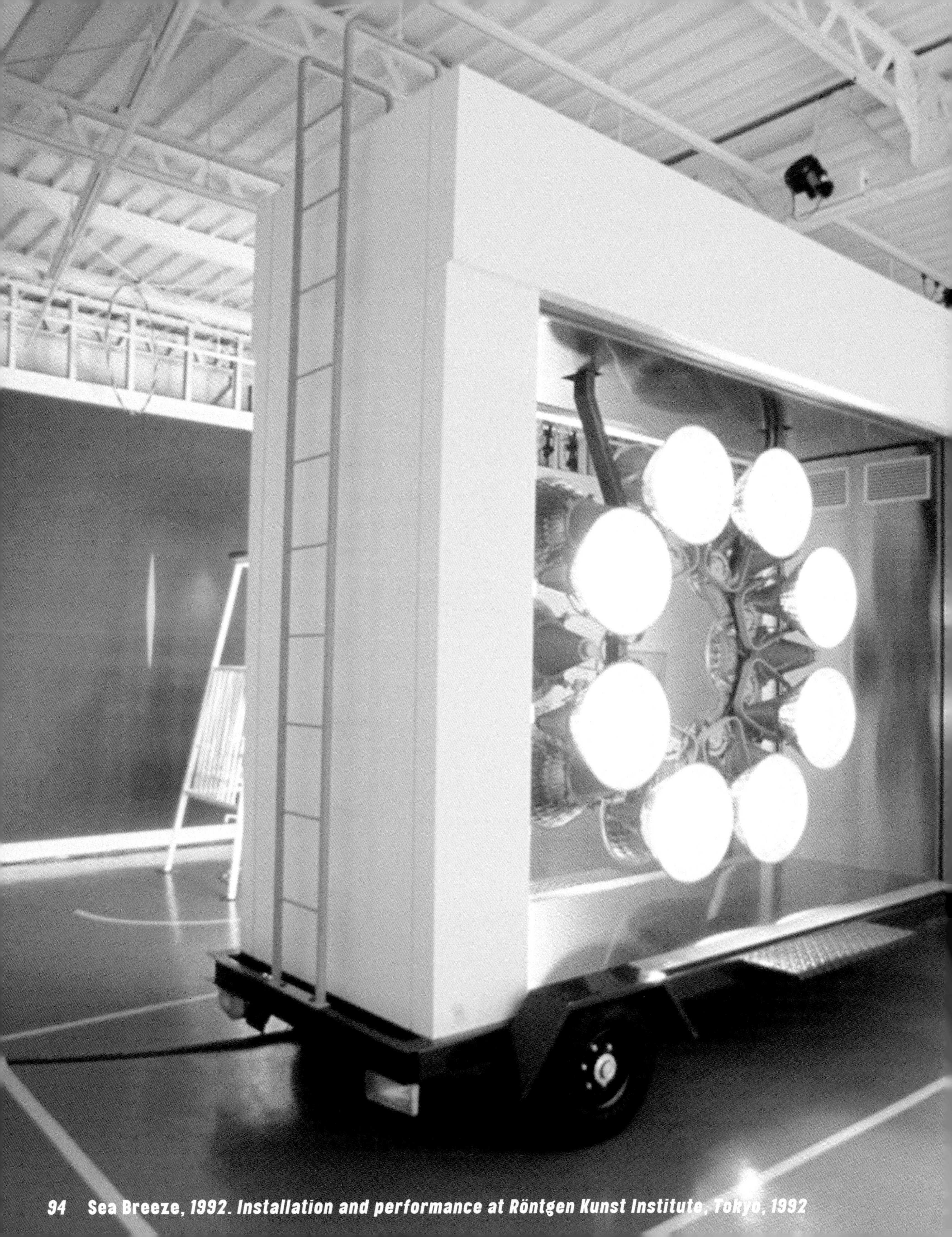

 Sea Breeze, 1992. Installation and performance at Röntgen Kunst Institute, Tokyo, 1992

Sea Breeze, 1992. Installation at Center for Contemporary Art, Art Tower Mito, Tokyo, 1999

During the mid-90s Yoshitomo Nara played a central role in the renewal of figurative painting on the Japanese art scene. His first solo show in Tokyo during the spring of 1995 signaled the return of emotional content and beauty as issues in contemporary Japanese art and heralded a fresh alternative to the ironic conceptualism of the early 90s. Nara's paintings have been described as "paintings of pleasure," referencing their immediate attractiveness. Featuring children with disproportionately large heads and expressively slanted eyes, they evoke the perceived duality of innocence and evil within children.

Alternately depicted as brandishing knives and bearing wounds, or singing and playing guitar, Nara's children are at once vulnerable and capable of violence towards themselves as well as others. Through bold elliptical strategies and figurative distortions that dissolve the distinction between human and animal, masculine and feminine, Nara also captures the dream-like qualities and state of indeterminacy embodied by the child.

¶ Although not directly related, Nara found counterparts in his American contemporaries Elizabeth Peyton and Karen Kilimnik. Emerging on the New York art scene around the same time, Peyton and Kilimnik represented the revived interest in emotion and figuration in contemporary art. Their deceptively naïve paintings incorporating popular kitsch unabashedly celebrated adolescent desire and androgyny through the juxtaposition of sensuous beauty and psychological violence.

YOSHITOMO NARA

¶ Like Peyton's and Kilimnik's, Nara's early paintings update the legacies of urban expressionists like Egon Schiele and George Grosz with a sensibility receptive to the impact of contemporary graffiti.

On the other hand, Nara's more recent paintings and sculpture cultivate the nuances of proto-Renaissance painting by simplifying the human form and adopting translucent pastel colors and luminous shadows, adding a veil of tranquility to his personal mythology.

¶ Made in 1995 as a three-dimensional rendition of his magical worldview and the faux-naïve aesthetic explored in his paintings, Cup Kids is Nara's first major sculptural piece. It features seven children, each contained in a cup and saucer, some in meditation and others wide awake. While all the children appear to possess wholeness and individuality, the diverse expressions on their faces suggest the range emotions a single person potentially contains.

Looking like a technological hybrid in an artificial womb or an alien in a spaceship hurtling towards an unknown future, Cup Kids reminds one of children's perceived vulnerability and strength; they also evoke Buddhist sculptures of minor deities representing various spiritual characteristics. Cup Kids is a hybrid of Western and Eastern figurative imaginations, conveying sacredness through the profane distortion and condensation of complex emotions in simple form. It represents an aspect of Nara's work that can be seen as a contemporary translation of folk sensibility.

Midori Matsui

100 Cup Kids, 1995. *Installation at Santa Monica Museum of Art, Santa Monica, California, 2000*

Chris Ofili introduced himself to the London artworld by trying to sell it shit—elephant shit.

Setting up a table at the pathetic end of a street market on Brick Lane, a worn-out area of the East End given a touch of arty glamour by the proximity of Gilbert and George's studio, Ofili offered fresh turds he had collected at the zoo. Only a few noticed. (Those who did might have drawn a connection to David Hammons's earlier sale of snowballs at an equally abject street market in New York.) Soon afterwards enigmatic stickers, saying only "Elephant Shit," appeared all over London, as well as painted graffiti—even an ad in the art magazine Frieze. There was "Elephant Shit" wherever you looked. A few more noticed. All the while, Chris Ofili was painting unabashedly gorgeous surfaces with translucent resins and multi-colored dots of paint.

¶ There is a deliberate contradiction at the heart of Ofili's presentation, between the immediate visual experience and the attitude behind it. On the surface, his paintings are light-filled and charming. Splashes of blue and gold paint, skeins of bright pigment, swirls of colored dots, swaths of gold leaf, constellations of heads and masks, are all brought to the service of a hallucinatory surface that glistens in the light, its luster creating a dizzying effect of other-worldliness. The paintings are never overworked, but passages in them build to a crescendo where strange dark lumps of organic matter sit, peculiar and unknowable. These lumps, of course, are clumps of elephant dung, glued to the canvas.

¶ Overall the paintings are decorative and pleasing, but these lumps create a different rhythm, a syncopated off-beat that saves the work from being too sweet. Hanging on the wall the paintings look dazzling, but more often they lean against it, propped up on little dung feet, looking very insouciant. While they stand very much on their own, they also recall the patterns of Vanessa Bell, the pop savvy of a young David Hockney, the dreamline landscapes of Australian aboriginal painting, various kinds of folk art, and some of the effects of Sigmar Polke. In short, Ofili's is a very Royal College kind of abstraction: layered with reference and full of wit, also cheeky and joyful, refusing to be too serious.

¶ Running counter to all this is a darker strain of anger fed by questions of racial identity and, one supposes, the ongoing sense of the inadequacy of painting.

Ofili is British-born, but his parents are African, and his doubt concerning the power and relevance of charming, witty paintings is palpable. After recognizing the potency of elephant dung, he began using this unknown and unexpected material during a residency in Zimbabwe, where it was readily available. Using dung, often in combination with torn photos of black cultural icons, is an aggressively love-filled act. It is echoed by the repetition of the word "shit" in some of Ofili's titles, like Painting with Shit on it and Shithead (both 1993), and recalls the early "Elephant Shit" stickers and graffiti. The dark underside of the paintings' shimmering beauty is what turns them into art.

Thomas Lawson

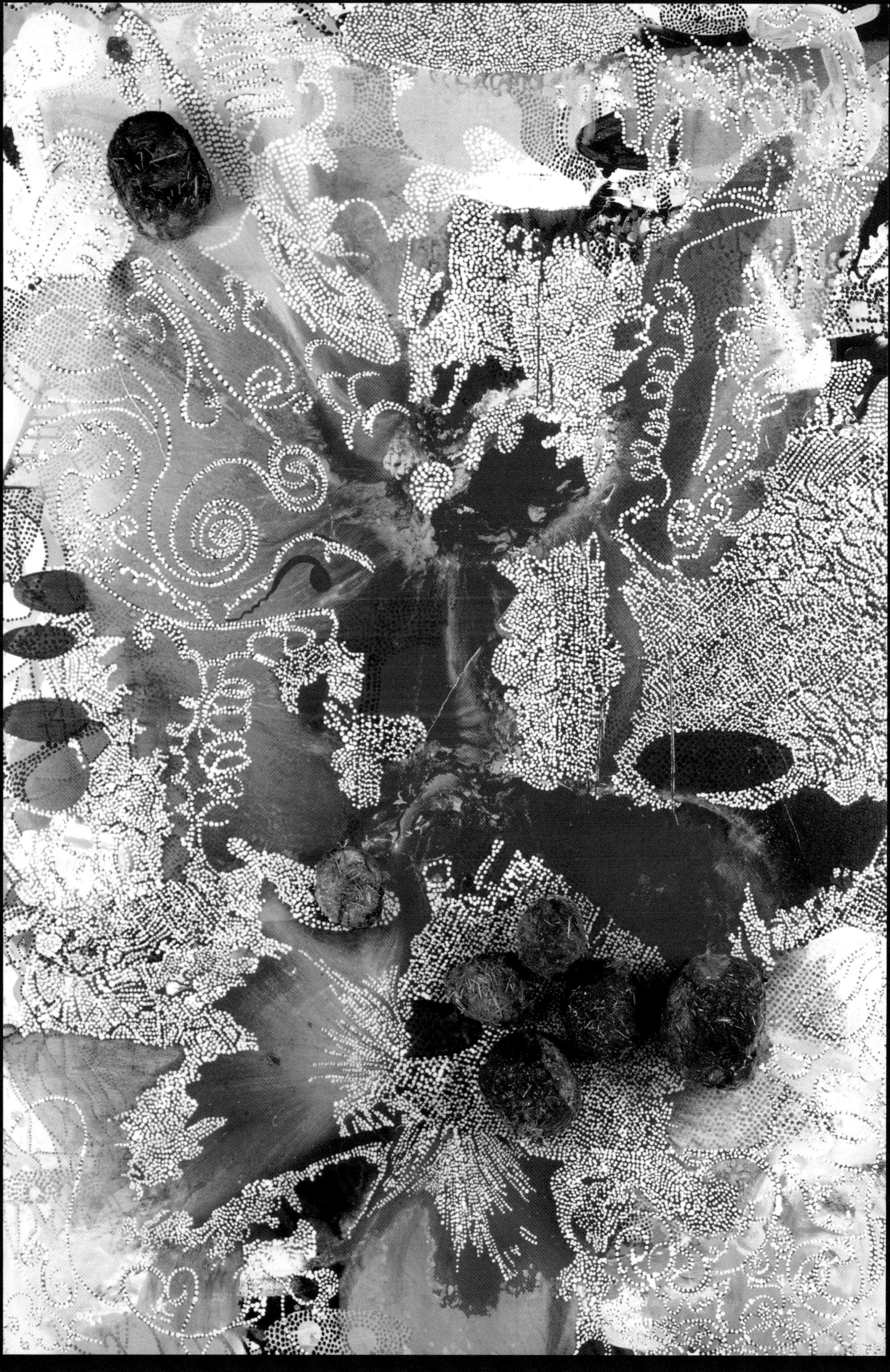

Open, *1993*

Shithead, *1993*

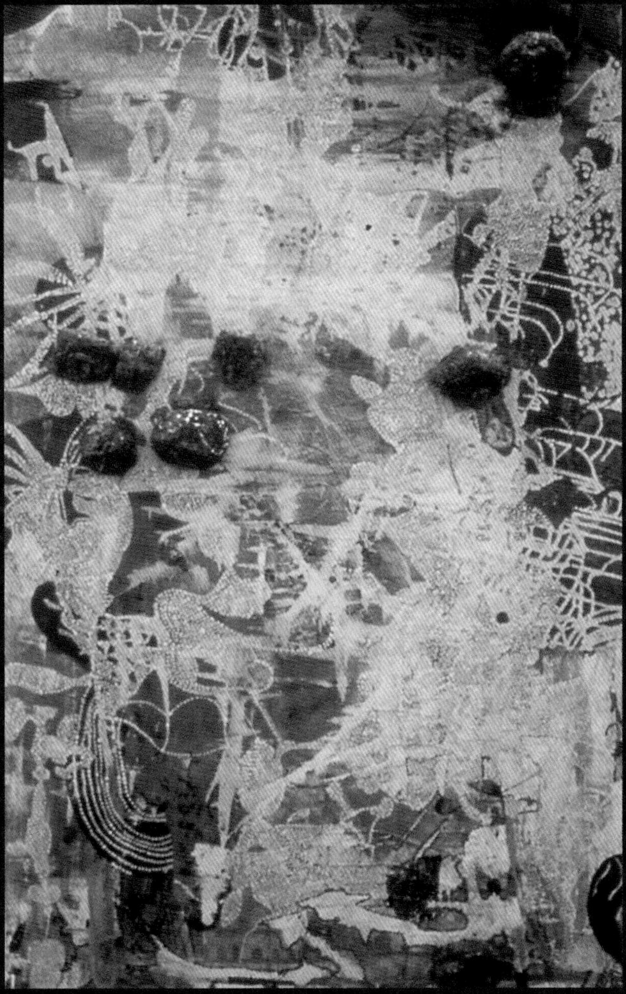

The Golden Age, *1993*

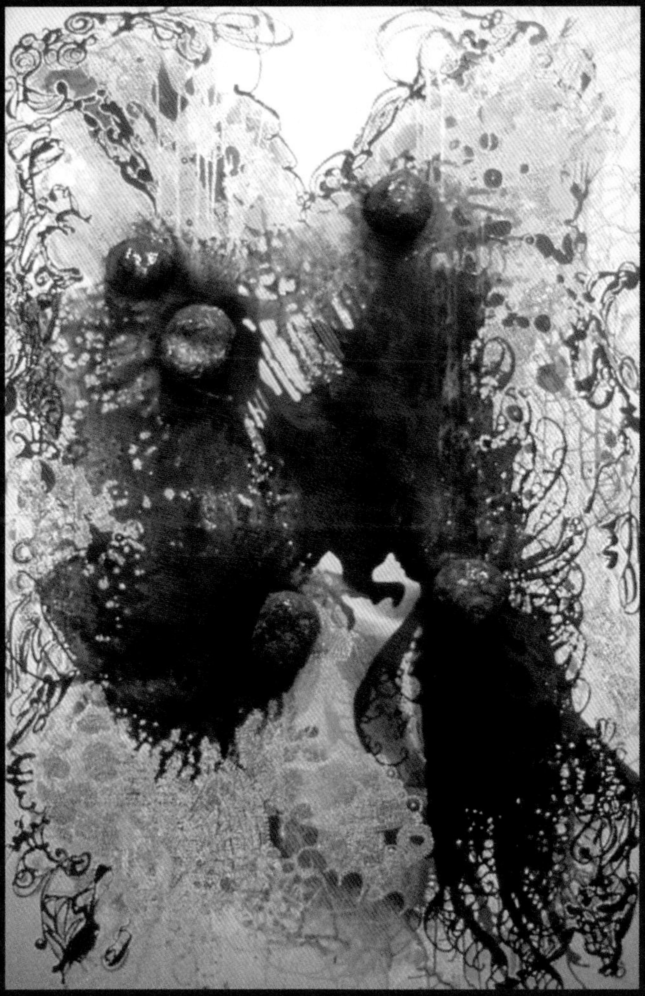

Mya, *1995*

Elephantastic, *1993*

One of Laura Owens's paintings from 1997 (all of her paintings are untitled) depicts what looks like a view down a big city street.

Against a sky-blue ground, tall glass buildings are rendered in schematic shorthand as mere vertical slats of blacks, blues, and beiges tapering in height and width, one behind the other, toward the bottom center of the canvas. It is an image you might encounter in a video game or, one might argue, it is the space between two stacks of monochromatic paintings. The first reading apparently liberates the work to refer beyond itself, to the culture at large—but so does, to a certain extent, the second.

The painting opens a visual path between monochromes; it literally stakes out a position just to the side of modernist painting's history. Rosalind Krauss once described this history as being "like a series of rooms en filade," in which "the effect of [the] pictorial act was to open simultaneously the door to the next space and close out access to the one behind."[1] An image of a long corridor is also featured in one of Owens's biggest works (Untitled, 1997), although her hallway leads not from one painting to the next but from one exhibition space to another, with only the edges of paintings visible through the doorway into each room. Here again the temporal succession Krauss evoked is spatialized, spread out into landscape, a scene.

LAURA OWENS

¶ As in the early *Untitled* (1995), included in this show, Owens often depicts the walls and floors around paintings, and she also likes to make canvases so big they fuse with the actual walls and floors of the space in which they're exhibited. As such, the work stresses its "situation"—one that "virtually by definition, includes the beholder," as Michael Fried famously wrote of Minimalist objects (another art that staked a position just to the side of modernist painting's history).[2]

The desire to exist just to the side of medium, history, discourse, etc. motivates much art today, and usually gets expressed in contradictory ways: either in a skeptical denial of discourse's power to transcend artworld contingencies, or in an attempt to transcend discourse itself in pursuit of the ineffable. Most often artworks try to do both simultaneously—to convey a hip shrug and appear deep.

Owens also juggles the contingent and its transfiguration, metonomy and metaphor, but not simply to hedge her bets. While she engages the literal space that frames painting, she does so not to gain a skeptical distance; there's too much inviting humor and sentiment at play in her work, and too much inviting illusionism as well, too many plunging views across floors and down corridors and streets.

Owens activates the real space in front of her work, the space of viewers and viewing, and ingests that space pictorially within the paintings themselves. She insists that her work's literal conditions be consequential (not apologize) for their figuration and vice versa (an insistence that aligns her practice with that of Felix Gonzalez-Torres and Lari Pittman).

Rather than coyly backpedal from painting, Owens's work is deeply concerned with the realities and possibilities of its reception.

Notes

1. Rosalind Krauss, "A View of Modernism," *Artforum* 11, no. 1 (September 1972): 49.
2. Michael Fried, "Art and Objecthood," *Artforum* 5, no. 10 (Summer 1967): 15.

Lane Relyea

Untitled, *1995*

Untitled, *1997*

Tsuyoshi Ozawa introduced a conceptual art radically different from the critical irony and materialism of Japanese New Pop.

In contrast to Takashi Murakami's predilection for anime, *a feature of mainstream Japanese popular culture, Ozawa's imagery frequently references 70s Japanese underground theater and comics, as well as the remains of landscapes scarred by systematic suburbanization. Ozawa's art is characterized by the subordination of object to act, the renunciation of creative control in favor of accidents and audience participation, and the reassertion of fragility and ephemerality as reminders of fortuity of human existence. These concerns can be observed in his early performative projects.*

¶ Nasubi Gallery, *first performed in 1993, modestly challenges the exclusively Japanese system of gallery rentals, where exhibition spaces are rented out to young and amateur artists. Ozawa invited his friends to install an "exhibition" in a small wooden box typically used to deliver milk, which he then showed on various streets in Tokyo. In* Sodan Art *(1989), Ozawa sought to transform his painting by incorporating the opinions of his audience, performing mock-university curriculum lessons at the Workshop of Art Tower Mito in 1995. As public art, both* Nasubi Gallery *and* Sodan Art *reflected the legacies of 60s Japanese conceptual art, particularly the Fluxus-like works of Genpei Akasegawa and Ushio Shinohara.*

¶ *In spite of the impact of* Nasubi Gallery *and* Sodan Art, *Ozawa's recognition as a forebear of lyrically suffused conceptual art is based on the emotionally evocative power of* Jizoing.

TSUYOSHI OZAWA

Between 1987 and 1992, Ozawa made drawings of jizo, the Japanese road deity, and installed them in various places throughout Asia. Jizoing is a series of photographs documenting these installations in which Ozawa's drawn effigies become traces of visits. For exhibition, they are hung above a mountainous pile of futons. Initially conceived as a prop for showing his photos, the futon installation is Ozawa's homage to a memorable scene in an underground comic by Yoshiharu Tsuge, as well as an evocation of childhood.

¶ Climbing up to view the Jizoing photos mounted high on the wall, the audience is disarmed as preconceptions about the critical discursivity of contemporary art fade away.The warmth and softness ofthe futons substitute for the maternal body and reflect the deeply private nature of Ozawa's encounter with Asia. However the images of jizo in such politically charged places as Tiananmen Square and the Korean border ominously convey inscrutable darkness, while the effigies indicate the paradoxical return of the artist's fragile human body to the landscape.

¶ In a second cycle of Jizoing, begun in 1996, the subject's private implications are accentuated. Twilight Jizoing consists of snapshots, taken at 6 P.M. every day wherever Ozawa found himself, accompanied by a drawing of jizo, each with the date attached. With this installation, the artist emphasizes his perception of art as part of the daily activity.

¶ Ozawa's humane conceptual work anticipated a pronounced return of emotion in Japanese contemporary art during the latter half of the 90s, while its relational potentialities and affirmation of banal details helped prepare for the late-90s world-wide reinstatement of the Fluxus spirit.

Midori Matsui

Twilight Jizoing ***(detail)*****, *1987–99***
Installation at Museum of Contemporary Art, Tokyo, 1999

Twilight Jizoing, *1987–99. Details and installation at Museum of Contemporary Art, Tokyo, 1999*

An independent Duchamp scholar, Rhonda Roland Shearer, has recently argued that the artist's readymades—the snow shovel, the coat rack he entitled Trébuchet, and others—were not mass-produced products straight off shop shelves, but intricately crafted duplicates, nearly identical save for a telling detail.

It's a strange and unconvincing theory for Marcel Duchamp in 1915 or 1917, but it seems to describe quite well the odd, doppelgänger objects of Jorge Pardo's first one-person show in 1990 at Thomas Solomon's Garage in Los Angeles. While it's probably not necessary to bring up Duchamp's name to talk about Jorge Pardo, it is interesting to think through the ways in which Pardo's remanufactured film splicer or paired baseball bats are not readymades—the rather specific ways in which Pardo gets Duchamp wrong.

¶ If the readymades were drawn directly from manufacturers' catalogues and shop windows, then what they signified was, in Thierry de Duve's words, "the abandonment of artisanal values in favor of industrial values, the substitution of an aesthetics of standardization for an aesthetics of the 'handcrafted.'"[1] Pardo's reconstructed ladder and his hand-milled, eight-foot long two-by-four of oiled African bubinga, on the other hand, clearly embrace the artisanal and the handcrafted, albeit oddly, as though the artisanal had been infected by the industrial culture that Duchamp's readymades were intended to acknowledge.

Pardo's choice of both materials and objects—a pallet and a router table join the ladder, boards, and planks—suggests a romance with the hardware store and lumberyard, but it does so differently. If Pardo's woods and oils and his involvement with them are drawn from the handicrafts, the objects he so carefully rebuilds, replacing standard woods—pine and fir—with oak and bubinga, beech and walnut, are taken from the same places as Duchamp's readymades. They are the manufactured objects of an industrial world.

JORGE PARDO

¶ Pardo's materials don't, in fact, refer back in time to the artisan of the Arts-and-Crafts movement or, before that, to preindustrial culture. Rather they point to contemporary design—Danish modern, perhaps—and to a clean, spare modernism that, if it borrows from the aesthetics of standardization and the values of industrialization, evades the factory's serial production. Quite unlike Duchamp's readymades, Pardo's work relies on taste. "The choice of these readymades was never dictated by esthetic delectation," Duchamp explained. "The choice was based on a reaction of visual indifference with at the same time a total absence of good or bad taste."[2] Pardo has, and maybe by now we all have, a certain nostalgia for taste, a taste not only for a now-old modernist design, but also for the insistent, out-of-category presence of the readymade.

Slowly and carefully replacing pieces of the industrial world with crafted pieces of a materially thicker and more peculiar one, Pardo marks the very small space left for the artisanal hand between the critical and deliberately de-skilled practice of art and the mass production and targeting of product design. His objects are figures for sensibility, the embedding of individual taste in industrial objects.

Notes

1. *Thierry de Duve,* Pictorial Nominalism: On Marcel Duchamp's Passage from Painting to the Readymade *(Minneapolis: University of Minnesota Press, 1991), 109.*

2. *Marcel Duchamp, "Apropos of 'Readymades,'" in Michel Sanouillet and Elmer Peterson, eds.,* Salt Seller: The Writings of Marcel Duchamp (Marchand du Sel) *(New York: Oxford University Press, 1973), 141.*

Howard Singerman

Installation at Thomas Solomon's Garage, Los Angeles, 1990

Ladder, *1989*

Pallate, ***1990***

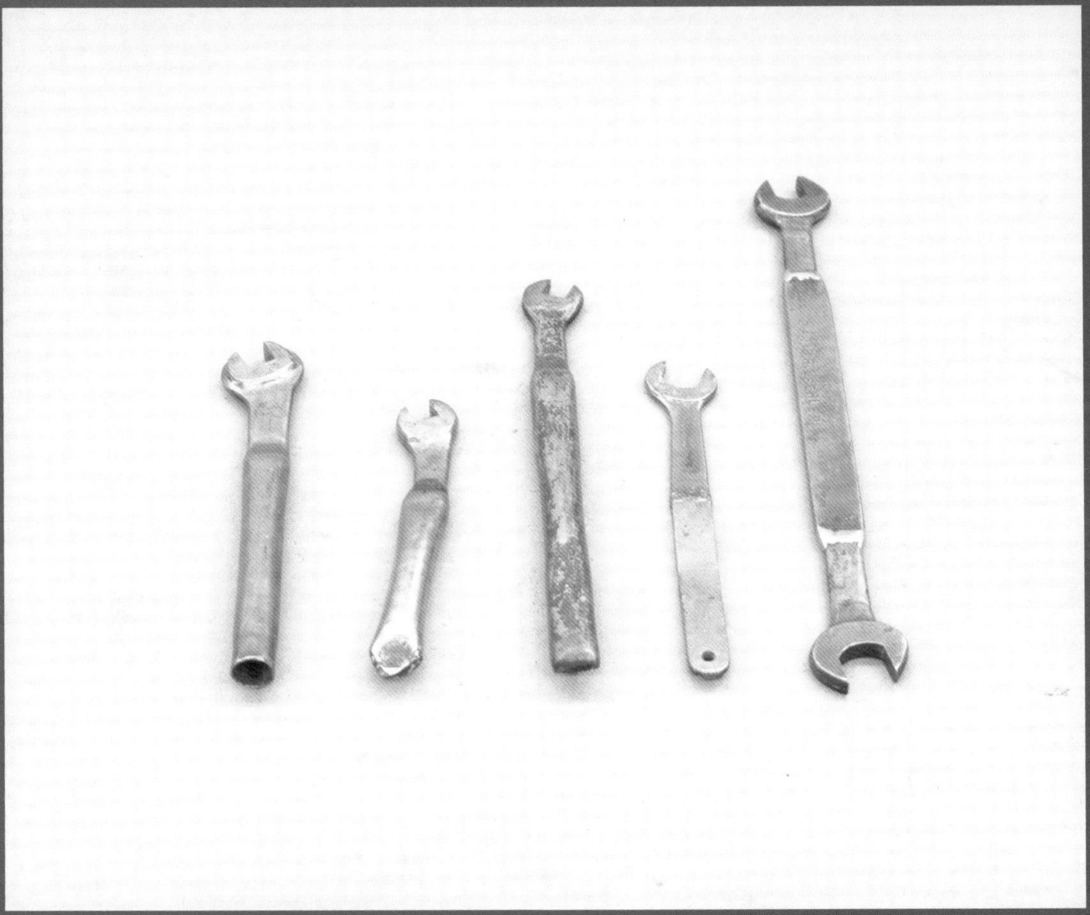

 Adjusted Wrenches, ***1990***

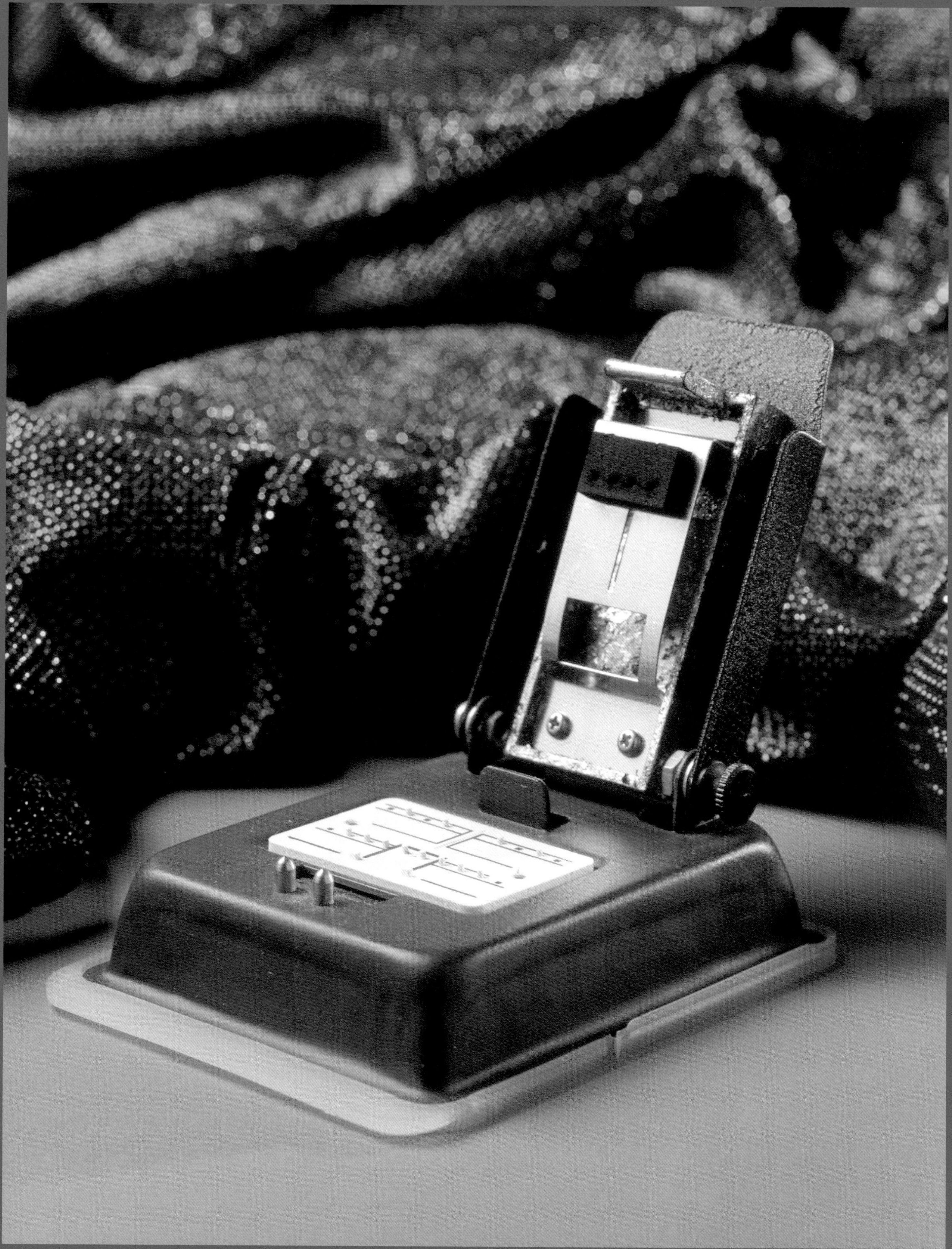

Splicer, ***1989***

When Manfred Pernice presented Sardinien *at Galerie NEU's booth at the European Art Forum in Berlin in 1996, it immediately got a lot of attention. The plywood construction took up the entire booth and left very little space for visitors. Its expanse and formal aspects gave the effect of both rejection and welcome. Even though the installation offered the viewer two visible sides with greatly differing structures, it let it be known that its interior was an area that could only be partially viewed—and that there was no entry.*

At the fair, Sardinien *seemed like a foreign body that compelled curious visitors to walk around it in the hopes of being able to enter the large hollow form or at least be able to look behind the façade.*

Walking along the outside of Sardinien, *one arrived at a small passage that, at first glance, suggested an entry to the fixture, but proved to be a dead end. This was not the only expectation that the construction masterfully circumvented.*

MANFRED PERNICE

¶ In view of many installations from the mid-90s that were interactive and designed for use (Tobias Rehberger's or Jorge Pardo's come to mind), Pernice's variation, reminiscent of a trailer, was frustrating because it seemed to deny direct access and be completely satisfied with itself. The surface of its plywood façade, partly untreated and partly painted white, seemed to ignore any demand for perfect craftsmanship.

Yet it constituted a subtly composed system of form and color in which curved and flat surfaces complemented each other in a balanced rhythm. Inside a small, eye-catching niche set into one wall stood a cup and a framed photograph of a landscape. The image suggested a holiday destination, not Sardinia specifically but somewhere in the Mediterranean with a view of mountains and a lake.

¶ Sardinien also attracted attention because Pernice, a relatively unknown artist, produced a work for the fair that was presumed unmarketable due to its size. However, one of Germany's most influential collectors of emerging artists' work reserved the piece, then a second collector bought it without hesitating despite the reservation. The question of why Sardinien created such a sensation can be answered in the context of the commercial fair and exhibition site; Pernice addressed the status of art as merchandise. He used the fair as a forum for his unwieldy installation and its implied associations with vacation—an alternative to a site connected to commerce and work.

¶ The installation's title, together with the framed landscape photograph, reinforce this association. In Sardinien Pernice sways between critical commentary on his own participation in the art fair and his absence while on vacation. In this context, vacation is a regenerative state—a set of spatial as well as temporal conditions ideally suited to the artist.

Yilmaz Dziewior

Sardinien, *1996*
Installation at European Art Forum, Berlin, 1996

132 Sardinien, *1996. Installation at European Art Forum, Berlin, 1996*

Jason Rhoades first attracted significant attention in the Los Angeles artworld while still a student at the University of California, Los Angeles (UCLA).

Works such as Jason the Mason and the Mason Dickson Linea *(1991) and his graduation show offering, the* Young Wight Grand Prix *(1993), announced the emergence of a talented and audacious artist. Rhoades began to show his work with Rosamund Felsen Gallery as early as 1992 (*Montgomery Ward Clinique Clinic*), and in 1994 he cemented his reputation with the installation of his largest and most ambitious project up to that time,* Swedish Erotica and Fiero Parts, *in Felsen's West Hollywood gallery.*

¶ Taking his cue from the gallery's distinctive yellow exterior, Rhoades filled the space with an array of crudely fabricated objects, most of them copies of Ikea furniture, most of them covered with yellow legal paper. The various components flowed into each other to compose a modular monochrome sculpture. A yellow Pontiac Fiero sports car was parked in the lot outside.

The chaotic assemblage overran the gallery, yet this apparent shambles came accompanied by extensive explanatory texts by the artist. Felsen was expected to read these to visitors who might be confused as they tried to follow the meandering path (modeled on the floorplan of an Ikea showroom) that wound through the space.

JASON RHOADES

¶ *The desire to fill any available space, no matter how large, has continued to be a hallmark of Rhoades's practice, most notably in his gigantic installation at the Deichtorhallen in Hamburg,* Perfect World *(1999). So too has his desire to explain the work, best expressed to date in the encyclopedia-like* Volume: A Rhoades Referenz *(1998). Almost all of Rhoades's work is surrounded by clouds of explanation from the artist. In conventional terms, however, these sincere attempts at explication tend to have the opposite effect, since Rhoades is committed to following whatever tangent crosses his mind at any given time. Such explanations explain nothing, but they are important nevertheless. They have the effect of extending the work into new realms. The mental process of explanation is thus directly related to the physical process of taking over space.*

¶ Swedish Erotica and Fiero Parts *was broken up and sold in units, most of which have been brought back together again for this exhibition. This pattern of disassembly and recombination has been a characteristic element of Rhoades's practice.* The Great See Battles of Wilhelm Schürmann, *for example, was first installed in 1994 spread out on and around a number of tables. In 1995 it was re-installed in the form of a ship, and then in 1997 the entire installation was shown packed up in a giant wooden container.*

For Rhoades this ongoing process is integral to his work. His exhibitions often include a workshop, as Swedish Erotica *did, and adjustments and additions to the work continue throughout the length of the show. After the exhibition is over, his fascination with archaeology and excavation result in a series of returns to the material, which will continue to be recycled in different contexts. No work by Jason Rhoades can ever be said to have reached an absolutely final stage.*

Russell Ferguson

Swedish Erotica and Fiero Parts, ***1994***
Installation at Rosamund Felsen Gallery, Los Angeles, 1994

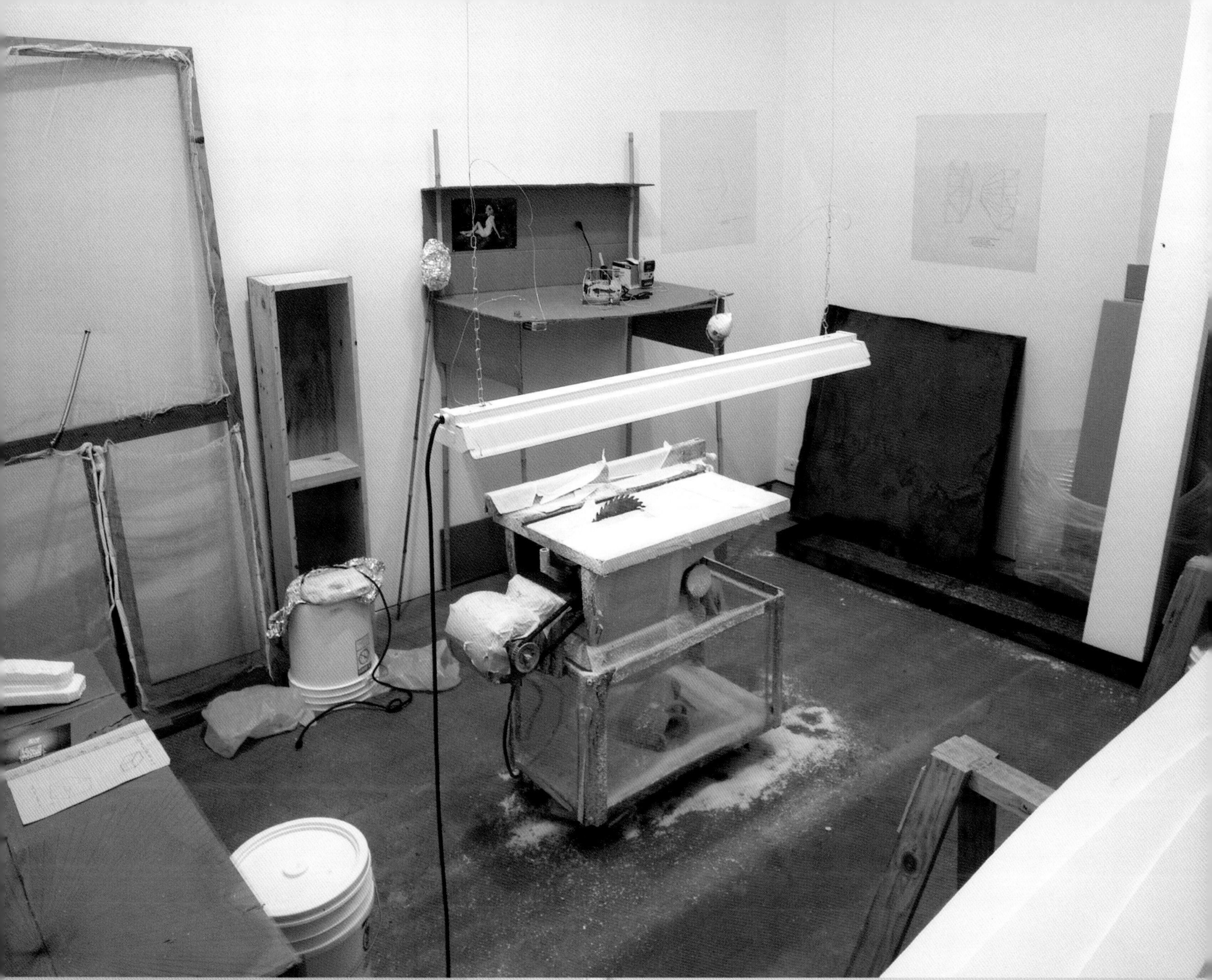

Swedish Erotica and Fiero Parts, ***1994***
Installation at Rosamund Felsen Gallery, Los Angeles, 1994

EX

Swedish Erotica and Fiero Parts, *1994*
Installation at Rosamund Felsen Gallery, Los Angeles, 1994

Ever since he emerged on the scene in 1993, Yutaka Sone has been noted for his highly individualistic style, indebted neither to the Japanese tradition of contemporary art nor to its vernacular pop culture.

Using banal objects and strenuous but comic performances, he has instead taken up late-modern Conceptualism's challenge to create metaphors for art's ability to regenerate itself.

In much the same way that Matthew Barney's eccentric vaseline artifact redefines the artist's desire for physical transcendence by transforming the meaning of exercise, Sone's work thematizes distance, with its necessary frustrations, as an intrinsic element of art. His audience enacts a process of connecting here and there, present and absent, through an installation that situates objects, performance, and ideas in multiple relationships. His objects are freestanding sculptures, but also function as performance props. Ultimately presented as the relics of a performance, frequently with video documentation, these objects evoke a larger narrative and philosophical content; the indeterminate details must be filled in by the audience.

¶ His debut work, Her 19th Foot *(1993), demonstrates Sone's central themes and the ongoing mechanism of his conceptual process. The eccentric sculpture becomes an occasion for transforming frustration into pleasure. Composed of nineteen modified unicycles chained together,* Her 19th Foot *stimulates the desire to ride, to set the work in motion, but technically it is extremely difficult to do; the weight of the riders, amplified by their own movements, functions as a constant burden. Deconstructing a familiar form through the negation of its use, the piece nonetheless offered an intense pleasure for both riders and audience during its initial performance at Art Tower Mito.*

YUTAKA SONE

The repeated failure to ride the unicycle-train—an expenditure of energy on a gratuitous act—turned the banal experience of riding a bicycle into pure play. Evoking an episode in Alfred Jarry's 1902 proto-surrealist novel* Le Surmâle, *in which a team of bachelors race against the Trans-Siberian Railway on chained bicycles,* Her 19th Foot *evokes the psycho-sexual dynamics underlying art—frustration fueling the desire for creation.

¶ The relation between distance and imagination introduced in Her 19th Foot *is explored in many of Sone's subsequent works, most notably in* Night Bus *(1995). For this "instruction" piece, Sone sent friends on a trip to Southeast Asia and to the West Coast of the United States to take video footage at night from the windows of buses while he remained in Tokyo, waiting to edit the results. The edited video is at once a trace of his imaginative attempt to reach across temporal and geographical distances and the substituted supplement to his own realized trip.*

This relationship between a complete blueprint and its modified execution suggests the influence of Sone's architectural training—particularly the idea of the architectural "unbuilt." Sone frequently conceives plans for nearly impossible acts or products, or puts objects to uses that challenge their conventionally set limits: take, for example, his plan for a camera with a 365-day-long exposure. Among the many discourses his elliptical expressions evoke, Sone's humorously ironic revelation of art's self-reflexivity seems most fundamental.

Midori Matsui

Her 19th Foot, 1993. Installation at Center for Contemporary Art, Art Tower Mito, Tokyo, 1993

146 **Her 19th Foot,** ***1993. Performance in Malmö, Sweden, 1995***

Diana Thater's work reconsiders and expands the medium of video and its possibilities for engaging pictorial, architectural, and temporal space, as well as interacting with the spectator. Thater's process of both inverting and merging interior and exterior space stems back to the early works that followed the completion of her M.F.A. at Art Center College of Design in Pasadena. The influence of Nam June Paik led her to "redirect [her]self toward space instead of the screen; real space indoors and outside the windows; other works of art instead of pitch black and memory, and interaction instead of presentation."[1]

¶ Thater's ongoing focus on landscape as a fusion of nature, culture, and technology was established in the 1992 works Oo Fifi, Five Days in Claude Monet's Garden, Part 1 *and* Oo Fifi, Five Days in Claude Monet's Garden, Part 2. Oo Fifi *was shot in five days, one per month, during a 1991 residency at the Musée Claude Monet in Giverny, France.*[2]

Named after the cat living at the museum, Oo Fifi *focuses on the flowers in Monet's famous gardens, which are used as the source for both versions of the work. Not unlike Monet's paintings of the gardens, the work is about "color and optics and light." Thater began with "light and the technology that produced it...consider[ing] it optically (technology), spatially (architecture-gels) and art historically (Claude Monet)."*

¶ The two parts of Oo Fifi *were first shown in successive exhibitions in the Los Angeles area during August and September of 1992. Both versions of the work use the same source tape/laserdisc, and are silent except for the sound of the equipment in operation. However,* Part 1 *is projected through a three-lens (red-green-blue) projector with the three lenses intentionally taken out of registration, whereas* Part 2 *"tries to put together what* Part 1 *took apart," using three of the same type of projector, each with only one of the respective lens/colors turned on.*[3]

DIANA THATER

Oo Fifi, Part 1 was shown at 1301 PE, Los Angeles, as part of "Into the Lapse," curated by Brian Butler and artist Jean Rasenberger. At 1301, *Part 1* was projected into a corner that included windows treated with neutral density gray gels that served to dim but not completely darken the space, allowing the projected images to overlay a legible interior architecture. The contrast between inside and out was further reduced by integrating the view of the garden outside the gallery window.

¶ Shortly after *Part 1* closed, *Oo Fifi, Part 2* opened at Shoshana Wayne Gallery in Santa Monica as part of the exhibition "VeryVeryVery." For *Part 2*, Thater increased the projection's scale and RGB (red-green-blue) gels on the windows to the street. Walking through the projections, the spectator passed through the beams of the projectors, at times blocking one of the three separated colors that were reconstituted on the wall.

¶ Within that group exhibition, *Oo Fifi, Part 2* was not shown in a separate space as would be expected for a video installation, but within the physical context of the other artists' works. Reflecting on the early decision to move out of the conventional video "black box," a move that still characterizes her work, Thater explained: "Now it could be in a space with other pieces, windows and walls (architecture could become part of it—so walls wouldn't just be screens but would be active in the work) and the work was open to inter-relationships with other works of art and to the architecture itself."

Notes

1. Letter from the artist, 3 October 2000. All further quotes are from this source.

2. 11 April; 30 May (videotaped by T. Kelly Mason); 26 June; 16 July; and 6 August 1991.

3. Thater acknowledges T. Kelly Mason, who shared the residency with Thater, for his influence on her ideas on color separation through the work he was doing while in Giverny.

Ann Goldstein

Oo Fifi, Five Days in Claude Monet's Garden, Part 1, ***1992***
Installation at 1301 PE, Los Angeles, 1992

Oo Fifi, Five Days in Claude Monet's Garden, Part 2, ***1992***
Installation at Shoshana Wayne Gallery, Santa Monica, California, 1992

Oo Fifi, Five Days in Claude Monet's Garden, Parts 1 & 2, ***1992***
Excerpt of accompanying text

Five days in Claude Monet's Garden**: 11 April, 30 May (videotaped by T. Kelly Mason), 26 June, 16 July, and 6 August 1991**

Acanthus (Acanthacees) S center
Acidanthena (Iridacees) *NW*
Age Vain (Danube Bleu) *SE corner*
Amarantoide (pour pre) *center*
Anacyclus (depressus) *S end*
Armeria (glorie de dusseldorf) *SE*
Arundinaria (Graminees) *SW*
Asclepias (Asciepiadacees) *S end*
Asperula (Odorata) *S end*
Astilbe (saxifragacees) *etang*

Berberis (Berberidacees) *center*

Catananche (Composees) (caerulea) *SE*
Celosie pl Hau (Forest Fire) *E end*
Centauree Barbeau (cyanus double bleu) *S*
Cercis (l egumineuse) *NW*
Chry Coronorarium (Double Hel) *N end*
Chry Paludosum (Blanc) *SW corner*
Cistus Cyprius *E*
Clematite (a grandes fleurs twilight) *W end*
Clematite (Mme. Lecoultre) *SE center*
Coreopsis (composees) *SW corner*
Coreopsis (Eleve Grand) *W center*
Cotinus (anacardiacees) *N*
Cotoneaster (rosacees) *W*
Cuphea (Ignea) *SE*

Dabocea (Scotica William buchanan) *etang*
Daboecia (cantabriac globosa pink) *etang*
Dahlia (Cactus M.E. Saweyer) *S end*
Dahlia (composees) (Pompon grenat) *W end*
Dahlia (composees) (promise) *N center*
Dahlia (pirouette) *S*
Dahlias (composee) *SW*
Del. Imperial (O Bleu-Spire) *NE center*
Delphinium (Renonculacees) (century) *SW*
Dianthus (caryophyllacees) (Barbatus) *SW*
Dianthus (caryophyllacees) (Newport Pink) *E center*
Digitalis (soraphulariacees) *E end*

Echinaceae (compositae) *W end*
Entourage *NW corner*

Forsythia (Oleacees) *S center*
Fuchsia (oenotheracees) magellanica *NE*

Gazania Mef (Daybreak) *NE*
Geranium (de bouture zonale) *SW center*
Geranium (Schone Helena) *N end*
Ginkgo Biloba *SW center*
Gladiolus (Classic) *SW*
Gladiolus (iridacees) *NE center*

Hemerocallis (liliacees) (Iron gate glacier) *NW*
Heracleum (ombelliferes) *SW end*
Huf Sonnet (Blanc) *SE*
Hydrangea (saxifragacees) *N end*

Impatiens (Accent Saumon) *W*
Impatiens (Balsaminacees) *etang*
Impatiens (Rose d Supertresor) *E end*
Iris (Iridacees) (Germanica Fifty Grand) *SW*
Iris (Iridacees) (Germanica Henry Shaw) *N*
Iris (Iridacees) (Germanica Son of Star) Iris *W*
(Iridacees) (germanica Brightside) *W*
Iris (Iridacees) (germanica Bristol Gem) *N*
Iris (Iridacees) (germanica Night Laughter) *S*

Iris (Iridacees) (germanica Sterling Silver) *N*
Iris (Iridacees) (germanicus Glistening Snow)*W*
Iris (Iridacees) (germanicus Golden Delight) *W end*
Iris (Iridacees) (Lilac Haze) *etang*
Iris (Iridacees) (Xiphion Hildegarde) *E*
Iris (iridacees) *NW corner*

Laratree (Lovliness) *etang*
Laratree (Mont Blanc) *SE*
Laratree (Silver cup) *NW corner*
Lathyrus (Legumineus) (Eleanor) *E end*
Liatris (composee) *SW end*
Lilium (Liliaceae) *etang*

Malope (Malvacees) *SW end*
Meconopsis (papaveracees) *etang*
Mirabilis (Nyctaginacees) *SW end*

Narcissus (Amaryllidaceea) (Gr. Coupes) *SW end*
Narcissus (Amaryllidaceea) (Scarlet Elegance) *E end*
Nerine (Amaryllydacees) *SW end*
Nigella (Renonculacees) (hispanica) *N*

Ornithogalum (Liliacae) *etang*
Ouillet Minde Jaune (cupidon) *E end*
Ouillet Minde Jaune (legion de honneur) *W*

Papaver (Catherina) *SW end*
Papaver (garden glory) *S end*
Papaver (lighthouse) *SE*
Papaver (papaveracee) (derwisch)
Papaver (papaveracee) (Grave. Witwe) *E end*
Papaver (papaveracee) (juliane) *SW end*
Papaver (papaveracee) (Suleika) *center*
Papaver (papaveracees) *NW corner*
Papaver (Rhoeas) *etang NW corner*
Passiflora (passifloraces) *SW end*
Pavot 4 Dislande (Gartenzwerg Melange) *W*
Petasites (composees) *W end*
Petu G.F.S. (Sprint Blue) *SW end*
Portlandrea (Souvenir de MacKinley) *W*
Portlandrea (Miranda) *NW corner*
Portlandrea (Rose de Roi) *center*

Rhododendron (ecicacees) *center*
Roi Madeleine (Bleu Fonce) *NW*
Rosa (Betty Herholdt Blanc) *etang*
Rosa (Ingrid Bergman) *NW corner*
Rosa (Messagerie) *SW end*
Rosa (PDT Leopola Senghor) *SW end*
Rosa (pink) *SW end*
Rosa (Robust Nirpaysage) *N*
Rosa (Rosacae) (Cent. Mucosa) *SW end*
Rosa (Rosacae) (Mistress Harkness) *SW end*
Rosa (Rosacae) (Mr. Loriol de Barny) *N*
Rosa (Rosacae) (Pink Cloud) *etang*
Rosa (Rosacae) Mm. Lucien Chaure) *E*
Rosa (rosacae) (Golden Showers) *SW end*
Rosa (Rosaceae) *E end*
Rosa (sissi) *E*
Rose I Eleve (Golden Jubilee) *SE*
Rose In Eleves (Orange Lady) *NE*
Rose Inde Eleves (Double Eagle) *etang*
Rosier (Nil Bleu) *SW end*
Rosier (White Dorothy Perkins) *SW end*
Rosier grimpant (Veilchenblau) *E end*
Rosier Tige (vent d'ete) *NW corner*
Rud O (marmalade) *SW end*

Salp:Glossis (Emperou SuperBissima) *N*
Salvia *NW corner*
Santolina (composees) *SW end*
Saponaire (caryophyllacees) *E*
Scabieuse Natur (Double Hel) *etang*
Staphylea (staphyleacees) *etang*
Statis Sinwata (Rose) *SW end*

Tabac Nicki (Rose Hi Fi) *SW end*
Tabac Nicki (Rouge Intense) *N*
Taxodium (Taxodiacees) *NW corner*
Tithonea (Torche) *NE*
Tulipa (Liliacees) *SW end*
Tulipa (Liliacees) (Per Black Parrot) *N*
Tulipa (liliacees) (Frangees Arma) *SW*
Tulipa (liliacees) (Princess Margreth) *center*
Tulipa (liliacees) (Trs. Aureola) *etang*

Verbascum (Scrophularacees) *SW end*
Verviene Naine (Etoile Bleue) *end*

Oo Fifi, Five Days in Claude Monet's Garden, Part 2 *(detail)*, 1992
Installation at Shoshana Wayne Gallery, Santa Monica, California, 1992

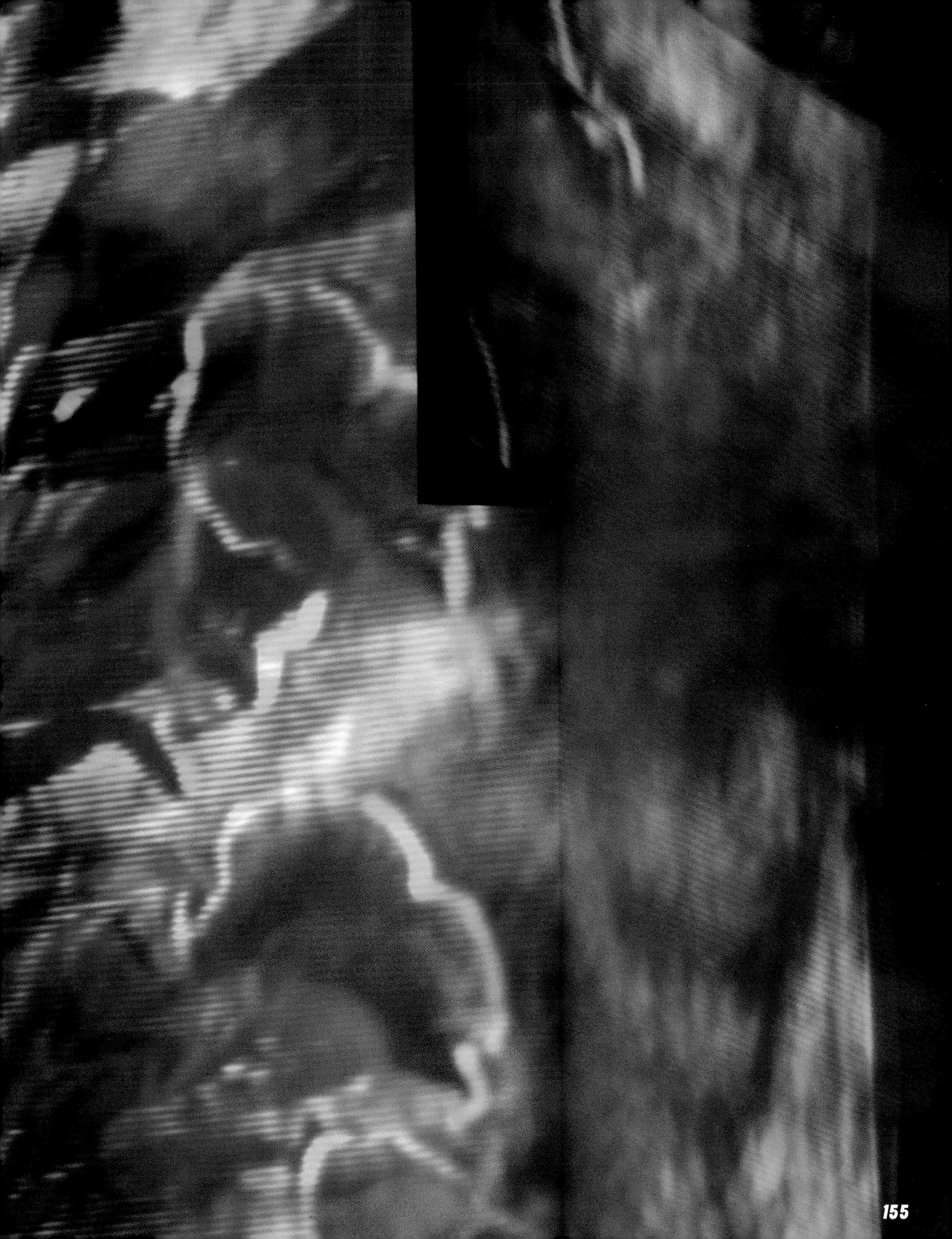

Transforming the semi-public spaces of art galleries and museums, normally reserved for the prescribed activities of art sales and aesthetic contemplation, into convivial places for informal gathering and socializing has become a trademark of Rirkrit Tiravanija's art practice. Through his many interactive performances and installations over the past decade, this artist of Thai descent has introduced cooking, eating, drinking, playing games, listening to music, reading, resting, and other ordinary pastimes into the austere context of modern art.

In doing so, Tiravanija has gently challenged the self-important hermeticism of art and its institutions. Through the assertion of activities associated with domesticity, in particular cooking, he has also provoked feminist issues concerning gendered labor and its function in the hierarchical separation of public and private.

¶ Pad Thai, presented at Paula Allen Gallery in New York in 1990, is a signal piece that helped to establish Tiravanija's artistic reputation. For the exhibition opening, the artist created a makeshift kitchen in the gallery to cook and serve visitors the Thai noodle dish of the title, effectively turning a standard gallery opening into a big dinner party. The used appliances, dishes, utensils, and discarded packaging of ingredients from the dinner/opening—some put into a large vitrine—remained on view throughout the duration of the show. But these objects were not conceived as works of art in themselves.

Rather, the exhibition, comprising a messy collection of material residue and detritus, served as a document or trace of the opening event, not unlike a photograph. The sharing of food and the social interactions that circumscribe, facilitate, and constitute that sharing became the artwork.

RIRKRIT TIRAVANIJA

¶ Tiravanija moved away from performing the role of chef/host of "exotic" Eastern cuisine in subsequent projects. Functioning more like an interior designer or architect in more recent years, he set up cafés in galleries in Cologne and Vienna and designed a lounge with game tables, sofas, and a refrigerator full of drinks for an exhibition in Dijon. He also presented scaled replicas of a two-story Swedish house inside the Rooseum in Malmö and of Philip Johnson's famous Glass House in the sculpture garden at The Museum of Modern Art in New York. His own East Village apartment was re-created full-scale, including kitchen, shower, and bath, for an exhibition at the Cologne Kunstverein in 1995.

¶ Projects such as these, fully functional as cafés, lounges, houses, and apartments, represent Tiravanija's shift from orchestrating events (around a meal) to creating physical environments. Both modes, however, provide a platform for the type of social situations that are, in their very ordinariness and banal pleasures, considered antithetical to an aesthetic experience. Picking up on different aspects of Tiravanija's practice—disinterest in making objects, emphasis on unorchestrated audience participation ("lots of people" is often listed as part of the medium for his work), and openness to chance—many critics have cited Marcel Duchamp and John Cage as important influences.

It is unclear though whether the stuff of everyday life is itself art in Tiravanija's view. But it is certain that his various stagings of the everyday within the context of high art throw into relief the very conventionality of both categories. Serving the audience and instigating their participation with free food, coffee, even shelter in certain instances, also foregrounds the changed role of the artist from object maker to provider of services and provisions. In Tiravanija's work art is not the assertion of an individual authorial voice but the provision of collective social experience.

Miwon Kwon

Dellwood
WOK
WOK

Pad Thai, ***1990. Performance at Paula Allen Gallery, New York, 1990***

160 Pad Thai, *1990. Performance at Paula Allen Gallery, New York, 1990*

Coca-Cola

***Rachel Whiteread's sculptures might be seen as the descendents of such American** postminimal works as Richard Serra's* **Castings** *(1969)—his hardened records of the act of casting molten lead at the intersection of the studio floor and the wall—or Bruce Nauman's fiberglass* **Platform Made Up of the Space between Two Rectilinear Boxes on the Floor** *(1966).*

What her sculptures share most obviously with these earlier works is casting, a rather traditional procedure but one that in the twentieth century is linked not to the constructivist mainstream of modernist sculpture—Naum Gabo and Vladimir Tatlin, David Smith and Anthony Caro, Tony Smith and Donald Judd—but to the alternative modernisms (and the not-quite sculpture) of Marcel Duchamp and Jasper Johns. **Unlike the constructed steel sculpture of Caro—the dean of British sculpture and an artist whom Whiteread and postminimalism in general can be read against—Whiteread's cast is necessarily doubled.**

This happens consistently and in a curious way—the way Nauman's titles make clear—referentially, even if only locally and indexically to the other of the mold. And unlike Tony Smith's black cube Die *(1962)—to which her black* Closet *(1988) makes implicit reference—Whiteread's casts, and Nauman's and Serra's, don't so much command or articulate space as mimic and mirror its boundaries. In Whiteread's case, in particular, they haunt it.*

RACHEL WHITEREAD

¶ At the same time Whiteread's sculptures are quite different from the casts of her predecessors. The space they describe is both more domestic and more public than either Serra's generic studio floor or Nauman's arbitrary constructions. The spaces she casts are recognizable, even familiar, and one might think of her castings as snapshots, negatives perhaps. They signify like photographs: they refer both to what they look like and what has caused them, iconic resemblance and indexical trace.

And as might be said of photographs—of snapshots of home, in particular—the real clings to them, held fast by the mechanics of their making. Or, one could say, their taking: for example *Flap* (1989), Whiteread's cast of the space beneath a dining-room table has refused to give up one of the table's wooden leaves.

¶ The space under a dining table or a fireplace mantel, the space inside a wardrobe, these are familiar, even homey, spaces. Dark and low to the ground, they are spaces that children inhabit, in which they hide. It is just there, inside the *heimlich*, in its concealed and enclosed spaces, and in their "coming to light," that Freud situated the experience of the uncanny. "The uncanny is nothing new or foreign, but something familiar and old—established in the mind that has been estranged.... An uncanny experience occurs... when repressed infantile complexes have been revived by some impression."[1] Ghostly presences whether or not they retain the plaster's white, Whiteread's doubled domestic interiors are at once perfectly visible and precisely estranged—and they are, of course, quite literally impressions.

Note

1. Sigmund Freud, "The Uncanny," *Studies in Parapsychology*, ed. Philip Rieff (New York: Collier Books, 1963), 47, 55.

Howard Singerman

Closet, *1988*

Mantle, *1988*

Untitled (Square Sink), *1990*

Cell, *1990*

The double estranges even the most comfortable objects; it renders them unfamiliar or, as Freud would have it, uncanny. In Jane and Louise Wilson's Normapaths (1995), the double comes naturally—the sisters are identical twins—but that doesn't make the work any less strange, any less haunted or marked. The work's title suggests a problem, a pathology of the normal; it echoes Freud's "psychopathology of everyday life."

¶ If they hear Baudelaire's insistence that the "artist can be an artist only on condition that he be double," or Rimbaud's "Je est un autre," Jane and Louise Wilson understand it as the norm. Since their concurrent, identical undergraduate thesis shows—Jane's at Newcastle Polytechnic, Louise's at Jordanstone College of Art in Dundee—they have played at and with the meaning and thickness of psychic otherness, staging it, like those first undergraduate shows, as theater. From the on-stage hypnosis of Hypnotic Suggestions 505 (1993) to the druggy, early 70s gothic of Crawl Space (1995) they have proffered the double in genre drag. For Normapaths they've picked a 60s television spy-thriller; the shiny black catsuits the twins and their stunt doubles wear as they jump and twist in slow motion in midair recall Diana Rigg in The Avengers. Like the catsuits and catwalks of the forebodingly empty industrial site in which Normapaths is filmed (a former brewery warehouse), the installation's double projection—an exaggeration of television's split screen—fits the period style.

But it belongs as well to the Wilsons' thematics of the everyday double. Sometimes a mirroring symmetry, at others a parallel space or shifted time, and still at others a continuous, if slightly off, lateral extension, it models the discontinuous relations between two identical things.

JANE AND LOUISE WILSON

¶ However well it mimics 60s television conventions, Normapaths is not plotted in any conventional sense. Rather, it is a montage of actions and locations that moves from the twisting, trampoline-launched figures to the darkened spaces of the factory stairwell, as those same figures fight with one another in mock karate style—on the open metal stairs—in a perfectly generic location.

The climax takes place in a flimsy kitchen set installed on the warehouse floor as the catsuited avengers chop their way through its polystyrene walls. These scenes belong to the genre; they owe it their appearance and style, but there are other scenes that seem to suggest a less banal and at least psychically stunt-free doubling. Between the opening jumps and the stairway fights, a single figure in flames strides across the work from one screen to another, swinging her burning handbag back and forth.

And when, in the wreck of the kitchen, the twins embrace in Normapaths' final scene, their coming together as one isn't any more natural, or less uncanny; indeed, there, in particular, the technological double is woven into the fabric of the biological one. Each caresses the other's face with feet—grown in the postproduction studio—where their hands should be.

Howard Singerman

172 *Stills from* Normapaths*, 1995. Installation at Chisenhale Gallery, London, 1995*

Still from Normapaths, 1995

Checklist of the exhibition

Janine Antoni

Gnaw, 1992
Three-part installation
Chocolate: 600 lbs. of chocolate gnawed by the artist
24 x 24 x 24 inches
Lard: 600 lbs. of lard gnawed by the artist
24 x 24 x 24 inches
Lipstick Display: Phenylethylamine; 27 heart-shaped packages made from chewed chocolate removed from chocolate cube; 130 lipsticks made with pigment, beeswax, and chewed lard removed from lard cube
19 x 5 x 80 inches
The Museum of Modern Art, New York
Mrs. John Hay Whitney Bequest Fund, 2000

Matthew Barney

REPRESSIA, 1991
Wrestling mat, pyrex, cast petroleum jelly and wax Olympic curl bar, socks, sternal retractor, skeet, salt water pearl, and petroleum jelly silicon gel pectoral form
168 x 216 x 150 inches
Collection Norman & Norah Stone, San Francisco
Courtesy Thea Westreich, Art Advisory Services, New York

Transexualis, 1991
Walk-in cooler, formed and cast petroleum jelly decline bench, human chrionic gonadotropin, and silicon gel pectoral form
144 x 168 x 102 inches
Videoactions: MILE HIGH Threshold: FLIGHT with the ANAL SADISTIC WARRIOR, 1991, and DELAY OF GAME, 1991
San Francisco Museum of Modern Art
Accessions Committee Fund, gift of Collectors Forum, Byron R. Meyer, Norman and Norah Stone, and Mr. and Mrs. Brooks Walker, Jr.

Thomas Demand

Fabrik (Mit Namen), 1994
C-print on photographic paper and Diasec
49 x 70 3/4 inches
Courtesy Victoria Miro Gallery, London, and 303 Gallery, New York

Sprungturm (Diving Platform), 1994
C-print on photographic paper and Diasec
42 x 46 1/2 inches
Andrew Silewicz, London

Archiv (Archive), 1995
C-print on photographic paper and Diasec
72 1/4 x 90 1/2 inches
The Saatchi Gallery, London

Flur (Corridor), 1995
C-print on photographic paper and Diasec
72 1/4 x 106 1/4 inches
The Saatchi Gallery, London

Treppenhaus (Staircase), 1995
C-print on photographic paper and Diasec
59 x 46 1/2 inches
Courtesy Victoria Miro Gallery, London, and 303 Gallery, New York

Ecke (Corner), 1996
C-print on photographic paper and Diasec
57 x 79 inches
Collection Michael and Judy Ovitz, Los Angeles

Renée Green

Import/Export Funk Office, 1992–93
Dimensions variable
The Museum of Contemporary Art, Los Angeles
Gift of Gabi and Wilhelm Schürmann

Michael Joaquín Grey

Burn (Orb) (Captured Heat), 1988
Photograph
9 3/4 x 7 3/4 inches
The Museum of Contemporary Art, Los Angeles
Gift of Thea Westreich and Ethan Wagner

Cast River, 1988
Photograph
9 3/4 x 7 3/4 inches (15 x 13 inches framed)
The Museum of Contemporary Art, Los Angeles
Gift of Thea Westreich and Ethan Wagner

The Drip, 1988
Hydrocal agar and marble dust
3 1/2 x 9 x 4 1/2 inches
Courtesy of the artist

L-River, 1989
Lacquered and galvanized steel, pump, and ballast
9 1/2 x 63 x 8 1/4 inches
Courtesy of the artist

Artificial Muscle Contraction, 1990
Video Actin Myosin
Courtesy of the artist

Electron M. (Microscope), 1990
Plasticine, steel, aluminum, and electron microscope
84 x 48 x 36 inches (steel base 34 x 30 x 51 1/2 inches)
Courtesy of the artist

Erosion Blocks: Units of Growth/Decay, 1990
Twenty pewter blocks
Overall dimensions variable
Collection of Markus Baenziger

Gametes (Sex Cells) [artificial life animation-neural network], 1990
Three sets of gametes, 3-D laser modeling, computer-aided design, stereo lithography, and laser-cured resin
4 x 6 x 1 inches
Private collection

Low Density Silicon Airgel (Solid Smoke), 1990
Low density silicon airgel
2 x 9 1/4 x 2 1/2 inches
Courtesy of the artist

My Sputnik, 1990
Aluminum, titanium steel, kevlar, and velvet
71 x 138 x 103 inches
Courtesy of the artist

Orange Between Orange, 1990
Photograph
16 x 14 inches
Collection Norman & Norah Stone, San Francisco
Courtesy Thea Westreich, Art Advisor Services, New York

Stool + Preposition, 1990
Cast-aluminum stool, orange bronze, and lead patina
8 x 13 1/2 x 7 inches
Clarissa Dalrymple, New York

Untitled (Captured Light), 1990
Ektacolor print
8 x 10 inches (13 x 15 inches framed)
The Museum of Contemporary Art, Los Angeles
Gift of Thea Westreich and Ethan Wagner

Damien Hirst

In & Out of Love, 1991
Eight paintings: household paint on canvas with butterflies
60 x 60 inches each
Four boxes
36 x 36 x 36 inches each
One table: formica top on steel base
42 x 84 x 36 inches
Four ashtrays: glass ashtrays filled with cigarette butts
Installation area: 96 x 480 x 240 inches
Collection Yale Center For British Art
Paul Mellon Fund

Gary Hume

Four Subtle Doors I, 1989/90
Household paint on canvas
94 x 234 inches
Helly Nahmad Gallery, London

Magnolia Door XI, 1989
Household paint on canvas
98 3/4 x 63 inches
Helly Nahmad Gallery, London

Magnolia Door XXIV, 1989/90
Household paint on canvas
100 x 64 inches
Courtesy Matthew Marks Gallery

Magnolia Door XXVI, 1989/90
Household paint on canvas
100 x 64 inches
Courtesy Matthew Marks Gallery

Toba Khedoori

Untitled (Train), 1993
Oil and wax on paper
132 x 240 inches
The Museum of Contemporary Art, Los Angeles
Purchased with funds provided by Clyde and Karen Beswick

Untitled (Windows), 1994
Oil and wax on paper
132 x 240 inches
Courtesy Jeffrey Deitch

Untitled (House), 1995
Oil and wax on paper
132 x 192 inches
Courtesy Sammlung Hauser und Wirth, St. Gallen, Switzerland

Untitled (Chain Link Fence), 1996
Oil and wax on paper
136 x 232 inches
Private collection, Germany
Courtesy David Zwirner Gallery, New York

Sharon Lockhart

Khalil, Shaun, A Woman Under the Influence, 1993
Director: Sharon Lockhart
16-mm color film
16 minutes
Courtesy of the artist and Blum & Poe, Santa Monica, California

Shaun, 1993
Framed C-prints, set of 5
14 x 10 inches each
Collection of Rachel & Jean-Pierre Lehmann

Audition One: Simone and Max, 1994
Framed C-print
49 x 61 inches
The Museum of Contemporary Art, Los Angeles
Purchased with funds provided by The Acquisition and Collection Committee

Audition Two: Darija and Daniel, 1994
Framed C-print
49 x 61 inches
The Museum of Contemporary Art, Los Angeles
Purchased with funds provided by The Acquisition and Collection Committee

Audition Three: Amalia and Kirk, 1994
Framed C-print
49 x 61 inches
The Museum of Contemporary Art, Los Angeles
Purchased with funds provided by The Acquisition and Collection Committee

Audition Four: Kathleen and Max, 1994
Framed C-print
49 x 61 inches
The Museum of Contemporary Art, Los Angeles
Purchased with funds provided by The Acquisition and Collection Committee

Audition Five: Sirushi and Victor, 1994
Framed C-print
49 x 61 inches
The Museum of Contemporary Art, Los Angeles
Purchased with funds provided by The Acquisition and Collection Committee

Sarah Lucas

Eating a Banana, 1990
Black-and-white photograph
29 1/2 x 32 1/4 inches
Courtesy Barbara Gladstone

28 Percent Bent, 1991
Letraset on paper
7 1/4 x 8 7/8 inches
Private collection
Courtesy Karsten Schubert, London

Divine, 1991
Photo and collage
32 x 36 1/4 inches
Collection Cerith Wyn-Evans, London

Figleaf in the Ointment, 1991
Plaster and human hair
Dimensions variable
The Saatchi Gallery, London

Mussolini Morning, 1991
Wire, ceramic vase, and C-prints on cards
23 x 16 x 16 inches
Sadie Coles HQ, London

The Receptacle of Lurid Things, 1991
Wax cast of the artist's finger
The Saatchi Gallery, London

1-123-123-12-12, 1992
Dr. Martens boots size 7 and razor blades
The Saatchi Gallery, London

The Old Couple, 1992
Two wood chairs, wax, and commercial false teeth
Dimensions variable
Collection Norman & Norah Stone, San Francisco
Courtesy Thea Westreich, Art Advisory Services, New York

Two Fried Eggs and a Kebab, 1992
Two fried eggs, photograph, kebab, and table
30 x 60 x 35 inches
The Saatchi Gallery, London

Steve McQueen

Bear, 1993
16-mm film
Courtesy Marian Goodman Gallery, New York

Takashi Murakami

Sea Breeze, 1992
Steel, stainless steel, shutters, mercury lamps, wheels, fans, and flashing lamp
138 x 189 x 98 inches
Collection Contemporary Art Museum, Kanazawa

Yoshitomo Nara

Cup Kids, 1995
Fiberglass, resin, wood, and lacquer paint
36 x 36 x 36 inches each
Collection of Ruth & Jake Bloom

Chris Ofili

Elephantastic, 1993
Oil paint, polyester resin, acrylic paint, and elephant dung on canvas
72 x 48 inches
Collection of Michael Lynne

The Golden Age, 1993
Oil paint, polyester resin, acrylic paint, and elephant dung on canvas
72 x 48 inches
Courtesy of the artist and Victoria Miro Gallery, London

Open, 1993
Oil paint, polyester resin, acrylic paint, and elephant dung on canvas
72 x 48 inches
Courtesy Peter Doig, London

Painting with Shit on it, 1993
Mixed media
72 x 48 inches
The British Council

Shithead, 1993
Dung ball, copper wire, and hair
10 x 8 x 8 inches
Collection of Marjory Jacobson

Shithead, 1993
Dung ball, Toma's teeth, and Chris's hair
10 x 8 x 8 inches
Courtesy of the artist and Victoria Miro Gallery, London

Harvest, 1994
Carton, paper, elephant dung, marker, watercolor, and pencil
5 1/4 x 4 1/4 x 3/4 inches
Courtesy Gavin Brown's enterprise, New York

Mya, 1995
Oil paint, polyester resin, acrylic paint, and elephant dung on canvas
72 x 48 inches
Susan & Michael Hort

Popcorn, 1995
Mixed media
72 x 48 inches
Private collection

Laura Owens

Untitled, 1994
Oil and acrylic on canvas
120 x 96 inches
Whitney Museum of American Art; Promised gift of Norman Dubrow

Untitled, 1995
Oil, acrylic, enamel, marker, ink, and colored pencil on canvas
72 1/4 x 84 1/4 inches
Collection of the artist

Untitled, 1995
Acrylic on canvas
72 x 60 inches
Collection of Jon Weaver

Untitled, 1996
Acrylic on canvas
120 x 96 inches
Courtesy of Claudio Guenzani, Milan

Untitled, 1997
Acrylic, oil, and modeling paste on canvas
96 x 120 inches
Private collection
Courtesy Thea Westreich, Art Advisory Services, New York

Tsuyoshi Ozawa

Twilight Jizoing, 1987–99
Futons, fluorescent lamps, and twenty-eight photographs
120 1/2 x 283 1/2 x 181 1/4 inches
Collection of the artist
Courtesy of Ota Fine Arts, Tokyo

Jorge Pardo

2 x 4, 1989
Bubinga wood and Danish oil
96 x 3 1/2 x 11 1/2 inches
Courtesy of Gil B. Friesen

Baseball Bats, 1989
Louisville Slugger, shop plywood, pine wood, cedar wood, mahogany wood, lacquer, and Danish oils
32 x 7 x 3 1/2 inches
Private collection, Los Angeles

Ladder, 1989
Fir wood, bubinga wood, redwood, veneered particleboard, dark Creosote bolts, and Danish oil
45 x 14 x 19 inches
Collection of Eileen and Peter Norton, Santa Monica, California

Shop Plywood, 1989
Birch plywood, oil ash burl veneer, oil paint, and Danish oil
96 x 17 x 16 inches
Private collection

Splicer, 1989
Metal, lacquer, and crinkle finish
3 1/2 x 3 1/2 x 5 1/2 inches
From the collection of Daniel Melnick

Adjusted Wrenches, 1990
Steel
5 parts: 19 x 1 1/4; 11 3/4 x 2 1/8; 14 3/8 x 1 5/8; 11 1/8 x 15/16; and 9 3/4 x 1 1/2 inches
Thomas Borgmann—Cologne

Pallate, 1990
Oak wood, sixteen penny nails, and Danish oil
40 x 27 1/4 x 5 inches
Collection Thomas Solomon

Prototype, 1990
Aluminum, bubinga wood, redwood, Plastikot Fleckstone, multi-hue texture spray, chrome-plated brass fitting, and plastic
12 x 9 x 4 inches
Collection of Eileen and Peter Norton, Santa Monica, California

Ultimate Router Table, 1990
Birch plywood, clear maple wood, poplar wood, pine wood, fir wood, bubinga wood, strand-oriented cedar board, Blum hinges, white plexiglass, oil finish, nutricellulose lacquer, water-base lacquer, and Danish oil
35 1/2 x 24 x 17 1/2 inches
Bunny and Jay Wasserman, Los Angeles

Manfred Pernice

Sardinien, 1996
Mixed media
79 7/8 x 256 x 177 inches
Collection Lohaus—De Decker, Antwerp

Jason Rhoades

Swedish Erotica and Fiero Parts, 1994
Mixed media
Dimensions variable
Courtesy of the artist and Falckenberg Collection; Galerie Hauser und Wirth, Zurich; Los Angeles County Museum of Art, purchased with funds provided by the Sadoff Collection, Beverly Hills; Collection of Gary and Tracy Mezzatesta; The Museum of Contemporary Art, Los Angeles, gift of Pablo M. Lawner; The Museum of Contemporary Art, Los Angeles, gift of Herbert and Lenore Schorr; The Museum of Contemporary Art, Los Angeles, purchased with funds provided by Councilman Joel Wachs; Collection of Lari Pittman and Roy Dowell; Clayton Press & Gregory Linn, Philadelphia; Private collection, New York; Private collection, courtesy Thea Westreich, Art Advisory Services, New York; Private collection, Sammlung Hauser und Wirth, St. Gallen, Switzerland; Whitney Museum of American Art, gift of Thea Westreich and Ethan Jay Wagner; Collection of Lorrin and Deane Wong Family Trust; and David Zwirner, New York

Yutaka Sone

Her 19th Foot, 1993
Nineteen connected bicycles and video
35 1/2 x 15 3/4 x 39 1/3 inches
Courtesy of Contemporary Art Center, Art Tower Mito

Diana Thater

Oo Fifi, Five Days in Claude Monet's Garden, Part 1, 1992
Video installation
Dimensions variable
Collection Brian D. Butler, Santa Monica, California

Oo Fifi, Five Days in Claude Monet's Garden, Part 2, 1992
Video installation
Dimensions variable
David Zwirner, New York

Rirkrit Tiravanija

Pad Thai, 1990
Mixed media
Dimensions variable
Private collection, Turin

Rachel Whiteread

Closet, 1988
Wood, felt, and plaster
63 x 34 5/8 x 15 3/8 inches
Courtesy of the artist

Mantle, 1988
Plaster and glass
24 x 47 1/4 x 20 7/8 inches
Courtesy of the artist

Flap, 1989
Plaster and wood
29 1/2 x 36 x 28 3/4 inches
Collection of Tony and Gail Ganz

Cell, 1990
Plaster
49 x 49 1/2 x 29 inches
Collection of Tony and Gail Ganz

Untitled (Square Sink), 1990
Plaster
42 1/2 x 40 1/4 x 34 inches
Collection of Tony and Gail Ganz

Jane and Louise Wilson

Normapaths, 1995
16-mm film
Dimensions variable
Courtesy Lisson Gallery, London

Artist Biographies

Janine Antoni

Janine Antoni was born in 1964 in Freeport, Bahamas, and received her M.F.A. from the Rhode Island School of Design in 1989. She had her first solo exhibition, entitled "Gnaw," in 1992 at Sandra Gering Gallery, New York; the following year she was chosen to exhibit in the Whitney Biennial and in the Aperto section of the Venice Biennale.

She has performed and shown her installations around the world in major group exhibitions including "Post Human," FAE Musée d'Art Contemporain, Lausanne (1992); "The Spine," De Appel, Amsterdam (1994); "Bad Girls," New Museum of Contemporary Art, New York (1994); "Young Americans," Saatchi Gallery, London (1996); and "NowHere," Louisiana Museum of Modern Art, Humlebaek, Denmark (1996).

Her solo exhibitions include "Slumber," Anthony d'Offay Gallery, London (1994); "Slip of the Tongue," Centre for Contemporary Arts, Glasgow (1995); "IMMA/Glen Dimplex Award Exhibition," Irish Museum of Modern Art, Dublin (1996); and "Swoon," Whitney Museum of American Art, New York (1998).

Janine Antoni lives and works in New York.

Selected Further Reading

Cottingham, Laura. "Janine Antoni: Biting Sums Up My Relationship to Art History." *Flash Art* 26, no. 171 (Summer 1993): 104–05.
Danto, Arthur C. "The 1993 Whitney Biennial." *The Nation* (19 April 1993).
Hall, James. *The Guardian*, 5 March 1994.
Horodner, Stuart. "Janine Antoni." *Bomb Magazine*, no. 66 (Winter 1999): 48–54.
Kandel, Susan. "The Binge Purge Syndrome." *Art Issues*, no. 28 (May/June 1993): 19–22.
Nesbitt, Lois E. "Janine Antoni at Sandra Gering Gallery." *Artforum* 30, no. 10 (Summer 1992): 112–13.
Ostrow, Saul, and Andrew Renton. "Spotlight: Janine Antoni." *Flash Art* 27, no. 177 (Summer 1994): 119.
Rathbone, Tina. "Janine Antoni." *Poliester* 2, no. 7 (Autumn 1993): 52–55.
Smith, Roberta. "Women Artists Engage the Enemy." *The New York Times*, 16 August 1992.
Taylor, Simon. "Janine Antoni at Sandra Gering." *Art in America* 80, no. 10 (October 1992): 149.

Matthew Barney

Matthew Barney was born in San Francisco in 1967 and attended Yale University, where he received his B.A. in 1989. In 1990 his work was included in "Viral Infection: The Body and its Discontents" at the Hallwalls Contemporary Arts Center, Buffalo, New York. In 1991 he was given solo shows at Barbara Gladstone in New York and Stuart Regen Gallery in Los Angeles. His work has been featured in numerous international exhibitions such as "Post Human," FAE Musée d'Art Contemporain, Lausanne (1992); Documenta IX, Kassel, Germany (1992); the Aperto section of the 1993 Venice Biennale; both the 1993 and 1995 Whitney Biennials; the Tenth Biennale of Sydney (1996); the 1997 Lyon Biennale; and the 1999/2000 Carnegie International, Pittsburgh.

Barney's solo exhibitions include "Field Dressing," Payne Whitney Athletic Complex, Yale University, New Haven (1989); "Matthew Barney: New Work," San Francisco Museum of Modern Art, San Francisco (1991); Tate Gallery, London (1995); "Matthew Barney: Cremaster 1," Kunsthalle, Vienna (1997); and "Cremaster 2: The Drones Exposition" at the Walker Art Center, Minneapolis (1999). In 1993 he was given the Europa 2000 Prize at the XLV Venice Biennale and received the Hugo Boss Prize in 1996.

Matthew Barney lives and works in New York.

Selected Further Reading

Bryson, Norman. "Matthew Barney's Gonadotrophic Cavalcade." *Parkett*, no. 45 (1995): 28–35.
Flood, Richard. "Rosebud, Anyone?" *Frieze*, no. 9 (March 1993): 35–36.
Johnson, Ken. "Matthew Barney at Barbara Gladstone." *Art in America* 80, no. 1 (January 1992): 113–14.
Madoff, Steven Henry. "Hallucinatory Acts." *Time* (30 August 1999).
O'Brien, Glenn. "Dividing the Sheep from the Goats." *Artforum* 31, no. 9 (May 1993): 8.
Pagel, David. "Notes Toward Art's Backside." *Shift 15* 7, no. 1 (1993): 16–23.
Relyea, Lane. "Openings: Matthew Barney." *Artforum* 30, no. 1 (September 1991): 124.
Saltz, Jerry. "The Next Sex." *Art in America* 84, no. 10 (October 1996): 82–91.
Siegel, Katy. "Nurture Boy: Matthew Barney's *Cremaster 2*." *Artforum* 37, no. 10 (Summer 1999): 132–35.
Sladen, Marc. "Assault Course: Marc Sladen Tackles Matthew Barney Head On." *Art Monthly*, no. 187 (June 1995): 8.
Vogel, Carol. "Bicoastal Ownership." *The New York Times*, 5 May 2000.
Wakefield, Neville. "Matthew Barney's Fornication with the Fabric of Space." *Parkett*, no. 39 (March 1994): 118–24.

Thomas Demand

Born in Munich in 1964, Thomas Demand studied at the Akademie der bildenden Künste, the Kunstakademie Düsseldorf, and Goldsmiths College in London, where he received his M.F.A. in 1994. His photographs of almost life-sized cardboard models have been exhibited widely in such early group shows as "Het Intelectuele Geweeten van de Kunst," Galerie D'Eendt, Amsterdam (1993); "Temples," Victoria Miro Gallery, London (1995); "Passions Prospect 96," Kunstverein Frankfurt, Frankfurt (1996); and "New Photography 12," The Museum of Modern Art, New York (1996). More recently, he participated in the 1999/2000 Carnegie International, Pittsburgh, and "The Mirror's Edge," which originated at the BildMuseet in Umeå, Sweden.

Demand's solo exhibitions include those at Förderkoje Art Cologne, Cologne (1992); Galerie Tanit, Cologne (1994); Galerie Guy Ledune, Brussels (1995); Victoria Miro Gallery, London (1995); Max Protetch Gallery, New York (1996); "Tunnel, Art Now 17," at the Tate Gallery in London (1999); and a recent exhibition at the Fondation Cartier Pour l'Art Contemporain, Paris (2000).

Thomas Demand lives and works in Berlin.

Selected Further Reading

Bonami, Francesco. "Thomas Demand at Max Protetch." *Flash Art* 29, no. 191 (November/December 1996): 106.

Enwezor, Okwui. "Spiral Village at Bonnefanten Museum, Maastricht." *Frieze*, no. 34 (May 1997): 82–83.

Grant, Simon. "Thomas Demand." *Art Monthly*, no. 184 (March 1995): 23.

Hoffmann, Justin. "Thomas Demand at Galerie Tanit." *Artforum* 31, no. 8 (April 1993): 107–08.

Levi Strauss, David. "Thomas Demand at Max Protetch." *Artforum* 35, no. 5 (January 1997): 83.

Morgan, Stuart. "Thomas Demand at Victoria Miro Gallery, London." *Frieze*, no. 23 (Summer 1995): 70–71.

Muniz, Vik, and Thomas Demand. "A Notion of Space, a Conversation." *Blind Spot*, no. 8 (1996).

Schjeldahl, Peter. "Real Again." *The Village Voice*, 14 January 1997, 85.

Schumacher, Rainald. "Thomas Demand at Tanit." *Flash Art* 27, no. 176 (May/June 1994): 118.

Smith, Roberta. "Around the World, Life and Artifice." *The New York Times*, 8 November 1996.

Renée Green

Renée Green was born in 1959 in Cleveland and graduated from the Whitney Independent Study Program in 1990. Subsequently, her work was featured in several major groups shows including "SITEseeing: Travel and Tourism in Contemporary Art," Whitney Museum of American Art, New York (1991); "New Generations: New York," Carnegie Mellon Art Gallery, Pittsburgh (1991); "Inheritance," Los Angeles Contemporary Exhibitions (1992); and "True Stories," Institute of Contemporary Arts, London (1992).

In 1993 she participated the Biennial Exhibition at the Whitney Museum of American Art, New York, and in the Aperto exhibition at the Venice Biennale. That same year she was awarded a DAAD Scholarship in Berlin, where she worked in residence until 1994.

Among her solo exhibitions are "Anatomies of Escape," The Clocktower Gallery, New York (1990); "World Tour: Souvenirs," Pat Hearn Gallery, New York (1992); "Import/Export Funk Office," Galerie Christian Nagel, Cologne (1992), and later at the Kunstraum, Universität Lüneburg, Germany (1997); and "World Tour," The Museum of Contemporary Art, Los Angeles (1993).

Renée Green lives and works in New York and Vienna.

Selected Further Reading

Brenson, Michael. "Renée Green–Anatomies of Escape." *The New York Times*, 25 May 1990.

Decter, Joshua. "Renée Green at Pat Hearn Gallery." *Artforum* 33, no. 1 (September 1994): 105–06.

Denson, G. Roger. "A Geneology of Desire: Renée Green Explores the Continent of Power." *Flash Art* 24, no. 160 (October 1991): 125–27.

Diederichsen, Diedrich, ed. "Conversation with Diedrich Diederichsen." In *Yo! Hermeneutics!* Berlin: Edition ID–Archiv, 1994.

Mercer, Kobena, and Joshua Decter. *Inheritance*. Exh. cat. Los Angeles: Los Angeles Contemporary Exhibitions, 1992.

Meyer, James. "Nomads." *Parkett*, no. 49 (Summer 1997).

Obrist, Hans-Ulrich. "The Installation Is Coming Through the Back Door." In *Meta 1–Die Kunst und ihr Ort*. Stuttgart: Künstlerhaus, 1992.

Prinzhorn, Martin. "Dauerhaftes Provisorium." *Texte zur Kunst*, no. 34 (June 1999): 193–96.

Wallis, Brian. "Excavating the 1970s." *Art in America* 85, no. 9 (September 1997): 96–99, 122.

Michael Joaquín Grey

Born in 1961 in Los Angeles, Michael Joaquín Grey received both a B.S. in Genetics and a B.A. in Art from the University of California, Berkeley, in 1984. He received his M.F.A. from Yale University in 1990. His breakthrough also came in 1990, with a solo show at Petersburg Gallery, New York. Since then, his work has been included in the 1993 Whitney Biennial; "A-Life" at the Tokyo International Arts Museum, Tokyo (1993); "The Final Frontier" at the New Museum of Contemporary Art, New York (1993); "Science Fair" at Thomas Solomon's Garage, Los Angeles (1993); "Some Went Mad, Some Ran Away" at the Serpentine Gallery, London (1994); and "Beyond Belief" at Lisson Gallery, London (1994). Early solo exhibitions also include those at Stuart Regen Gallery, Los Angeles (1992); Barbara Gladstone Gallery, New York (1992); Lisson Gallery, London (1993); and Kunsthalle Loppem, Belgium (1994).

In 1997 Grey founded Primordial, a company that manufactures *ZOOB*, a children's play system he invented based on the movements of and our connections to the natural world.

Michael Joaquín Grey lives and works in San Francisco.

Selected Further Reading

Avgikos, Jan. "Michael Joaquín Grey at Petersburg." *Artforum* 29, no. 7 (March 1991): 127–28.

Bonami, Francesco. "Dion, Grey, Joo, Pardo, Pippin, Tiravanija: The Right Stuff." *Flash Art* 26, no. 170 (May/June 1993): 80.

Decter, Joshua. "Michael Joaquín Grey." *Flash Art* (Summer 1992).

Jana, Reena. "Toying with Science." *The New York Times Magazine*, 4 October 1998.

Pagel, David. "A Mix of Romper Room and Science Lab." *Los Angeles Times*, 13 February 1992.

Ritchie, Matthew. "Michael Joaquín Grey: Five of a Kind." *Artext*, no. 58 (August/October 1997): 52–57.

Rees, Michael. "Yale Sculpture: A Recent Breed of Critically Trained Artists from the Noted School of Art." *Flash Art* 26, no. 170 (May/June 1993): 65–67.

Saltz, Jerry. "Big Science: Michael Joaquín Grey's *Electron M.*, 1990." *Arts Magazine* 65, no. 7 (March 1991): 13–14.

Smith, Roberta. "Echoes of 60s and 70s Among the Young and Little Known." *The New York Times*, 30 November 1990.

Weissman, Benjamin. "Michael Joaquín Grey at Stuart Regen Gallery." *Artforum* 30, no. 9 (May 1992): 123–24.

Damien Hirst

Born in 1965 in Bristol, England, Damien Hirst graduated from Goldsmiths College in London in 1989. While still a student, in 1988 he curated the seminal exhibition "Freeze" for a disused building space in the Docklands area of East London.

His work quickly garnered notoriety and was featured in such group shows as "Modern Medicine" at Building One, London (1990); "Posthuman" at the FAE Musée d'Art Contemporain in Lausanne (1992); the Aperto section of the 1993 Venice Biennale; "Some Went Mad, Some Ran Away," curated by Hirst for the Serpentine Gallery, London (1994); and "Sensation," which premiered at the Royal Academy of Arts, London (1997).

Notable solo shows include "In & Out of Love," at Woodstock Street, London (1991); "Internal Affairs" at the Institute of Contemporary Arts, London (1991); "Visual Candy" at Regen Projects, Los Angeles (1993); "Pharmacy" at the Tate Gallery, London (1999); and more recently "Theories, Models, Methods, Approaches, Assumptions, Results and Findings" at Gagosian Gallery, New York (2000).

Damien Hirst lives and works in Devon, England.

Selected Further Reading

Bonami, Francesco. "Damien Hirst: The Exploded View of the Artist." Flash Art 29, no. 189 (Summer 1996): 112–16.

Graham-Dixon, Andrew. "Hatching a Scheme." The Independent, 16 July 1991.

Groys, Boris. "Decadent Geometry." Parkett, no. 40/41 (1994): 74–75.

Hill, Peter. "In and Out of Love." Artext, no. 43 (September 1992).

Hirst, Damien, with Liam Gillick. "It's a Maggot Farm: The B-Boys and Fly Girls of British Art" (interview). Artscribe, no. 84 (November/December 1990): 56–62.

Kent, Sarah. Shark Infested Waters: The Saatchi Collection of British Art in the 90s. London: Zwemmer, 1994.

Renton, Andrew. "Modern Medicine at Building One, Tower Bridge Business Square, London." Flash Art 23, no. 153 (Summer 1990): 182.

Rugoff, Ralph. "Damien Hirst at Regen Projects." Artforum 32, no. 2 (October 1992): 100.

Schjeldahl, Peter. "He Loves You." The Village Voice, 21 May 1996, 65.

Tomkins, Calvin. "After Shock." The New Yorker (20 September 1999): 84–93.

Whiteread, Rachel. "My Choice." The Telegraph, 27 July 1991.

Gary Hume

Born in Kent, England, in 1962, Gary Hume attended Goldsmiths College in London, where he participated in the legendary "Freeze" exhibition curated by Damien Hirst. He began working on the Magnolia series while still in school. After graduating in 1988, Hume's work was featured in group shows such as "Broken English" at the Serpentine Gallery, London (1991); "Lea Andrews, Keith Coventry, Anya Gallaccio, Damien Hirst, Gary Hume, Abigail Lane, Sarah Lucas, Steven Pippin, Mark Quinn, Marcus Taylor, Rachel Whiteread" at Barbara Gladstone Gallery, New York (1992); "Brilliant! New Art from London" at the Walker Art Center, Minneapolis (1995); and "Fiona Rae/Gary Hume" at The Saatchi Gallery, London (1997).

Hume's solo exhibitions include shows at Karsten Schubert, London (1989, 1991); Galerie Tanja Grunert, Cologne (1991); Daniel Weinberg Gallery, Santa Monica, California (1992); and Matthew Marks Gallery, New York (1992, 1994, 1997, 1998). In addition his work was featured in the 23rd International Bienal de São Paulo, and in 1999 he was chosen to represent Britain at the Venice Biennale.

Gary Hume lives and works in London.

Selected Further Reading

Adams, Brooks. "Gary Hume at Matthew Marks." Art in America 80, no. 5 (May 1992): 134–35.

Archer, Michael. "Ian Davenport, Gary Hume, Michael Landy at Karsten Schubert." Artforum 27, no. 6 (February 1989): 147.

Batchelor, David. "Behind a Painted Smile." Frieze (May 1994): 20.

Bush, Kate. "The British Art Show 1990 at McLellan Galleries." Artscribe, no. 81 (May 1990): 70–71.

Craddock, Sasha. "Freeze: The Fast Dockland Train to Simplicity." The Guardian, 13 September 1988.

Dannatt, Adrian. "Gary Hume: The Luxury of Doing Nothing." Flash Art 28, no. 183 (Summer 1995): 96–99.

Liebmann, Lisa. "Gary Hume: Matthew Marks Gallery." Artforum 30, no. 8 (April 1992): 94.

Renton, Andrew. "East Country Yard Show, London." Flash Art 23, no. 154 (October 1990): 191.

Schjeldahl, Peter. "Down Swinging." The Village Voice, 13 May 1997.

Searle, Adrian. "Shut That Door." Frieze, no. 11 (Summer 1993): 46–49.

Toba Khedoori

Born in Sydney, Australia, in 1964, Toba Khedoori received her M.F.A. from UCLA in 1994. While still a student she participated in "Invitational '93" at Regen Projects, Los Angeles (where she also had her first solo show in 1995). Two years after graduation, she mounted a solo exhibition at David Zwirner Gallery, New York.

She has exhibited widely in group shows including "Toba Khedoori/Rachel Khedoori," David Zwirner Gallery, New York (1994); the 1995 Whitney Biennial, New York; "Everything That's Interesting Is New," The Dakis Joannou Collection, DESTE Foundation and Athens School of Fine Arts, Athens, Greece (1996); "Some Recent Acquisitions," The Museum of Modern Art, New York (1996); "Architecture as Metaphor," The Museum of Modern Art, New York (1997); and "Elusive Paradise: Los Angeles Art from the Permanent Collection," The Museum of Contemporary Art, Los Angeles (1997).

Recent solo exhibitions include those at The Museum of Contemporary Art, Los Angeles (1997); David Zwirner Gallery, New York (1999); and the Museum für Gegenwartskunst, Basel (2000).

Toba Khedoori lives and works in Los Angeles.

Selected Further Reading

Anderson, Michael. "Invitational '93 at Regen Projects." Art Issues, no. 31 (January/February 1994): 43.

DiMichele, David. "Fresh Work: Invitational '93 at Regen Projects." Artweek 24, no. 21 (4 November 1993): 22.

Stein Greben, Deidre. "Toba Khedoori at David Zwirner." Art News 98, no. 9 (October 1999): 189.

Kimmelman, Michael. "A Whitney Biennial That's Generous, Sensuous, and Quirky." The New York Times, 24 March 1995, B-1.

Pagel, David. "A Model World View." Frieze (May 1995).

Relyea, Lane. "Toba Khedoori at the LA Museum of Contemporary Art." Artforum 35, no. 10 (Summer 1997): 131.

Saltz, Jerry. "Critic's Diary. A Year in the Life: Tropic of Painting." Art in America 82, no. 10 (October 1994): 90–101.

Van de Walle, Mark. "Toba Khedoori at David Zwirner Gallery." Artforum 35, no. 2 (October 1996): 117–18.

Vine, Richard. "Rachel Khedoori and Toba Khedoori at David Zwirner." Art in America 82, no. 10 (October 1994): 137–38.

Wakefield, Neville. "Openings: Toba Khedoori." Artforum 34, no. 2 (October 1995): 94–95.

Sharon Lockhart

Sharon Lockhart was born in 1964 in Massachusetts and received her M.F.A. in 1993 from Art Center College of Design, Pasadena, California. She began to exhibit widely before graduation, gaining the attention of the artworld upon presenting *Shaun* at Art Center in 1993 and *Auditions* at neugerriemschneider, Berlin, in 1994.

Since that time she has exhibited all over the world including solo shows at Friedrich Petzel Gallery, New York (1994); "Sharon Lockhart," Künstlerhaus Stuttgart, Stuttgart (1995); Blum & Poe, Santa Monica (1996, 1998); and the Museum Boijmans van Beuningen, Rotterdam (1999).

Significant group shows include "Underthings," Bliss, Pasadena (1992); "Ba Ba Baby," The Knitting Factory, New York (1993); "Nor Here Neither There," Los Angeles Contemporary Exhibitions (1994); "The Freed Weed," Richard Telles Fine Art, Los Angeles (1994); "Human/Nature," New Museum of Contemporary Art, New York (1995); "Campo 95," Venice, Italy (1995); "a/drift: Scenes from the Penetrable Culture," Center for Curatorial Studies Museum, Annandale-on-Hudson, New York (1996); "Scene of the Crime," UCLA Armand Hammer Museum of Art, Los Angeles (1997); "Cinema Cinema," Van Abbemuseum, Eindhoven (1999); and the 2000 Biennial Exhibition at the Whitney Museum of American Art, New York.

Sharon Lockhart lives and works in Los Angeles.

Selected Further Reading

Aukeman, Anastasia. "Sharon Lockhart at Friedrich Petzel." *Art in America* 83, no. 4 (April 1995): 112–13.

Bonami, Francesco, ed. *Echoes: Contemporary Art in the Age of Endless Conclusions*. New York: Monacelli Press, 1996.

Brougher, Kerry. *Art and Film Since 1945: Hall of Mirrors*. Exh. cat. Los Angeles: The Museum of Contemporary Art; and New York: Monacelli Press, 1996.

Diederichsen, Diedrich. "Oostende." *Texte zur Kunst*, no. 14 (June 1994): 214–17.

Greenstein, M. A. "Sharon Lockhart at Blum & Poe." *Art Issues*, no. 43 (Summer 1996): 37.

McDonald, Daniel. "Sharon Lockhart at Friedrich Petzel Gallery." *Frieze*, no. 20 (January/February 1995): 63–64.

Martin, Timothy. "Documentary Theater." In *Sharon Lockhart: Teatro Amazonas*, Exh. cat. Rotterdam: Museum Boijmans Van Beuningen Rotterdam and NAi Publishers, 2000.

Myers, Terry R. "Sharon Lockhart." *New Art Examiner* (Summer 1996): 45–46.

Relyea, Lane. "Openings: Sharon Lockhart." *Artforum* 33, no. 3 (November 1994): 80–81.

Scanlan, Joe. "Let's Play Prisoners." *Frieze*, no. 30 (September/October 1996): 60–67.

Sarah Lucas

Born in 1962, Sarah Lucas graduated from Goldsmiths College in 1987, and was one of the artists in the exhibition "Freeze," curated by former College schoolmate Damien Hirst. In 1992 she mounted two London exhibitions, "The Whole Joke" at Kingly Street and "Penis Nailed to a Board" at City Racing. In 1993 Lucas co-founded "The Shop," a London boutique she organized and operated with artist Tracey Emin that sold multiples made by her and her friends.

Her sculptures and installations has been featured in a number of group exhibitions including "Sarah Lucas and Steven Pippin" at The Museum of Modern Art, New York (1993); "Young British Artists II" at Saatchi Gallery, London (1993); "Brilliant! New Art from London" at the Walker Art Center, Minneapolis (1995); "Material Culture" at the Hayward Gallery, London (1997); and "The Anagrammatical Body" at the ZKM Centre for Media Art and Technology, Karlsruhe (2000).

Other important solo shows include "Got a Salmon On (Prawn)" at Anthony d'Offay Gallery, London (1994); "Sarah Lucas" at the Museum Boymans-van Beuningen, Rotterdam, and Portikus, Frankfurt (both 1996); "The Law," organized by Sadie Coles at St. Johns Lofts, London (1996); "The Old In Out" at Barbara Gladstone Gallery, New York (1998); and "Sarah Lucas: Beyond the Pleasure Principle," one of a series of interventions at The Freud Museum in London.

Sarah Lucas lives and works in London.

Selected Further Reading

Bishop, Claire. "Sarah Lucas at Sadie Coles HQ, London, and Freud Museum, London." *Artext*, no. 70 (August/October 2000): 78–79.

Buck, Louisa. "Sarah Lucas Lights Up and Gets Freudian." *The Art Newspaper*, no. 101 (March 2000): 72.

Collings, Matthew. "The New Establishment." *The Independent on Sunday*, 31 August 1997.

Daly, Pauline, and Brendan Quick. "Crazy Tracey, Sensible Lucas." *Purple Prose* (Summer 1993).

Freedman, Carl. "A Nod's as Good as a Wink." *Frieze*, no. 17 (Summer 1994).

Lucas, Sarah, and Tracey Emin. "How We Met." *The Independent on Saturday Magazine*, 12 October 1997.

Muir, Gregor. "Warning: Sarah Lucas's Art May Seriously Damage Your Health." *Dazed and Confused* (July 1997).

Saltz, Jerry. "She Gives as Good as She Gets." *Parkett*, no. 45 (1995): 76–85.

Schjeldahl, Peter. "Those Nasty Bits." *The New Yorker* (1999).

Schorr, Collier. "Sarah Lucas at Barbara Gladstone Gallery, New York." *Frieze*, no. 23 (Summer 1995): 65.

Steve McQueen

Born in London in 1969, Steve McQueen received his M.F.A. from Goldsmiths College in 1993. Subsequently he attended the Tisch School of Arts at New York University, where he began working on *Bear*. Since then he has participated in numerous group shows including "Acting Out: The Body in Video, Then and Now" at the Royal College of Art, London (1994); "X/Y" at the Centre Georges Pompidou, Paris (1995); "The British Art Show" in Manchester (1995); "Mirage: Enigma of Race, Difference, and Desire" at the Institute of Contemporary Arts, London (1995); "Life/Live" at the Musée d'Art Moderne de la Ville de Paris (1996); and "Spellbound" at the Hayward Gallery in London (1996).

McQueen has mounted solo exhibitions at Anthony Reynolds Gallery, London (1996); Museum of Contemporary Art, Chicago (1996); Stedelijk Van Abbemuseum, Eindhoven (1997); Portikus, Frankfurt (1997); Institute of Contemporary Arts, London (1999); and Marian Goodman Gallery, New York (2000). In 1999 he won the coveted Turner Prize.

Steve McQueen lives and works in Amsterdam.

Selected Further Reading

Elwes, Catherine. "Acting Out, The Body in Video: Then and Now." *Art Monthly* (April 1994): 23–24.

Frankel, David. "Opening: Steve McQueen." *Artforum* 36, no. 3 (November 1997): 102–03.

Gbadamosi, Raimi. "Am I Black Enough?" *Third Text*, no. 44 (Autumn 1998): 69–78.

Haye, Christian. "Just an Illusion." *Frieze*, no. 24 (September 1995): 52–53.

McQueen, Steve, with Patricia Bickers. "Let's Get Physical" (interview). *Art Monthly* (December 1996/January 1997): 1–5.

Scott, Whitney. "Must Picks of the Week: Must Museum." *New York Post*, 6 December 1997.

Searle, Adrian. "Let Me Through—I'm a Critic." *The Guardian*, 31 December 1996.

Smith, Roberta. "Steve McQueen at Marian Goodman Gallery." *The New York Times*, 6 June 1997.

Williams, Gilda. "Steve McQueen at Anthony Reynolds." *Art in America* 85, no. 4 (April 1997): 125.

Winkelmann, Jan. "Steve McQueen at Portikus, Frankfurt." *Artext*, no. 58 (August/October 1997): 97–98.

Takashi Murakami

Born in 1962 in Tokyo, Takashi Murakami received his Ph.D. in 1993 from Tokyo National University of Fine Arts and Music. A leading figure of the Neo-Pop movement in Japan, Murakami has exhibited in group shows around the world, including "Anomaly," Röntgen Kunst Institute, Tokyo (1992); "Nakamura and Murakami," SCAI The Bathhouse, Tokyo (1992); Mars Gallery, Tokyo (1992); Tokyo Metropolitan Art Museum, Tokyo (1993); "Cutting Up," Max Protetch Gallery, New York (1995); "Japan Today," Louisiana Museum of Modern Art, Humlebaek, Denmark (1995); "Cities on the Move," Wiener Secession, Vienna (1997); and "Colour Me Blind!" at the Stadtische Ausstellungshalle am Hawerkamp, Munster, and Dundee Contemporary Arts, Dundee (2000). Most recently, he curated the exhibition "Superflat," which was presented at The Museum for Contemporary Art, Los Angeles, in early 2001.

Solo exhibitions include "A Very Merry Unbirthday" at the Hiroshima City Museum of Contemporary Art, Hiroshima (1993); "Which Is Tomorrow?—Fall in Love" at SCAI The Bathhouse, Tokyo (1994); and "Takashi Murakami" at Ynglingag 1, Stockholm (1995). Murakami has also shown at Gavin Brown's enterprise, New York (1996); Blum & Poe, Santa Monica, California (1997); and P.S.1 Contemporary Art Center, New York (2000).

Takashi Murakami lives and works in Tokyo and New York.

Selected Further Reading

Blum, Timothy, and Jon Kessler. "Made in Japan. Otaku: Home Alone." *Documents*, no. 2 (February 1993): 31–36.

Darling, Michael. "The Fire Hose Lariats of Takashi Murakami at Blum & Poe in Santa Monica." *d'Art International* 1, no. 3 (Fall 1998).

Friis-Hansen, Dana. "Japan Today: Empire of the Goods, Young Japanese Artists and the Commodity Culture." *Flash Art* (March/April 1992): 78–81.

Joyce, Julie. "Star Blazers: New Pop from Japan." *Art Issues*, no. 54 (September/October 1998): 23–25.

Matsui, Midori. "Japanese Innovators: Fruitful Transformations of the Modernist Aesthetic." *Flash Art* 33, no. 210 (January/February 2000): 90–91.

Munroe, Alexandra. "Hinomaru Illumination: Japanese Art of the 1990s." In *Japanese Art After 1945: Scream Against the Sky*. New York: Harry N. Abrams, 1994.

Rimanelli, David. "Takashi Murakami at Bard Center for Curatorial Studies, Annandale-on-Hudson, New York." *Artforum* 38, no. 3 (November 1999): 134–35.

Sawaragi, Noi, and Fumio Nanjo. " Japan Today: Dangerously Cute." *Flash Art* (March/April 1992): 75–77.

Yoshitomo Nara

Born in 1959 in Japan, Yoshitomo Nara received his M.F.A. in 1987 from Aichi Prefectural University of Fine Arts and Music and later attended Kunstakademie Düsseldorf until 1993.

His work has been featured in group shows such as "Endless Happiness" at SCAI The Bathhouse, Tokyo (1995); "Tokyo Pop" at The Hiratsuka Museum of Art, Hiratsuka City, Japan (1996); "New Modernism for a New Millenium" at San Francisco Museum of Modern Art (1999); "Continental Shift" at Ludwig Forum, Aachen, Germany (2000); and "Presumed Innocent," which originated at CAPC Musée d'Art Contemporain, Bordeaux, and toured to the Hayward Gallery, London.

Solo exhibitions include "Hula Hula Garden," Galerie d'Eendt, Amsterdam (1994); "In the Deepest Puddle," SCAI The Bathhouse, Tokyo (1995); and "Cup Kids," Museum of Contemporary Art, Nagoya (1995); as well as those at Blum & Poe, Santa Monica, California (1997), and The Ginza Art Space, Tokyo (1999). In 2001 Nara will mount a one-person show at the Yokohama Museum of Art.

Yoshitomo Nara lives and works in Cologne and Nagoya, Japan.

Selected Further Reading

"Exhibitions Held Last Month Nara Declares The End of the Girl Civilian." *Gekkan Bijutsu* (February 1994).

"Gangster Girls by Nara Yoshitomo." *Geijutsu Shincho* (January 1994).

"Harmlos." *Neue Rheinische Zeitung*, 26 January 1991.

Inoue, Takao. "Art Space." *Asahi Shimbun*, 16 April 1994.

"Kunst mit Kinder." *Westdeutsche Zeitung*, 28 January 1991.

Nara, Yoshitomo. "The Ordinary Life of an Ordinary Person." *Bijutsu Techō* (July 1995).

Nishihara, Min. "Suburbia Baby, The Suburbs of Art." *Silvester Club* (July 1994).

Shimizu, Minoru. "Nara Yoshitomo at Itoki Crystal Hall—Review." *Bijutsu Techō*, no. 703 (March 1995): 175–77.

Tager, Alisa. "Yoshitomo Nara—Pacific Babies." *Poliester* 4, no. 13 (Fall 1995): 64.

Chris Ofili

Born in 1968 in Manchester, Chris Ofili received his M.A. from the Royal College of Art in London in 1993. Prior to graduating he showed in the "Whitworth Young Contemporaries" exhibition in Manchester (1989), for which he was the prizewinner. Later he organized "Shit Sale," which he staged on Brick Lane in London, and later on Strasse des 17. Juni, Berlin (1993). Subsequent group shows include "To Boldly Go..." at Cubitt Street Gallery, London (1993); "BT New Contemporaries" at the Cornerhouse Gallery, Manchester (1993–94); "Cocaine Orgasm" at Bank Space, London (1995); "'Brilliant!' New Art from London," which was initiated at the Walker Art Center, Minneapolis (1995); and the exhibition "Sensation," which began at the Royal Academy of Arts, London (1997).

Ofili has mounted solo exhibitions at Kepler Gallery, London (1991); Gavin Brown's enterprise, New York (1995, 1999); and Victoria Miro Gallery, London (1996, 2000), to name a few. His work has also appeared in the 6th International Instanbul Biennial (1999); the 1999/2000 Carnegie International, Pittsburgh; and the Sydney Biennial (2000). In 1998, he won Britain's prestigious Turner Prize.

Chris Ofili lives and works in London.

Selected Further Reading

Buck, Louisa. "Openings: Chris Ofili." *Artforum* 36, no. 1 (September 1997): 112–13.

Hilton, Tim. "The Best Painting in Britain." *The Independent on Sunday*, 17 November 1996.

MacRitchie, Lynn. "Ofili's Glittering Icons." *Art in America* 88, no. 1 (January 2000): 96–101.

Maloney, Martin. "Dung & Glitter." *Modern Painters* (Autumn 1998): 41–42.

Morgan, Stuart. "The Elephant Man." *Frieze*, no. 15 (March/April 1994): 40–43.

Myers, Terry R. "Chris Ofili: Power Man." *Artext*, no. 58 (August/October 1997): 36–39.

Ofili, Chris. "The Rumor Is..." (interview). *Dazed and Confused*, no. 21 (June 1996).

Ofili, Chris, with Paul D. Miller. "Deep Shit: An Interview with Chris Ofili." *Parkett*, no. 58 (May 2000): 164–69.

Searle, Adrian. "Going Through the Motions." *The Independent*, 27 December 1994.

Smith, Roberta. "Chris Ofili at Gavin Brown's enterprise." *The New York Times*, 2 December 1995.

Worsdale, Godfrey. "Chris Ofili at Victoria Miro Gallery." *Art Monthly*, no. 198 (July/August 1996).

Laura Owens

Born in 1970 in Ohio, Laura Owens received her M.F.A. from the California Institute of the Arts in 1994 and attended the Skowhegan School of Painting and Sculpture that same year. Also in 1994, her paintings were included in the "L.A.C.E. Annuale," curated by Dave Hickey for Los Angeles Contemporary Exhibitions. Other significant group shows include "Painting Show" at Regen Projects, Los Angeles (1995); "Wunderbar" at Kunstverein, Hamburg, Germany (1996); "Exterminating Angel" at Galerie Ghislaine Hussenot, Paris (1998); "Nach-Bild" at the Kunstalle Basel (1999); and "Examining Pictures: Exhibiting Paintings," which originated at Whitechapel Art Gallery in London and traveled in 2000 to the Museum of Contemporary Art, Chicago, and UCLA Hammer Museum in Los Angeles.

She has had solo exhibitions at Rosamund Felsen Gallery, Santa Monica, California (1995); Sadie Coles HQ, London (1997, 1999); Gavin Brown's enterprise, New York (1997); and Inverleith House, Royal Botanical Garden, Edinburgh (2000).

Laura Owens lives and works in Los Angeles.

Selected Further Reading

Avgikos, Jan. "Laura Owens at Gavin Brown's Enterprise." Artforum 37, no. 5 (January 1999): 118–19.

Cruz, Amada. "Laura Owens." In Fresh Cream. London: Phaidon Press, 2000.

Hainley, Bruce. "Sharon Lockhart, Laura Owens, Frances Stark at Blum & Poe." Artforum 36, no. 3 (November 1997): 119–20.

Owens, Laura, and Susan Morgan. "A Thousand Words: Laura Owens Talks About Her New Work." Artforum 37, no. 10 (Summer 1999): 130–31.

Owens, Laura, with Russell Ferguson. "Exchange of Ideas Among the Living" (interview). Cakewalk (Fall 2000): 26.

Relyea, Lane. "Virtually Formal." Artforum 37, no. 1 (September 1998): 126–33, 173.

Schjeldahl, Peter. "Hot Coffee." The Village Voice, 18 February 1997.

Smith, Roberta. "Laura Owens at Gavin Brown's Enterprise." The New York Times, 18 April 1997.

Tumlir, Jan. "Gentle Purpose." New Art Examiner 26, no. 8 (May 1999): 45–46.

Weissman, Benjamin. "Openings: Laura Owens." Artforum 34, no. 3 (November 1995): 84–85.

Tsuyoshi Ozawa

Born in 1965 in Tokyo, Tsuyoshi Ozawa graduated from the M.F.A. program at Tokyo National University of Fine Art and Music in 1990. In 1989, while still a student, he began working on part one of his epic project Jizoing. Early groups shows include "Fo(u)rtunes" at the Röntgen Kunst Institute, Tokyo (1993); "Liquid Crystal Futures" at Fruitmarket Gallery, Edinburgh (1995); and "Little Aperto," a series of parallel presentations on the streets of Venice, Italy, during the 1995 Biennale. More recently Ozawa's work has been featured in "Cities on the Move," curated by Hans-Ulrich Obrist and Hou Hanru for the Vienna Secession; the Taipei Biennale (1998); and "Dark Mirrors from Japan" at the De Appel Foundation, Amsterdam.

Solo exhibitions include a show at Hosomi Gallery, Tokyo (1992); Trance X Trance Vision, Tokyo (1993); Asian Fine Arts Factory, Berlin (1998); and Ota Fine Arts, Tokyo (1999, 2000). From 1996 to 1997 Ozawa lived in New York on a residency sponsored by the Asian Cultural Council.

Tsuyoshi Ozawa lives and works in Tokyo.

Selected Further Reading

1998 Taipei Biennial: Site of Desire. Exh. cat. Taipei: Taipei Fine Arts Museum, 1998.

Bellars, Peter. "Documented History—Photos Tell the Stories of the Times." Asahi Evening News, 12 December 1992.

Hanru, Hou, and Hans-Ulrich Obrist, eds. Cities on the Move. Exh. cat. Ostfildern, Germany: Hatje Cantz, 1997.

Hara, Makiko. "Contemporary Japanese Art: Young Artists, Consumer Culture, and Internationalization." Parachute, no. 88 (October/December 1997): 36–42.

Hasegawa, Yuko. "Pleasure in Nothingness." In Liquid Crystal Futures: Contemporary Japanese Photography. Exh. cat. Edinburgh: Fruitmarket Gallery, 1994.

Miyatake, Miki. "A Jizo Here and a Jizo There: The Smallest Galleries Anywhere." The Japan Times, 17 March 1996.

Ryan, Lorna. "Manga, TV, and Tinker Games: Masterpieces of Modernity." The Japan Times, 31 January 1993.

Silva, Arturo. "The Good, the Bad, and the Insecure." The Japan Times, 17 September 1995.

The Smallest Gallery in the World. Tokyo: Nasubi Gallery, 1996.

Tsuyoshi Ozawa. Exh. cat. Tokyo: Ota Fine Arts, 1998.

Jorge Pardo

Born in Havana in 1963, Jorge Pardo received his B.F.A. in 1988 from Art Center College of Design, Pasadena, California, and had his first solo exhibition at Bliss in Pasadena the following year. Subsequently his solo show at Thomas Solomon's Garage, Los Angeles (1990), was met with critical acclaim. Since then his installations and sculptures have been featured in various group exhibitions including "VeryVeryVery" at Shoshana Wayne Gallery, Santa Monica, California (1992); "Backstage" at Kunstverein Hamburg (1993); "Pure Beauty: Some Recent Work From Los Angeles," The Museum of Contemporary Art, Los Angeles (1994); "Traffic," CAPC Musée d'Art Contemporain in Bordeaux (1996); Skulptur Projekte in Münster (1997); and "What If" at the Moderna Museet, Stockholm (2000). Other solo exhibitions include those at Person's Weekend Museum, Tokyo (1993); "Lighthouse" at Museum Boijmans Van Beuningen in Rotterdam (1997); and "Swish I'm a Fish" at Museum Abteiberg in Mönchengladbach, Germany (1999). Pardo recently developed a major installation for the ground floor of the Dia Center for the Arts in New York.

Jorge Pardo lives and works in Los Angeles.

Selected Further Reading

Avgikos, Jan. "Jorge Pardo at Petzel/Borgmann Gallery." Artforum 32, no. 9 (May 1994): 101.

Bush, Kate. "4166 Sea View Lane." Parkett, no. 56 (September 1999): 152–55.

Fricke, Harald. "Kunst in Berlin jetzt: Jorge Pardo." Die Tageszeitung, May 1994.

Greene, David A. "Jorge Pardo at Thomas Solomon's Garage." Art Issues, no. 29 (September/October 1993): 38.

Hainley, Bruce. "Jorge Pardo at Patrick Painter." Artforum 37, no. 4 (December 1998): 135–36.

Kornblau, Gary. "Jorge Pardo at Thomas Solomon Gallery." Art Issues (September/October 1990): 35.

Miles, Christopher. "Flat Wares." Artforum 38, no. 9 (May 2000): 67.

Musgrave, David. Review. Art Monthly, no. 209 (September 1997): 40–42.

Pagel, David. "Young Lamplighter." Los Angeles Times, 12 April 1993, F-8.

Schmidt-Wulffen, Stephan. "Notizen zu Skulptur und Gegenwart." Neue bildende Kunst (February/March 1994): 16–21.

Manfred Pernice

Manfred Pernice was born in 1963 in Hildesheim, Germany. He attended Studium Grafik/Malerei in Braunschweig, as well as the Studium der Bildhauerei and Meisterschüler of the Hochschule der Künste in Berlin. Even before completing his studies in 1994, Pernice was exhibiting in shows such as "Kunst-aufstellung Aufgub," Frontart, Berlin (1993). Since then, Pernice has added a number of group exhibitions to his credit, including "Steglitz I," FBK, Berlin (1994); "Something Changed," Galerie Klosterfelde, Hamburg, Germany (1996); the Biennale de Lyon, France (1997); "Heaven," at P.S.1, Long Island City, New York (1997); and "Side Construction," at South London Gallery, London (1998).

Among his solo exhibitions are "Zeichnungen & Modelle," Galerie NEU, Berlin (1995); an installment of the Migrateurs series at the Musée d'Art de la Ville de Paris (1998); "Bad, Bath" at Anton Kern Gallery, New York (1998); and a show at the Institute of Visual Arts, Milwaukee, Wisconsin (1999).

Manfred Pernice lives and works in Berlin.

Selected Further Reading

Archer, Michael. "Manfred Pernice at Asprey Jones." Artforum 37, no. 3 (November 1998): 125–26.
Dziewior, Yilmaz. "Openings: Manfred Pernice." Artforum 37, no. 8 (April 1999): 112–13.
Fricke, Harald. Die Tageszeitung, 14 November 1996.
Last, Bogumil. Hamburger Morgenpost, 6 October 1996.
Meyer-Hermann, Eva. Surprise II. Nurnberg, Germany: Kunsthalle Nürnberg, 1997
Obrist, Hans-Ulrich. Unbuilt Roads: 107 Unrealized Projects. Ostfildern, Germany: Hatje Cantz, 1997.
Schmidt, Eva. Fiat. Exh. cat. Zwickau, Germany: Städtisches Museum Zwickau, 1997.
Szeemann, Harald. In 4e Biennale d'art contemporain de Lyon. Paris: Réunion des Musées Nationaux, 1997.
Williams, Gregory. "Manfred Pernice at Anton Kern Gallery, New York." Frieze, no. 42 (September/October 1998): 97–98.

Jason Rhoades

Jason Rhoades was born in Newcastle, California, in 1965. He attended the Skowhegan School of Painting and Sculpture in 1988 before receiving his M.F.A. from UCLA in 1993.

He has shown in numerous group exhibitions including "Going Down Stairs Diagonally," curated by Paul McCarthy at Rosamund Felsen Gallery, Los Angeles (1993); "Don't Look Now," Thread Waxing Space, New York (1994); "Ripple Across the Water '95," The Watari Museum of Contemporary Art, Tokyo (1995); and "Defining the Nineties: Consensus-Making in New York, Miami, and Los Angeles," Museum of Contemporary Art, Miami (1996). Rhoades was selected for inclusion in the Whitney Biennial in both 1995 and 1997 and was also included in the 1997 exhibition "Sunshine & Noir: Art in Los Angeles 1960–1997" which originated at the Louisiana Museum of Modern Art, Humlebaek, Denmark.

Solo exhibitions include "Cherry Makita—Honest Engine Work," David Zwirner Gallery, New York (1993); "Swedish Erotica and Fiero Parts," Rosamund Felsen Gallery, Los Angeles (1994); Kunsthalle Basel, Switzerland (1996); "The Purple Penis and the Venus (and Sutter's Mill) for Eindhoven," Stedelijk Van Abbemuseum, Eindhoven, The Netherlands (1998); and "Propposition" with Paul McCarthy at David Zwirner Gallery, New York (1999).

Jason Rhoades lives and works in Los Angeles and Munich.

Selected Further Reading

Adams, Brooks. "Jason Rhoades at David Zwirner." Art in America 81, no. 11 (November 1993): 126–27.
Cameron, Dan. "Son of 'Scatter.'" Art & Auction 16, no. 5 (December 1993): 52–56.
Duncan, Michael. "L.A. Rising." Art in America 82, no. 12 (December 1994): 72–83.
Miller, John. "Openings: Jason Rhoades." Artforum 32, no. 5 (January 1994): 86.
Myers, Terry R. "Jason Rhoades at Rosamund Felsen." Art Issues, no. 33 (May/June 1994): 45.
Ostrow, Saul. "Jason Rhoades: In a Field of Signs." Bomb, no. 62 (Winter 1998): 104–06.
Rhoades, Jason, and Daniel Birnbaum. "A Thousand Words: Jason Rhoades Talks About His Impala Project." Artforum 37, no. 1 (September 1998): 134–35.
Schorr, Collier. "Jason Rhoades at David Zwirner." Frieze, no. 13 (November/December 1993): 57–58.
Schaffner, Ingrid. "Deep Storage." Frieze, no. 23 (Summer 1995): 58–61.
Smith, Roberta. Review. The New York Times, 8 October 1993.

Yutaka Sone

Yutaka Sone was born in Shizuoka, Japan, in 1965. He received his B.F.A. in 1988 and his M.A. in Architecture in 1992, both from Tokyo Geijutsu University.

A series of solo exhibitions followed graduation, including "One Hand Clapping," Yokohama Galleria, Yokohama, Japan (1993); "Her 19th Foot," which premiered at the Contemporary Art Center in Mito (1993); and "Departures," Röntgen Kunst Institute, Tokyo (1995). More recently Sone showed at Navin Taxi Gallery, Bangkok (1998), and at David Zwirner Gallery, New York (1999).

Group shows include one at Shinjuku Shonen Art in Tokyo (1994); "Ripple Across the Water" at The Watari Museum of Contemporary Art, Tokyo (1995); Skulpturen Projekte, Münster (1997); and "Cities on the Move," Wiener Secession, Vienna (1997). In late 2000, Sone was an artist-in-residence at ArtPace, San Antonio, along with Jason Rhoades and John Hernandez.

Yutaka Sone lives and works in Los Angeles and Tokyo.

Selected Further Reading

Hasegawa, Yuko. The Man Who Digs a Bottomless Swamp, or an Absurd Duchamp. Exh. cat. Yokohama: Yokohama Galleria, 1994.
Hanru, Hou, and Hans-Ulrich Obrist, eds. Cities on the Move. Exh. cat. Ostfildern, Germany: Hatje Cantz, 1997.
Grabner, Michael. "Unfinished History." Frieze (May 1999): 95.
Bonami, Francesco. Unfinished History. Minneapolis: Walker Art Center, 1998.
Lind, Maria. "Nutopi (Nowtopia) at Rooseum, Malmö." Frieze, no. 24 (September 1995): 73–74.
Kurosawa, Shin. Desire, Impossibility and the Other Being. Exh. cat. Tokyo: Art Tower Mito, 1993.
Nishizawa, Miki. "Artist Steps Up Plans for Alpine Attack." The Japan Times, 14 February 2000, 14.
Nittve, Lars, and Shin Kurosawa. Nutopi. Malmö, Sweden: Rooseum, 1995.
Obrist, Hans-Ulrich. Unbuilt Roads: 107 Unrealized Projects. Ostfildern, Germany: Hatje Cantz, 1997.
Zaya, Octavio. Interzones. Copenhagen: Kunstforeinengen, 1995.

Diana Thater

Diana Thater was born in San Francisco in 1962. After receiving her B.A. in Art History from New York University in 1984, and her M.F.A. from Art Center College of Design in Pasadena, California, in 1990, she began presenting her video installations to international audiences. In her graduating year she was included in the group show "Heart in Mouth" at the Fahey/Klein Gallery in Los Angeles. Early solo ventures include "Dogs and Other Philosophers" at Dorothy Goldeen Gallery in Santa Monica (1991) and "Up the Lintel" at Bliss, Pasadena (1992). Subsequent solo exhibitions include "Abyss of Light" at 1301 PE, Santa Monica (1993); "Diana Thater and Stan Douglas," Witte de With, Rotterdam (1994); "China," The Renaissance Society at the University of Chicago (1995); "Electric Mind," Salzburger Kunstverein, Austria (1996); "The best space is the deep space," Carnegie Museum of Art, Pittsburgh (1999); and, more recently, "Delphine," Vienna Secession (2000).

Her work was included in both the 1995 and 1997 Whitney Biennial exhibitions, the 1997 Johannesburg Biennale, and the 1999/2000 Carnegie International.

Diana Thater lives and works in Los Angeles.

Selected Further Reading

Avgikos, Jan. "Sense Surround: Diana Thater." *Artforum* (May 1996): 74–77, 118.

Cameron, Dan. "Glocal Warming." *Artforum* 36, no. 4 (December 1997): 17–22, 130.

Cooke, Lynne. "Diana Thater: On Location." *Parkett*, no. 56 (September 1999): 177–182.

Frank, Peter. "Diana Thater at The MAK Center for Art and Architecture and Patrick Painter." *Art News* 98, no. 3 (March 1999): 139.

Gardner, Colin. "Diana Thater at Dorothy Goldeen Gallery." *Artforum* 29, no. 9 (May 1991): 152–53.

Gilbert-Rolfe, Jeremy. "Slaves of L.A. and Others," *Artspace* (Summer 1991).

Lunenfeld, Peter. "Diana Thater: Constraint Decree." *Artext*, no. 62 (August/October 1998): 66–72.

Ross, Adam. "Diana Thater at Bliss, 1301 Franklin, and Shoshana Wayne." *Art Issues*, no. 26 (January/February 1993): 45.

Salvioni, Daniela. "The Whitney Biennial: A Post 80s Event." *Flash Art* 30, no. 195 (Summer 1997): 114–17.

Smith, Roberta. "Diana Thater." *The New York Times*, 24 December 1993, C-25.

Rirkrit Tiravanija

Rirkrit Tiravanija was born in 1961 in Buenos Aires and graduated from the Whitney Independent Studies Program in New York in 1988. His works span a range of media and are interactive, inviting the public to eat, cook, and sleep. They have been featured in an exhaustive list of group exhibitions including "Work on Paper," Paula Allen Gallery, New York (1990); "The Big Nothing or Le Presque Rien," New Museum of Contemporary Art, New York (1991); "Spielhölle," Grazer Kunstverein, Graz, Austria (1993); Künstlerhaus Bethanien, Berlin (1993); "Migrateurs," Musée d'Art Moderne de la Ville de Paris, Paris (1993); "Don't Look Now," Threadwaxing Space, New York (1994); and "Truce: Echoes of Art in an Age of Endless Conclusions," SITE Santa Fe (1997).

In addition he has participated in numerous international exhibitions including the Berlin Biennale (1998), the Carnegie International (1995), the Kwangju Biennale (1995), the Johannesburg Biennale (1995), the Sydney Biennial (1998), and "dAPERTutto" at the 1999 Venice Biennale, to name but a few.

His solo projects include "Pad Thai," Paula Allen Gallery, New York (1990); Randy Alexander Gallery, New York (1991); 303 Gallery, New York (1992); a one-person exhibition at the Kunstverein, Hamburg (1996); and "Untitled (tomorrow can shut up and go away)" at Gavin Brown's enterprise, New York (1999).

Rirkrit Tiravanija lives and works in Berlin and New York.

Selected Further Reading

Bonami, Francesco. "Dion, Grey, Joo, Pardo, Pippin, Tiravanija: The Right Stuff." *Flash Art* 26, no. 170 (May/June 1993): 80.

Hainley, Bruce. "Where Are We Going? And What Are We Doing? Rirkrit Tiravanija's Art of Living." *Artforum* 34, no. 6 (February 1996): 54–59, 98.

Heartney, Eleanor. "Rirkrit Tiravanija at Randy Alexander." *Art in America* 79, no. 6 (June 1991): 142.

Hess, Elizabeth. "The White Rabbit (Among Other Alternatives)." *The Village Voice*, 17 December 1991.

Hixson, Kathryn. "Trouble in Paradise: Musing on the 1993 Venice Biennale." *New Art Examiner* 21, no. 2 (October 1993): 28–32.

Melo, Alexandre. "Guess Who's Coming to Dinner." *Parkett*, no. 44 (July 1995): 101–05.

Saltz, Jerry. "Resident Alien." *The Village Voice*, 7 July 1999, 157.

Siegel, Katy. "Rirkrit Tiravanija at Gavin Brown's Enterprise." *Artforum* 38, no. 2 (October 1999): 146.

Smith, Roberta. "The Gallery Is the Message." *The New York Times*, 4 October 1992, 35.

Weil, Benjamin. "Ouverture." *Flash Art* (January/February 1993): 79.

Rachel Whiteread

Born in 1963 in London, Rachel Whiteread received her M.A. from the Slade School of Art in London in 1987. In 1993 she received international recognition for *House*, a plaster cast of a Victorian Terrace house installed in a park in East London that was later demolished. That same year she won the Turner Prize for *House*.

Whiteread's early group exhibitions include Whitworth Young Contemporaries, Manchester (1987); Riverside Open, London (1988); Deichtorhallen, Hamburg (1989); "The British Art Show" McLellan Galleries, Glasgow (1990); and "A Group Show," Karsten Schubert, London (1990). Solo exhibitions include "Ghost," Chisenhale Gallery, London (1990); Karsten Schubert, London (1991); Luhring Augustine, New York (1992); Fundació "la Caixa," Barcelona (1992); "House," organized by ARTangel Trust, London (1993); DAAD Galerie, Berlin (1993); Kunsthalle Basel (1994); and Tate Gallery, London (1997). More recently she mounted the *Water Tower* project for the Public Art Fund, New York (1998).

In addition, Whiteread has participated in the 1992 Biennale of Sydney, the 1995 Istanbul Biennale, and the 1995 Carnegie International. In 1997 she was chosen to represent Britain at the Venice Biennale.

Rachel Whiteread lives and works in London.

Selected Further Reading

Archer, Michael. "Ghost Meat." *Artscribe*, no. 87 (Summer 1991): 35–38.

Bickers, Patricia. "Rachel Whiteread at the Arnolfini, Bristol and Karsten Schubert Ltd., London." *Art Monthly*, no. 144 (March 1991): 15–17.

Bush, Kate. "The British Art Show 1990 at McLellan Galleries." *Artscribe*, no. 81 (May 1990): 70–71.

Kimmelman, Michael. "Turning Things Inside Out." *The New York Times*, 5 February 1995, sec. 2: 1, 35.

Morgan, Stuart. "The Turner Prize." *Frieze*, no. 1 (October 1991): 4–6.

Renton, Andrew, and Liam Gillick, eds. *Technique Anglaise: Current Trends in British Art*. London: Thames and Hudson, 1991.

Searle, Adrian. "Rachel Doesn't Live Here Anymore." *Frieze*, no. 14 (January/February 1994): 26–29.

Smith, Roberta. "Rachel Whiteread at Luhring Augustine Gallery." *The New York Times*, 17 January 1992, C-38.

Storr, Robert. "Remains of the Day." *Art in America* 87, no. 4 (April 1999): 104–09, 154.

Wakefield, Neville. "Rachel Whiteread: Separation Anxiety and the Art of Release." *Parkett*, no. 42 (December 1994): 76–89.

Jane and Louise Wilson

Twins Jane and Louise Wilson were born in Britain in 1967 and each received an M.F.A. from Goldsmiths College in London in 1992.

The Wilsons' first solo show, "Route 1 & 9 North," took place in 1994 at the AC Project Room in New York, followed by "Normapaths" at Chisenhale Gallery and "Crawl Space" at Milch Gallery (both in London, 1995).

Their collaborative videos and installations have also been featured in a number of group exhibitions, including "Inside a Microcosm, Summer Show," Laure Genillard Gallery, London (1992); "Barclays Young Artists," Serpentine Gallery, London (1993); "Beyond Belief," Lisson Gallery, London (1999); "Wild Walls," Stedelijk Museum, Amsterdam (1995); "NowHere," Louisiana Museum of Modern Art, Humlebaek, Denmark (1996); "Hyperamnesiac Fabulations," The Power Plant, Toronto (1997); and "Spectacular Optical," Threadwaxing Space, New York (1998).

Jane and Louise Wilson live and work in London.

Selected Further Reading

Archer, Michael. "Home and Away." Art Monthly, no. 188 (July/August 1995): 8–10.

Baerwaldt, Wayne. "Crawl Space: Jane & Louise Wilson." Artext, no. 52 (September 1995): 45–47.

Cottingham, Laura. "Wonderful Life at Lisson Gallery, London." Frieze, no. 12 (September/October 1993): 56–57.

Hilty, Greg. "Beside Themselves." Frieze, no. 18 (September/October 1994): 40–43.

Kent, Sarah. Here and Now. Exh. cat. London: Serpentine Gallery, 1995.

Morgan, Stuart. BT New Contemporaries. London: New Contemporaries, 1994.

Renton, Andrew. Over the Limit. Bristol: Arnolfini, 1993.

Stallabrass, Julian. "Beyond Belief." Art Monthly, no. 177 (June 1994): 29–30.

Wakefield, Neville. "Openings: Jane and Louise Wilson." Artforum 37, no. 2 (October 1998): 112–13.

Wilson, Jane, and Louise Wilson. Block Notes, no. 8 (Winter 1995): 62–63.

Photo Credits

All photographs appear courtesy of the artists and/or lenders of the works. The following list, keyed to page numbers, applies to photographs for which a separate acknowledgement is due:

Courtesy Luhring Augustine Gallery, pp. 16-19, 166-67, 268. Courtesy Regen Projects, pp. 68-69; photograph by Susan Einstein, pp. 22-23; photograph by Zeif-Fridlizius, p. 25; photograph by Robert Wedemeyer, p. 66; photograph by Josh White, pp. 70-71, 100-01; and photograph © Douglas M. Parker Studio, p. 261. Courtesy Barbara Gladstone Gallery, pp. 26-27; photograph by L. Lame, p. 24; and photograph by Adam Reich, pp. 45-49. Courtesy 303 Gallery, pp. 33, 204. Courtesy Andrew Silewicz, London, pp. 30-32, 34-35. Courtesy Pat Hearn Gallery, pp. 38-41. Courtesy Jay Jopling/White Cube, London, pp. 52-53. Courtesy Matthew Marks Gallery, pp. 62-63; and photograph by Brian Forrest, p. 67. Courtesy Blum & Poe, Santa Monica, pp. 74-75, 96-97, 256, 260. Courtesy of Sharon Lockhart, p. 76. © Sarah Lucas, Courtesy Sadie Coles HQ, London, pp. 80, 82-85. Courtesy Marian Goodman Gallery, New York, photograph by Attilio Maranzano, p. 202. Courtesy Röntgen Kunstraum; photograph by Mikio Kurokawa, pp. 94-95, 239, 242, 244, 245 bottom; and photograph by Yuko Yamamoto, p. 240. Courtesy Victoria Miro Gallery, London, pp. 104-07, 214. Courtesy Rosamund Felsen Gallery, Los Angeles, photograph © Douglas M. Parker Studio, pp. 111-12, 113 bottom, 137-41. Courtesy Gavin Brown's enterprise, pp. 113 top, 158-60. Courtesy Friedrich Petzel Gallery, New York, pp. 122-27. Courtesy Galerie NEU, Berlin, pp. 131-33, 230 bottom. Courtesy David Zwirner, New York, p. 144-45, 259; and photograph by Yumiko Kojima, pp. 146-47. Courtesy Shoshana Wayne, Santa Monica, pp. 150-55, back cover. Courtesy Renato Alpegiani, p. 161. Courtesy Anthony d'Offay Gallery, pp. 164, 168-69. Courtesy Andrea Rosen Gallery, New York, p. 198 top; and in representation of The Estate of Felix Gonzalez-Torres, photograph by Stephen Rohner, p. 205. Courtesy of Chris Burden, p. 198 bottom. Courtesy of Michael Joaquín Grey, p. 196 top. © 2001 The Museum of Modern Art, New York; © Jasper Johns/licensed by VAGA, New York, NY, p. 206; and p. 207. Courtesy South London Gallery, p. 212 all. Courtesy Tate Gallery, London, p. 210. Courtesy The Saatchi Gallery, p. 221; and photograph by Anthony Oliver, p. 216, front cover. Photograph © Edward Woodman, London, p. 217. Courtesy Thomas Dane Limited, London, p. 219. © Mark Wallinger, Courtesy Anthony Reynolds Gallery, London, p. 220. Courtesy of Markus Selg, p. 225 top. Courtesy Galerie Martin Klosterfelde, Berlin, p. 225 bottom. Courtesy Galerie Christian Nagel, Cologne, p. 226 all. Courtesy Schipper + Krome, Berlin, 230 top. Courtesy neugerriemschneider, Berlin, p. 231. Courtesy Shiraishi Contemporary Art, Inc., photograph by Norihiro Ueno, p. 237 top. Courtesy Tomio Koyama Gallery, pp. 237 bottom, 247. Courtesy of Frances Stark and MARC FOXX Gallery, p. 265. Courtesy ACME., p. 266. Courtesy of California Institute of the Arts, photograph by Steven A. Gunther, p. 273. Courtesy of the Renaissance Society at The University of Chicago, p. 277. Courtesy of San Francisco Art Institute, photograph by William R. Heick, p. 278. Courtesy of Mike Kelley and Rosamund Felsen Gallery, Los Angeles, p. 290.

List of Contributors

Essays

Yilmaz Dziewior is the director of the Kunstverein in Hamburg and has worked as a freelance writer for Artforum, neue bildende kunst, and Texte zur Kunst. As an independent curator he organized "Sarah Lucas" (1997) and co-curated "Art-Worlds in Dialogue: From Gauguin to Global Present" (1999), both for Museum Ludwig, Cologne.

Midori Matsui is Associate Professor of American Studies at Tohoku University, Japan. She has published extensively on contemporary art and artists in such journals as Flash Art and Parkett, and in exhibition catalogues including Carnegie International 1999/2000 (2000), and Dark Mirrors of Japan (2000). Her essay on contemporary Japanese painting is published in Painting at the Edge of the World (New York: D.A.P., 2001).

Lane Relyea has written essays and reviews for numerous magazines including Artforum, Parkett, Frieze, Art in America, and New Art Examiner. He has contributed essays to such exhibition catalogues as Colour Me Blind! (1999) and Helter Skelter (1992). From 1987 to 1991 he served as editor of Artpaper. After teaching for a decade at the California Institute of the Arts in Valencia, he is currently Director of the Core Program in Houston. He is also finishing work on a doctoral degree in art history from the University of Texas at Austin.

Paul Schimmel, Chief Curator at The Museum of Contemporary Art, Los Angeles, has also organized such exhibitions as "Out of Actions: Between Performance and the Object, 1949-1979"; "Helter Skelter: L.A. Art in the 1990s"; and "Hand-Painted Pop: American Art in Transition, 1955-62" (co-curated with Donna De Salvo).

Katy Siegel is Assistant Professor of contemporary art history and criticism at Hunter College, City University of New York. A frequent contributor to Artforum, she has recently written catalogue essays on Lisa Yuskavage and Rineke Djikstra.

Howard Singerman taught in Los Angeles from 1979 to 1989 at Art Center College of Design, California Institute of the Arts, and the University of California at Los Angeles, and currently teaches at the University of Virginia. He has published criticism in Artforum, October, and Parkett, and written catalogue essays on Chris Burden, Mike Kelley, and Sherrie Levine, as well as for MOCA's "Forest of Signs" exhibition. He is the author of Art Subjects: Making Artists in the American University (1999).

Jon Thompson was formerly Head of Department and Reader in Fine Art at Goldsmiths College, and afterwards Head of Department at the Post-graduate Workplatz–the Jan van Eyck Akademie–at Maastricht. Presently, he is Research Professor in Fine Art at Middlesex University in England. He exhibits with Anthony Reynolds Gallery in London.

Artist entries

Leslie Dick is a writer whose books include Kicking (1992) and The Skull of Charlotte Corday (1995). She has taught in the Art Program at California Institute of the Arts since 1992, and currently is Co-Director of the Art Program.

Ciara Ennis is Associate Curator at the Santa Monica Museum of Art. She graduated from the contemporary curating program at the Royal College of Art, London, and has worked as an independent curator both in London and Los Angeles. In addition to serving as Project Director of "Public Offerings," Ennis is currently co-curating an exhibition for TENT in Rotterdam.

Russell Ferguson is Deputy Director for Exhibitions and Programs and Chief Curator at the UCLA Hammer Museum, Los Angeles. Formerly Associate Curator at The Museum of Contemporary Art, Los Angeles, he organized "In Memory of My Feelings: Frank O'Hara and American Art" (1999) and is currently working on exhibitions of the work of Douglas Gordon and Liz Larner for MOCA.

Ann Goldstein is Curator at The Museum of Contemporary Art, Los Angeles. Her exhibitions have included "A Forest of Signs: Art in the Crisis of Representation" (1989, co-curated with Mary Jane Jacobs); "Pure Beauty: Some Recent Work from Los Angeles" (1994); "1965-1975: Reconsidering the Object of Art" (1995, co-curated with Anne Rorimer); "Christopher Wool" (1998); and "Barbara Kruger" (1999).

Miwon Kwon is Assistant Professor in the Department of Art History at University of California at Los Angeles. She is also a founding editor and publisher of Documents, a journal of art, culture, and criticism. Her book One Place after Another: Essays on Site-specific Art and Locational Identity is forthcoming from MIT Press.

Thomas Lawson is an artist who undertakes a broad variety of projects; some of these are art, and some are about art. An example of the latter is his participation in the selection of "The British Art Show 4" in 1995, which included Chris Ofili. Lawson is currently Dean of the Art School at California Institute of the Arts.

Matthew Ritchie is an artist and writer currently living and working in New York. His work explores the nature of cultural information through painting, installation, drawing, sculpture, and narrative and has been widely exhibited in the United States and Europe. Recent exhibitions include solo shows at the Dallas Museum of Art (2001), Miami Museum of Contemporary Art (2000), and Andrea Rosen Gallery, New York (2000).

Lenders to the Exhibition

303 Gallery, New York
Markus Baenziger
Ruth & Jake Bloom
Blum & Poe, Santa Monica, California
Thomas Borgmann–Cologne
The British Council
Gavin Brown's enterprise, New York
Brian D. Butler, Santa Monica, California
Sadie Coles HQ, London
Contemporary Art Center, Art Tower Mito
Contemporary Art Museum, Kanazawa
Clarissa Dalrymple, New York
Jeffrey Deitch
Peter Doig, London
Falckenberg Collection
Galerie Hauser und Wirth, Zurich
Gil B. Friesen
Tony and Gail Ganz
Barbara Gladstone
Marian Goodman Gallery, New York
Michael Joaquin Grey
Claudio Guenzani, Milan
Sammlung Hauser und Wirth, St. Gallen, Switzerland
Susan & Michael Hort
Marjory Jacobson
Lisson Gallery, London
Rachel & Jean-Pierre Lehmann
Sharon Lockhart
Lohaus–De Decker, Antwerp
Los Angeles County Museum of Art
Michael Lynne
Matthew Marks Gallery
Daniel Melnick
Gary and Tracy Mezzatesta
Victoria Miro Gallery, London
The Museum of Contemporary Art, Los Angeles
The Museum of Modern Art, New York
Helly Nahmad Gallery, London
Eileen and Peter Norton, Santa Monica, California
Chris Ofili
Michael and Judy Ovitz, Los Angeles
Laura Owens
Tsuyoshi Ozawa
Lari Pittman and Roy Dowell
Clayton Press & Gregory Linn, Philadelphia
Private collection
Private collection, Germany
Private collection, Los Angeles
Private collection, New York
Private collection, Turin
Jason Rhoades
The Saatchi Gallery, London
San Francisco Museum of Modern Art
Karsten Schubert, London
Andrew Silewicz, London
Thomas Solomon
Norman & Norah Stone, San Francisco
Bunny and Jay Wasserman, Los Angeles
Jon Weaver
Rachel Whiteread
Whitney Museum of American Art
Lorrin and Deane Wong Family Trust
Cerith Wyn-Evans, London
Yale Center for British Art
David Zwirner, New York

public

JANINE ANTONI
MATTHEW BARNEY
THOMAS DEMAND
RENÉE GREEN
MICHAEL JOAQUIN GREY
DAMIEN HIRST
GARY HUME
TOBA KHEDOORI
SHARON LOCKHART
SARAH LUCAS
STEVE McQUEEN
TAKASHI MURAKAMI
YOSHITOMO NARA
CHRIS OFILI
LAURA OWENS
TSUYOSHI OZAWA
JORGE PARDO
MANFRED PERNICE
JASON RHOADES
YUTAKA SONE
DIANA THATER
RIRKRIT TIRAVANIJA
RACHEL WHITEREAD
JANE AND LOUISE WILSON

HOWARD SINGERMAN

LANE RELYEA

offerings

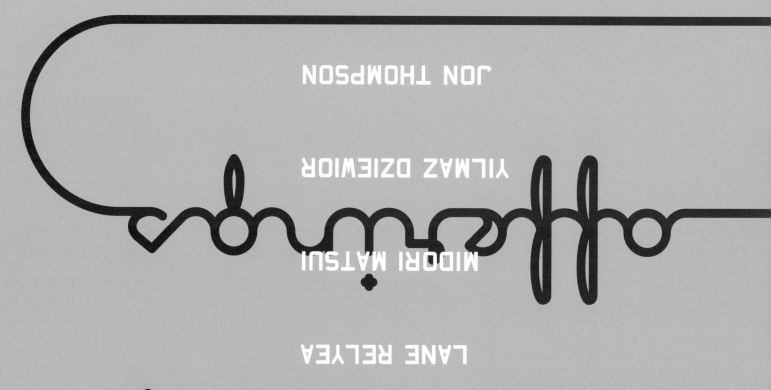

MIDORI MATSUI

YILMAZ DZIEWIOR

JON THOMPSON

KATY SIEGEL

1. Harold Rosenberg, "The American Action Painters" (1952), in Rosenberg, The Tradition of the New (New York: Grove Press, 1959), 37.
2. Lawrence Alloway, "The Past Decade," Art in America 4, no. 4 (August 1964): 21.
3. William Seitz, "The Rise and Dissolution of the Avant-Garde," Vogue 142 (September 1963): 231.
4. "Reviews and Previews: New Names this Month," ArtNews 57, no. 6 (October 1958): 16-17, 48.
5. Bourdieu, The Field of Cultural Production: Essays on Art and Literature (New York: Columbia University Press, 1993), 106.
6. In 1950, discussing the Abstract Expressionists showing at the Venice Biennale alongside more traditional European painters, Alfred Barr could say that there was a new "spirit" in American art after World War II, to be found in the "younger generation of today. In the United States, three of the younger leaders have been Gorky, de Kooning and Pollock." At the time, de Kooning was 46. Alfred H. Barr, Jr. in "7 Americans Open in Venice," ArtNews 49, no. 4 (Summer 1950): 60.
7. Rosenberg, "American Action Painters," 29-30.
8. Thomas B. Hess, "Great Expectations, Part I," ArtNews 55, no. 4 (Summer 1956): 36-37, 59-61; Thomas B. Hess, "Younger artists and the unforgivable crime," ArtNews 56, no. 2 (April 1957): 46-49, 64-65; and Reinhardt, "44 Titles for Articles for Artists Under 45," It Is 1 (Spring 1958): 22-23.
9. Herman Cherry, "Letter to the Editor," ArtNews 59, no. 6 (October 1960): 6.
10. Hess, "Great Expectations, Part I," 59.
11. Ben Heller, "Jasper Johns," in B. H. Friedman, School of New York: Some Younger Painters (New York: Grove Press, 1959), 64.
12. Dorothy C. Miller, Sixteen Americans (New York: The Museum of Modern Art, 1959); and B. H. Friedman, School of New York.
13. In fact, Thomas B. Hess, reviewing the 1956 exhibition, had complained that the museum, while preserving its historical responsibilities, was neglecting its duty to living artists (a familiar complaint). Hess, "Great Expectations, Part I," 36.
14. Rubin, "Younger American Painters," Art International 4 (1960): 25.
15. And of course, Rubin himself curated not one but two retrospectives of Frank Stella, the first in 1970 and, confirming the earlier judgment, the second in 1987.
16. "Pop Art-Cult of the Commonplace," Time (3 May 1963): 72.
17. Max Kozloff, "'Pop' Culture, Metaphysical Disgust, and the New Vulgarians," Art International 6, no. 2 (March 1962): 34-36.
18. Sidney Tillim, "Further Observations on the Pop Phenomenon," Artforum 4, no. 3 (November 1965): 17.
19. Robert Indiana, in Swenson, "What Is Pop Art? Answers from 8 Painters, Part I," ArtNews 62, no. 7 (November 1963): 27.
20. Interview with the author, 12 December 2000.
21. This split is also expressed by Buchloh against the retrograde return of figurative painting. Benjamin Buchloh, "Figures of Authority, Ciphers of Repression: Notes on the Return of Representation in European Painting," October, no. 16 (Spring 1981).
22. Andreas Stephanson, "Interview with Craig Owens" (1987), reprinted in Owens, Beyond Recognition: Representation, Power, and Culture (Berkeley: University of California Press, 1992), 298-99.
23. For an interesting oral history of these events from several perspectives, see Amy Newman, Challenging Art: Artforum 1962-1974 (New York: Soho Press, 2000), 383-425.
24. The Editors, "About October," October, no. 1 (Spring 1976): 5.
25. For more information, see Scott Gutterman, "A Brief History of the ISP," in Independent Study Program: 25 Years (New York: Whitney Museum of American Art, 1993), 14-40.
26. Miwon Kwon, "Reflection on the Intellecual History of the ISP," in Independent Study Program: 25 Years, 54-55.
27. Hal Foster, "Who's Afraid of the Neo-Avant-Garde?," in Return of the Real: The Avant-Garde at the End of the Century (Cambridge, Mass.: The MIT Press, 1996), 1-33.
28. Quoted in Kay Larson, "Women's Work (or Is It Art?) Is Never Done," The New York Times, 7 January 1996, sect. 2, 35.
29. Ibid.
30. Benjamin Weil, "Matthew Barney," Flash Art 25, no. 162 (January 1992): 102.
31. Demonstrating the ubiquity of these references among a wide range of artists, in 1990 Roberta Smith subtitled a New York Times review article "Echoes of 60s and 70s Among the Young and Little Known." Smith, "Reviews," The New York Times, 30 November 1990, C-24.
32. Clark, in Gutterman, " A Brief History of the ISP," 37-38.
33. For example, the artists Clegg and Guttmann asked, "What if critique itself were a desirable commodity, not in spite of its content, but because of it?" Clegg and Guttmann, "On Conceptual Art's Tradition," Flash Art, no. 143 (November/December 1988): 99. See also Michael Leja, "Debilitating Binaries: Theory/History, Theory/Practice, Theory/Object," and Allan Wallach, Response. Unpublished papers, Association of Historians of American Art, CAA Annual Meeting, 27 January 1995, San Antonio, Texas.
34. Masheck, in "Critics and the Marketplace," Art in America 76, no. 7 (July 1988): 110. Masheck, although himself left-wing, sounds not unlike Hilton Kramer railing against Rosenberg's characterization of the Abstract Expressionists as transgressive pioneers long after their success: "Let's face it: the man in the Coonskin hat has a dry martini in his hand!" Hilton Kramer, "Month in Review," Arts Magazine 33, no. 10 (September 1959): 59.
35. Quoted in "Rirkrit Tiravanija: In and Around Minneapolis, March, 1995. Interview by Rochelle Steiner," in Art Recollection: Artists' Interviews and Statements in The Nineties, ed. Gabriele Detterer (Ravenna: Danilo Montanari & Exit & Zone Archives Editore, 1997), 220.
36. The specter of the nouveau-riche collector (literally "new," if not literally young) reappeared in the art boom of the 80s. If the former as an All-American instance could seem sexist or anti-Semitic, the latter often seemed racist, as people complained about foreign investors driving up Van Gogh prices. The complaints, made by those such as Time magazine critic Robert Hughes (who called the Sunflowers sale a mark of "the new vulgarity," much as Kozloff decried Pop's audience as "new vulgarians"), were rebutted in Craig Owens, "The Yen for Art," in Owens, Beyond Recognition, 316-23.
37. Thomas Crow, "The Graying of Criticism," Artforum 32, no. 1 (September 1993): 188. One could also say that if theory is global then, like the international Pop Art phenomenon of the 60s, it's more of a sign of the problem than a solution to it, unless the critics critique themselves and use their "globalized" theory to recognize that there's no escaping globalization.
38. O'Brien, "Think or Thwim," Artforum 32, no. 1 (September 1993): 186; and Liebmann, in "Critics and the Marketplace," 107.
39. O'Brien, "Think or Thwim," 186.
40. Carter Ratcliff, "The Marriage of Art and Money," Art in America 76, no. 7 (July 1988): 81.
41. Nancy Sullivan, "Inside Trading: Postmodernism and the Social Drama of Sunflowers in the 1980s Artworld," in George E. Marcus and Fred R. Myers, eds., The Traffic in Culture: Refiguring Art and Anthropology (Berkeley, Calif.: University of California Press, 1995), 256-301.
42. Raymonde Moulin, "The Museum and the Marketplace" (1986), The International Journal of Political Economy 25, no. 2 (Summer 1995): 38.
43. Sullivan, "Inside Training," 273.
44. In 1990, ArtNews published special issues on Latin America, Europe, and L.A.; in 1991, Art in America published issues devoted to Latin America, the Pacific Rim, and L.A.
45. Moulin, "The Museum and the Marketplace," 46-48.
46. Daniel Pinchbeck, "NY Artist Q & A: Rirkrit Tiravanija," The Art Newspaper 10, no. 94 (July/August 1999): 69.
47. Ibid.
48. On his generosity as an artist, see Janet Kraynak, "Rirkrit Tiravanija's Liability," Documents, no. 13 (Fall 1998): 26-40.
49. Daniel Buren, "The Function of the Studio," October, no. 10 (Fall 1979): 51-58; and Craig Owens, "Bibliography for Contemporary Art and Art Criticism," in Owens, Beyond Recognition, 334-38.
50. Jack Bankowsky recalls coming to the Whitney in 1980 as a young painter, excited to have a studio in Manhattan, only to discover that painting was distinctly persona non grata in the program. Author's interview, 30 November 2000.
51. Interview with Tim Rollins, in Felix Gonzalez-Torres (Los Angeles: A.R.T. Press, 1993), 6-7. Charles Long recalls that the only thing in Gonzalez-Torres's studio was a pornographic snapshot tacked to the wall. Author's interview.
52. "Maurizio Cattelan with Bob Nickas" (interview), Index (September/October 1999): 58.
53. Hilton Kramer, "Month in Review," Arts Magazine 35, no. 1 (October 1960): 52-55.
54. Robert Storr, "An Interview with Mike Kelley," Art in America 82, no. 6 (June 1994): 91.
55. Jack Bankowsky, "Slackers," Artforum 30, no. 3 (November 1991): 96-100.
56. In fact, many have argued that the category "teenager" was invented by advertisers as a marketing device. As PTA Magazine put it in 1956, "The trouble with teenagers started when some smart salesman made a group of them in order to sell bobby sox." Cited in Michael Barson and Steven Heller, Teenage Confidential (San Francisco: Chronicle Books, 1998), 22.
57. Interview with Jerry Saltz, 29 November 2000.
58. Dalrymple has made a career championing young artists in various capacities; a recent Artforum profile comments on her "reputation as a bellwether of new art." Avant-garde or alternative galleries show young artists not only because of their cutting-edge sensibility, but because their art is available to low-budget operations, and affords what Bourdieu referred to as "symbolic capital." Clarissa Dalrymple, "First Take: Richard Wright," Artforum 39, no. 5 (January 2001): 118.
59. Michael Rees, "Yale Sculpture: A Recent Breed of Critically Trained Artists from the Noted School of Art," Flash Art 26, no. 170 (May/June 1993): 65-67.
60. Interview with author, 8 December 2000.
61. See for example Margaret Mead, Culture and Commitment: A Study of the Generation Gap (New York: American Museum of Natural History, 1970); and Frank Musgrove, Youth and the Social Order (Bloomington: Indiana University Press, 1965).
62. Julien LaVerdiere, Randall Peacock, and Vincent Mazeau, in Robyn Dutra, "Big Room: Taking Fashion from Behind," Surface, no. 26 (December 2000): 133.
63. Marc Selwyn, "Michael Joaquin Grey: Dysfunctional Playground," Flash Art 25, no. 164 (May/June 1992): 106.
64. Evident not only in their often biomorphic sculpture, but in the interest of Barney and Grey in elementary biological forms, which Grey has called a "state of preposition" and Barney a "state of potential." Grey, quoted in Matthew Ritchie, "Michael Joaquin Grey: Five of a Kind," Artext, no. 58 (August/October 1997): 53; and Barney, in "Travels in Hypertrophia," interview with Thyrza Nichols Goodeve, Artforum 33, no. 9 (May 1995): 68.
65. See Weil, "Matthew Barney," 102. Jerry Saltz wrote about Barney's M.F.A. show in Arts Magazine, "Wilder Shores of Art: Matthew Barney's Field Dressing (orifill), 1989," Arts Magazine 65, no. 9 (May 1991): 29-31.
66. Antoni is called "slim and agile" in The New York Times, while Vogue magazine says she has the "quiet allure of a Pre-Raphaelite Madonna." Larson, "Women's Work (or Is It Art?) Is Never Done," 35; and George Melrod, "lip schtick," Vogue (June 1993): 90.
67. Roberta Smith, "Critic's Notebook: Portrait of the Artist as a Young Woman," The New York Times, 5 July 2000.
68. Sherrie Levine, of course, being the most obvious example of an individual rewarded for making anti-authorial art.
69. Interview with Tim Rollins, in Felix Gonzalez-Torres, 23.
70. Cattelan, "Maurizio Cattelan with Bob Nickas," 58.
71. The parallel idea of turning the gallery into a living space, as in the recent work of Jorge Pardo, Tiravanija, and Andrea Zittel, is acutely addressed in Lane Relyea's essay.
72. "Work? Work in Progess? Work?" exhibition press release, Andrea Rosen Gallery, November 1990. This condition rhymes oddly with Barney's and Grey's previously mentioned interest in suspended or undeveloped biological states.
73. Jorge Pardo's and Maurizio Cattelan's appropriation of other artists' life stories in interviews (Phillipe Parreno and Ange Leccia, respectively) may be an acknowledgement of the stress on the artist's identity, but it comes across less as institutional critique and more as adolescent prankishness.
74. Apollinaire's remark was often cited in art publications of the 50s: "Is Today's Artist With or Against the Past? Part I," ArtNews 57, no. 4 (Summer 1958): 26; and Robert Motherwell, in P. G. Pavia and Irving Sandler, eds., "The Philadelphia Panel," It Is 5 (Spring 1960): 35. For examples of the latter phrase, see Jerry Saltz, "Babylon Calling," The Village Voice (19 September 2000): 71; and Dodie Kazanjian, "The Scene Setter," Vogue 190, no. 9 (September 2000): 624-27, 681-82.

¶ Whether the artist is competitive,

"self-critical"

like Green and Fraser,

"generous"

like Gonzalez-Torres and Tiravanija, or

"narcissistic"

like Barney, Antoni, and Landers, much of the art of the early 90s centers on the display of the self to the point where even private moments become public.[73] Here two points converge: the theoretical conceit that the private is always formed and determined by public forces, and the cultural demand for the glamorized display of the desirable, private self.

These developments don't necessarily signal a new generation (or style) of art, but a new generation of people entering the artworld.

People as well as objects can be a new model or have a new style, so that eventually the biggest difference between one artist and another may be in how the artist behaves as opposed to how he or she paints or makes installations. Therefore, the ethos of a given art-school program might be more important than what kind of work the school actually produces, as if the students were more involved in how they looked and talked—their self-presentation—than in their artistic production.

¶ And it is that self that goes on the market. The avant-garde of the first half of the century made its stand on "the corpse of the father": today's savage, Oedipal truism is

"the artworld eats its young."[74]

If you didn't envy them, you might feel sorry for them.

¶ In any case, it is a short distance from the death-of-the-author/ birth-of-the-reader to the artistic life lived totally in public. In 1993, Gonzalez-Torres said "I need the viewer, I need the public's interaction. Without a public, these works are nothing, nothing."[69] A few years later, Maurizio Cattelan seemed to echo this sentiment, but with far more commercial overtones:

"If I didn't have any shows, and there wasn't any interest, I wouldn't do anything."[70]

All of the artist's efforts go straight to market—nothing is made unless intended for the public sphere. We have come a very long way from the Abstract Expressionists' experiments with new ways of applying paint that were highly unlikely to appeal to public taste or interest.

"Work? Work in Progress? Work?"
exhibition at Andrea Rosen Gallery, New York, 1990

¶ In a 1990 show at Andrea Rosen titled "Work? Work in Progress? Work?" six artists occupied the gallery for a month, including Laurie Parsons, who worked as a gallery assistant. The gallery became a studio, the place where they worked, and spectators could see the art being made, recalling Chris Burden's 1975 Natural Habitat in which he moved the studio he shared with Alexis Smith into a gallery.[71] While the exhibition's press release stressed the aspect of process, even more than that this studio activity displaced to the public space of the gallery seems to depict art's potentiality, the state of being promising.

The object was not so much rejected or critiqued as half-baked, like the artists themselves, still in progress. The press release alluded to the problem of the artist's ego or identity, nominally put aside by avant-garde artists during the 60s and 70s: "The gallery will act as a hot house—as the artists vie for space and attention, potential collaboration or confrontation could ensue."[72] Did this put the ultimate burden of creation on the viewer? At the least, the public was being called upon to support the artists by giving all of them attention, volunteering to play the voyeur to the artist's narcissist.

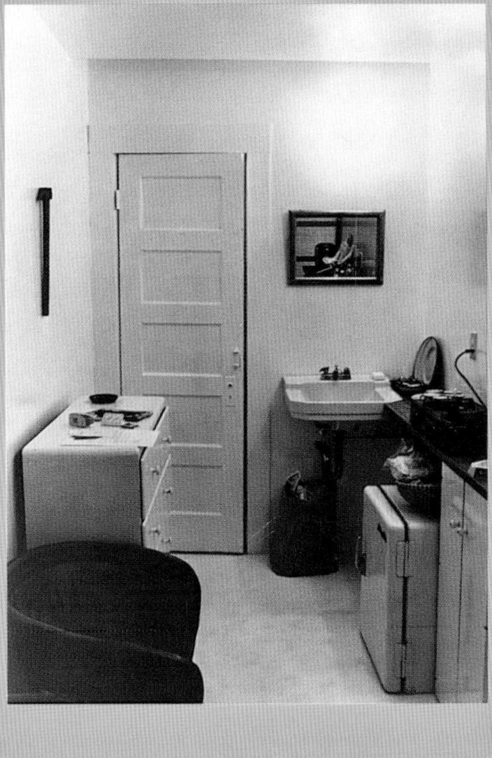

Chris Burden
Natural Habitat, 1975
Photograph
8 x 10 inches

¶ Barney was clearly the star of the Yale group; by the time he appeared at Barbara Gladstone Gallery in 1991, many people had already heard about him.[65]

In the exhibition "Transexualis," gym equipment cast in petroleum jelly was installed in the gallery, along with the video MILE HIGH Threshold: FLIGHT with the ANAL SADISTIC WARRIOR (1991), which showed the near-naked artist climbing the gallery walls with a harness and cleats.

Despite (or because of) its much-remarked opacity—like his 1989 B.F.A. show—Barney's video seemed to be an allegory for the artist's process of creation, his physical struggle with material. The piece revealed in fantastic, exaggerated form what we imagine might happen in an artist's private studio; further confusing things, the activity took place in the gallery.

¶ Where the work emerging from the Whitney actively referred to Conceptualism and Minimalism, Barney's work referenced performance; critics repeatedly invoked Joseph Beuys, Chris Burden, Bruce Nauman, and Vito Acconci when discussing him. Articles about Janine Antoni and Barney alike emphasized endurance (a return to the physical body, converted into a semiological, social signifier by theoretical concerns); their personal, gendered obsessions (food and sex for her, sports and sex for him); and the artists' physical beauty.[66]

Today, we have not only the seemingly ubiquitous fashion spreads of cute young artists in the popular press, but articles chastising us for our obsession with the image of the artist.[67]

¶ Barney replaces the artist's mark (his "signature") as the sign of authority with a performance that somehow reveals who the artist really is. But if the real person is a product of social and semiotic forces—as "theory" claims—then the acting-out in performance has to have something of the look of the general commodity. This is true of works such as Andrea Fraser's performances as museum docent Jane Castleton and Gonzalez-Torres's untitled self-portrait in text that combines historical events (the Bay of Pigs) with the more personal (meeting his boyfriend Ross). Here the human being appears as a social commodity attempting to discover and represent the social forces that have formed it; ironically though, in the end individual artists are almost always credited for revealing what are purported to be social truths.[68] To the extent that Barney comes across as a strange individual, he resists (perhaps passively, because non-theoretically) what theory since the 60s has been arguing.

It seems that he's doing something slightly different, even if he's not particularly aware of its precise significance.

ZOOB®, DNA Creation;
Courtesy Primordial™ LLC, 1997

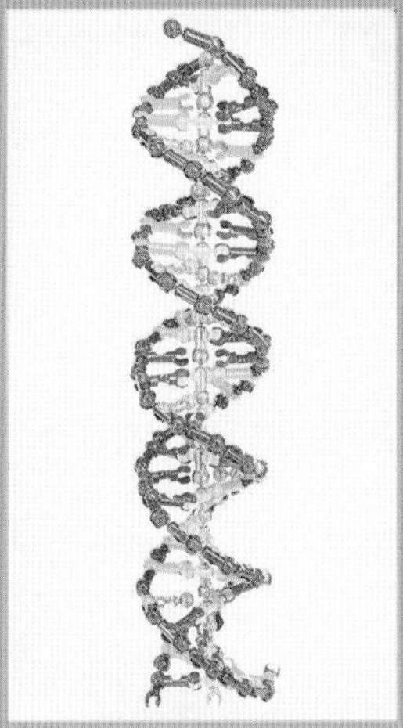

¶ **Despite his "loser" pose, Landers's blatant careerism seemed to play into Yale's reputation as a place for ambitious artists as opposed to the Whitney's high-mindedness.**
This reputation grew throughout the 90s, as graduates from the painting (John Currin, Lisa Yuskavage) and photography departments (Anna Gaskell and Dana Hoey, among others) were often accused of making fashionable objects too easily complicit with the market—and of being too marketable themselves. Critics often note (admiringly or derisively) Matthew Barney's ambition in producing large-scale, high-quality films; his classmate, Michael Joaquín Grey, left the artworld's confines in the mid-90s to form a corporation, Primordial, which designs and manufactures the very successful toys called ZOOBs.

¶ **The reorientation toward the market seems to have occurred in Yale's sculpture program during the mid-80s. Charles Long recalls that when he came to Yale in 1986 as a graduate student, director David von Schlegell was adamant about not inviting the artworld into the school: no curators, dealers, not even critics. During Long's second year (when he ran the visiting artist program with Michael Rees), von Schlegell reversed his position. That year artist Ashley Bickerton visited, bringing Clarissa Dalrymple of the Petersburg Gallery to see several students including Barney, Rees, and Grey.[58]**

Charles Long
Special, 1987–89
Hydrocal and mirrored plexiglas
98 x 60 x 81 inches

¶ In 1993, Rees published an article titled "Yale Sculpture," which made playful reference to the Yale "pedigree," interspersing a discussion of himself and four classmates with descriptions of purebred dogs.[59] Rees speaks of them as a community of peers, not of teachers and students; Barney similarly recalls von Schlegell's strength as being that he allowed them to do what they wanted.[60] It is a postwar commonplace that rapid social and technological change has rendered teachers and parents obsolete as models for young people.[61] The imperative to be socially synchronized means that we learn more from peers, with whom we find either community or competition: recent graduates of Yale sculpture have described the experience as being not unlike *Lord of the Flies*.[62] How should the professors respond? Perhaps to behave like the students, joining the community of the young.
¶ If there was certainly a Yale pedigree, was there a Yale style as well? In a 1992 review of Grey's solo show at Stuart Regen Gallery, the writer discerned "the initial manifestations of a 'Yale aesthetic'" in Grey's scientific interests (shared by Barney, Rees, Long, and Katy Schimert).[63] Grey had studied genetics at Berkeley as an undergraduate, and his first solo at Petersburg Gallery, in 1990, was based on the history of science. He created a model of a Russian rocket in *My Sputnik* (1990) and covered a large electron microscope with gray modeling clay in *Electron M. (Microscope)* (1990). *Erosion Blocks: Units of Growth/Decay* (1990) put a basic rectangular form through twenty sculptural variations in pewter. The combination of materiality and abstraction in both art and popular science links Grey to his Yale peers; they share a fundamental opacity of form, as well as an interest in the unformed.[64]

New and Young

"There is no such thing as an unsophisticated art student anymore."[53]—Hilton Kramer, 1960

"Five years ago I never would have expected to see SoHo full of scatter art and body art, junk art and adolescent art, bad-girl art or whatever. It's shocking to me that this has happened, and now universities are turning out people making this stuff. So already my work doesn't mean what it meant five years ago."[54]—Mike Kelley, 1994

Karen Kilimnik
John & Paul, 1990
Crayon on paper
35 x 23 inches

¶ Locally, following the art market crash of summer 1990, what was quickly termed "Slacker" art followed on the 80s go-go art market and its stars.[55] Walking around Soho in November of 1990, one could see young artists Michael Joaquín Grey, Sean Landers (in three places), Lily van der Stokker, Richard Phillips, Karen Kilimnik, Laurie Parsons, Rirkrit Tiravanija, John Currin, Simon Leung, and Gavin Brown. Many of these artists were making their first appearances; the sudden lack of money in New York created a certain sense of room in the artworld because nothing was selling.

¶ The artists of the early 90s were not only young but often took youth as their subject. Much of the art referred to popular culture, which is after all created for (not by) the young.[56] Richard Phillips curated an exhibition called "Total Metal" at Simon Watson in 1990, which featured art inspired by the loud and aggressive (yet relatively mainstream) music, as well as a selection of the clothing and records usually associated with heavy metal, a form of popular culture that targets youth culture at its most alienated.

¶ A still more specific approach was taken by Sean Landers, a recent Yale graduate who made the young artist's struggles the subject of his widely shown scrawlings on yellow notebook paper. As critic Jerry Saltz put it, "Sean Landers was one of the artists who really started the '90s."[57] For his first solo show in 1990, Landers created an alter ego, the sculptor Chris Hamson, and in this voice rambled on about his desire for greatness and anxiety about his art; this self-expression was not heroic but intentionally pathetic and petty. Landers's show at Andrea Rosen in 1992 featured his correspondence with student loan officers in **"Attn. Miss Gonzales"** (1991), which alternated between shame about his poverty, delusions of future greatness, and hostility.

Sean Landers
"Attn. Miss Gonzales", 1991
Ink on paper
8 leaves: 11 x 8½ inches each

¶ Artists noticed and commented on this global cultural exchange. Renée Green, whose work often parodies the role of the visiting artist, installed Import/Export Funk Office (1992) in Cologne. The piece examined the exchange between black American culture and Germany, as exemplified by particular people such as Theodor Adorno; his student Angela Davis; a German music critic, Diedrich Diederichsen; and the artist herself. Green's large-scale installation featured shelves filled with books, cassettes, and videotapes (owned by Green and/or Diederichsen), as well as photos of Green's and Diederichsen's apartments. Hip-hop and political speeches played in the background. Earlier, in 1990, Andrea Fraser (a fellow Whitney graduate) had made a scrapbook tracing the reception of American art in Germany; she implicated herself in that history by including her curriculum vitae as the frontispiece.

¶ Rirkrit Tiravanija's art seemed more happily embracing of diversity. Usually described by critics and curators as a Thai artist, Tiravanija himself emphasizes his experiences in Thailand. He is decidedly less forthcoming about his New York artworld experiences, including those at the Whitney program: asked if he had any important encounters with teachers, Tiravanija replied,

"My schooling has always been more on my own. I learn through the friends I make along the way."[46]

(Nonetheless, his ideal catalogue juxtaposes a "few words from a grandmother who saw a piece somewhere, and then ten densely written pages by Benjamin Buchloh."[47]) The most famous of his works, in which he served pad thai at Paula Allen's gallery in 1990 (a piece that has been repeated several times in later years), determined the dominant reading of Tiravanija's art as "generous" rather than critical.[48] Tiravanija's culinary generosity neatly fits the gastric cosmopolitanism of his audience, even if it is intended to lampoon it.

¶ The political, theoretical interest in the "other" oddly coincided with the expanding global art market; so did the critique of the "romance of the studio." Daniel Buren's essay on the studio appeared in October in 1979 and was included on Craig Owens's syllabus[49]; Michael Asher (an October favorite) teaches a course on "Post-Studio Production" at Cal Arts. The argument against fetishizing the private, expressionist struggle of the individual extended through the artworld concurrent with the "end of painting" in the 70s and early 80s.[50] Throughout his career, Gonzalez-Torres was adamant about not having a studio, eschewing the constant production of objects.[51] But artists of the past decade are also more likely to keep moving. Tiravanija lives all over the world, as do many contemporary artists like Gabriel Orozco and Maurizio Cattelan, who both declare they have no studio. As Cattelan said recently of his constant travel and decision against having a studio:

"This is the condition of everybody lately."[52]

Maurizio Cattelan
Mini-me, 1999
Resin, rubber, fabric, hair, and paint
13¾ inches tall

Market

If the 70s introduced theory to the artworld, the booming art market of the 80s provided an ever-larger object to resist.[36]

"That's why I live in New York, because it's one place where you can go easily to anywhere you want."[35]*—Rirkrit Tiravanija*

Thomas Crow has argued that theory was an appropriately international response by critics trying to hold their own against globalization.[37] But the reliance on theoretical arguments was also a sign of critics' irrelevance in the face of the market, which pushed the critic out of the real center of producing art and legislating taste. Non-academic critics who worked through this period often blamed theory, jargon, and the academicization of criticism for the displacement of critics. Glenn O'Brien suggested that art critics became irrelevant because their writing was impenetrable, while Lisa Liebmann insisted that when critics turned toward theory and away from the "object," they allowed the market to rush into the artworld.[38] Of course, precisely the reverse was true: theoretical discourse responded to the dominance of the market, rather than creating that dominance.

¶ While O'Brien argued that "dealers wielded whatever power the critics once had," some found a different culprit.[39] As Carter Ratcliff put it in 1988:

"Paradoxically, as the '80s art market flourishes, galleries seem to come in for less blame. Flashier, more aggressive players have begun to assume some of that burden. Sleek with profits, they inspire moralistic fingers to shift direction, like weathervanes. Dealers, too, have begun to point. Their targets are the auction houses."[40]

¶ Auction houses, recently the site of enormous sales and speculation in modern and even contemporary art, led some to argue that they had diminished not only critics but dealers.[41] In this atmosphere of short-term speculation—often compared to the stock market—new dealers needed new artists for maximum return—"new" could simply mean "another."[42]

¶ Indeed, another figure of rising power—a new force in the expanding field—was the international curator, jetting around to biennials, fairs, and other international art events, as if to discover new sources of product as well as new markets.[43] The art market crash of 1990 only seemed to increase the importance of these international, state-supported venues, as well as the New York artworld's interest in "other" places.[44] Anticipating trends (whether in young artists or work from other countries) confirmed the role of curators as taste-makers, particularly if the work seemed difficult or anti-market like installation art, and allowed their museums to benefit, eventually, from their "prescient" acquisitions.[45]

¶ Among others who employed this strategy, Janine Antoni, a Rhode Island School of Design M.F.A. graduate, had perhaps the most memorable debut. In 1992 (at age 27), she showed *Gnaw*, a deliberate quotation of Minimalism and, in particular, Tony Smith's *Die*: two giant cubes, one of chocolate, the other of lard, that she had "carved" using her mouth. As Antoni put it,

"I had an incredible self-consciousness about everything: the fact that I couldn't make a mark that didn't have some roots in art history."[28]

One article put this self-consciousness at the feet of "eleven years of expensive American schooling."[29]

¶ Artists like Frank Stella had studied modernism in school and learned what "the next step" was; as Howard Singerman has pointed out, school has absorbed the modernist self-critique. But because the pointed references of young artists of the late 80s and early 90s to earlier avant-gardes often served as testaments to authenticity, the artists were often subject to an interrogation of their motives. One critic voiced his suspicion that Matthew Barney (along with "other artists" left unnamed) had borrowed from more obviously political artists who were pursuing:

"a practice closer to that of minimal and conceptual art, rendering the marketing strategies of the eighties all the more obsolete. Meanwhile, other artists appropriated the new languages of this 'political' art, 'gentrifying' this work to reintroduce political issues as yet another market-oriented art form."[30]

¶ Already, this "new language" could be "appropriated," imitated inauthentically. The critic Benjamin Weil was a 1989 graduate of the Whitney, and presumably found a more genuine use of the historical avant-garde in Whitney instructors such as Jenny Holzer or fellow alumni such as Renée Green.[31]

¶ By the 80s, theory was being disseminated more widely throughout American art schools and universities, largely in anthologies that mixed post-structuralist texts and art criticism. Collections by Hal Foster (*The Anti-Aesthetic*, 1983) and Brian Wallis (*Art After Modernism*, 1984) were required reading in my college classes of the mid-80s. Theoretical commonplaces—particularly those generated by Jean Baudrillard and Guy Debord—also clearly influenced museums, spawning exhibitions such as "A Forest of Signs" (at The Museum of Contemporary Art, Los Angeles, in 1989) and "Image World" (at the Whitney in 1990). Clark himself alluded to the Whitney program's reputation for "orthodoxy" in matters of ideology and pedagogy.[32] As in the earlier case of Abstract Expressionism, it seems that here a school of thought could be defined leading to a certain continuity, but also to increasing standardization and perhaps even a rigidity and dogmatism ("orthodoxy"). In turn, the school produced an intellectual, cultural commodity: the Whitney program style.

¶ The objectification and commodification of theory with a capital "T" has been widely commented on.[33] Joe Masheck, a former *Artforum* editor, referred angrily to "Millionaire Marxists," unnamed critics who lined their pockets while writing left-wing polemic.[34] Much like the contradiction of an art of free expression converted into a new academy, the conversion of an anti-capitalist critique into a fashionable object was too much of an irony for many to bear.

Theory

"It seemed like every week Derrida or Deleuze would be talking at public panel discussions at NYU and we went, and that's what we thought being in the artworld was, and we thought it would never end."[20]
—Andrea Rosen

¶ Clearly, the 50s and 60s already featured many complaints that we usually consider as contemporary: an emphasis on publicity, self-replication in the art schools, far too many artists, a cyclical demand for newness, and the rise of the art market. So what's new? A few interrelated developments of the 70s and 80s stand out: an increasing emphasis on theoretical concerns in art and criticism, the acceleration of the art market through auctions, and the globalization of the artworld. Theory and the market are often opposed, analogous to the perceived splits between October and Artforum, Appropriation Art and Neo-Expressionism, Whitney and Yale.[21]

¶ The advent of "theory" within the American university system, which came to mean French structuralist and post-structuralist writings across the fields of anthropology, linguistics, literature, film studies, history, sociology, and other disciplines, can be dated to the late 60s. Within the artworld, however, the phenomenon wasn't particularly strong until the mid-70s.[22] In 1976, Rosalind Krauss and Annette Michelson, along with Jeremy Gilbert-Rolfe, left Artforum to start the journal October amidst editorial disputes about the direction of the older magazine.[23] October's content was also, like many essays published in Artforum during the early 70s, a reaction to the low intellectual content of graduate art-history programs; even at Harvard and Yale, much of the curriculum was devoted to looking at slides and discussing stylistic relationships. In the mission statement published in the first issue of October, the editors wrote that the journal would use limited illustrations, to be "determined by considerations of textual clarity," stressing "the primacy of text" over images.[24]

¶ If October was the place to read theory in New York, the Whitney Museum's Independent Study Program was the place to study it.

Founded in 1968 and still in operation, it incorporated both a Studio Program and an Art History/Museum Studies Program (renamed Curatorial and Critical Studies in 1987).[25] From the beginning, there was a clear interest in theoretical structures and an avant-garde position towards the larger culture; director Ron Clark characterized its identity as "defined in great measure by its critical relationship to the existing ideological imperatives of the artworld."[26] The historians and critics teaching at the Whitney shared (then and now) an interest in the Frankfurt school of criticism (the "critical theory" of Walter Benjamin and Theodor Adorno, German in origin) and French post-structuralism and psychoanalysis (Jacques Derrida, Jacques Lacan, and others). The artists invited to the program largely practiced various forms of conceptual art, addressing issues of representation and modernist history.

¶ During the 80s and 90s, the number of soon-to-be-prominent alumni included artists Felix Gonzalez-Torres, Andrea Fraser, Mark Dion, Ashley Bickerton, Glenn Ligon, Rirkrit Tiravanija, and Renée Green, as well as dealers, editors, critics, curators, and historians of modernism. Much of the art produced and promoted by the alumni references the strategies and forms of the avant-gardes of the 60s and 70s.[27] Most notably, Gonzalez-Torres set the standard for taking on Minimalist form, not in parody but to infuse it with a personal and more obviously political content.

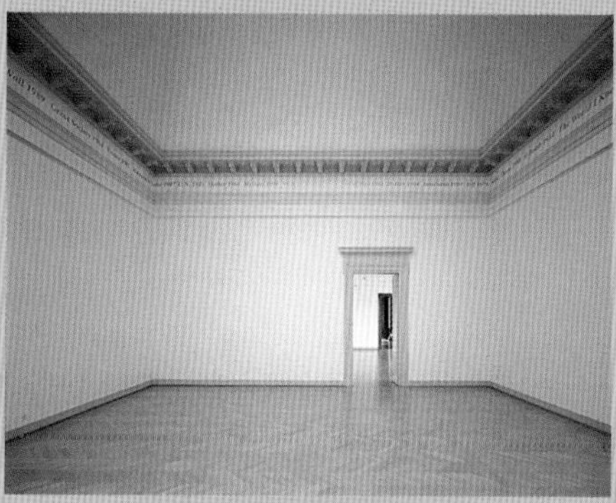

Felix Gonzalez-Torres
Untitled, 1989/1995, at Kunstmuseum St. Gallen, Switzerland, 1997
Paint on wall
Dimensions variable

¶ In 1965 critic Sidney Tillim went so far as to characterize the whole of Pop Art by its relationship with its audience. Rather than falsely credit the artists with a ponderous social critique, Tillim located the importance of Pop Art in its reception. In his account, the entire American culture adheres to the model of the rebellious and most often fun-loving adolescent, rather than the more sophisticated adult or even the more innocent child of European modernism:

"We are witnessing...a release from the conventions, values and consciousness of a culture...grown men and women have thrown off the trappings of 'respectability,' i.e., the serious side of culture, auctioned off their collections of Abstract Expressionism and rolled out the American flag."[18]

¶ Tillim is describing a change in a certain group of established art collectors who—in acting young, going for the next thing, and throwing out European culture—formed "the new audience." The flag of course, represents not only Jasper Johns, but also America: the new, the young, the non-European. Pop Art succeeded because it gave people precisely what they already wanted but weren't prepared to acknowledge; they could enjoy Pop Art because it was fun, and because it seemed to have been made for their generation. If they had any self-reflective tendencies, they would realize that Pop's values were what their culture, even the serious side of it, was all about.

¶ Robert Indiana tied the Pop Artist's representational interest in death to the realization of a limited future: "Pop does admit Death in inevitable dialogue as Art has not done for some centuries; it is willing to face the reality of its own and life's mortality. Art is really alive only for its own time; that eternally-vital proposition is the bookman's delusion."[19]

Jasper Johns
Flag, 1954-55
Encaustic, oil, and collage on fabric mounted on plywood
$42^{1/4}$ x $60^{5/8}$ inches
The Museum of Modern Art, New York
Gift of Philip Johnson in honor of Alfred H. Barr Jr.

¶ Pop Art showed us, then, what was profoundly real in our culture (the commodity, the sign, the socially induced desire, fashion), as opposed to some fantasy about the eternal beauties of nature or history.

¶ Critics in the late 50s and 60s, including Hess, often reiterated this cliché of acceleration to condemn what was perceived as the premature success of younger artists; the Abstract Expressionists themselves—"old" before their "time"—were considerably more bitter about it. Events such as Jasper Johns's tremendously successful first one-man show, held in 1958 when he was twenty-eight years old, drew considerable attention and comment. The Museum of Modern Art (MOMA) bought three works—its first purchase of a major Hans Hofmann had been made only two years earlier in 1956, when that artist was already seventy-six years old.[11]

Frank Stella
The Marriage of Reason and Squalor, II, 1959
Enamel on canvas
90¾ x 132¾ inches
The Museum of Modern Art, New York
Larry Aldrich Foundation Fund

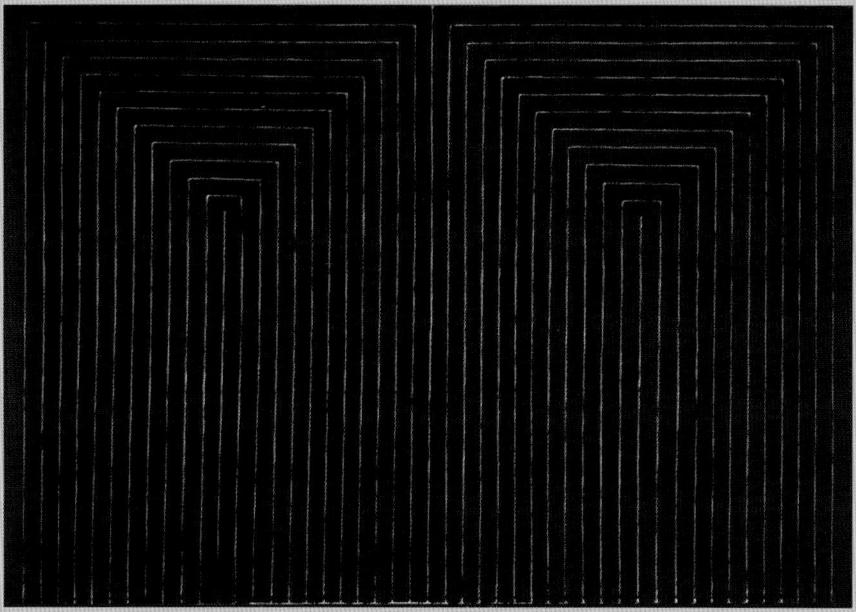

¶ In 1959, MOMA's "Sixteen Americans" exhibition opened.[12] The fourth of the museum's postwar "group" exhibitions, held at irregular intervals since 1946, "Sixteen Americans" caused quite a stir, largely because of the youth of the artists, in particular Frank Stella, then twenty-three years old with one gallery show to his credit. The museum had waited until 1952 to include Pollock in one of its group shows, and until 1956 to recognize Franz Kline—both five years after the artists' seminal moments of invention—and was criticized for its slowness.[13] William Rubin, discussing the museum's shifting criteria in his appropriately titled essay "Younger Artists," wrote of the previous MOMA exhibitions:

"Whether the Museum intended it or not, inclusion in them constituted a kind of official sanction. In view of the youth, relative inexperience, and in some cases total lack of reputation of the 'Sixteen Americans,' no such canonization can possibly be implied."[14]

¶ Of course, official sanction was implied: MOMA was not generously offering unknown artists their chance for exposure. Rather, the province of "official sanction" had moved from the canonization of successful, mature artists to the coronation (and some would say, creation) of young artists as stars of the future.[15]

¶ Youth culture extended not just to young artists but also to a young audience and to young collectors. Designed to introduce its broad national readership to Pop Art, a 1963 article in Time magazine, "Pop Art: Cult of the Commonplace," described its viewers as "decorous teenage girls" from prestigious private schools giggling at the Guggenheim Museum.[16] Similarly, art critic Max Kozloff, in an early review of Pop Art, referred to its supporters as "vulgarians" and "bobby soxers."[17]

At least in description, art's new audience of high schoolers and bobby soxers was the same age as the audience for movies, top-forty music, and comic books—the products of popular culture.

"With a few important exceptions, most of the artists of this vanguard found their way to their present work by being cut in two. Their type is not a young painter but a re-born one. The man may be over forty, the painter around seven. The diagonal of a grand crisis separates him from his personal and artistic past."[7]

¶ These artists, for Clement Greenberg and other critics as well as for Rosenberg, presented a new model for the artist, one most often represented by Jackson Pollock. This "new" artist experienced long stretches of seemingly unproductive time; he or she did not slowly evolve into a master, but rather abruptly burst into greatness, into a signature style that might have little apparent connection to previous and perhaps otherwise undistinguished work.

¶ During the mid-50s, there appears to have been a sharp rise in self-consciousness about the category of "younger"; between 1956 and 1958, several articles satirized the idea.[8] The term was primarily comparative, defining artists as separate from and in relation to those already established. "Younger" covered a multitude of art practices, such as the popular imagery of Jasper Johns and Robert Rauschenberg (whom critics found particularly difficult to place); the Color-Field painting of Morris Louis and Kenneth Noland; and the more easily assimilated second-generation Abstract Expressionist painting of Joan Mitchell and Milton Resnick.

¶ These artists didn't have to be substantially younger chronologically than established artists, only to have not yet received the rewards of career success. Herman Cherry's plaintive and amusing letter in a 1960 issue of *ArtNews*:

"I think this myth about me being a 'younger artist' has reached a point of no return. It has become absurd. Writers on art have been pigeonholing me as a youth (alas, some of the writers have since passed on) despite the greying hair, arthritis, gout, glasses and subsequent middle-age ailments...I am becoming suspicious that 'younger' means 'lesser reputation.'"[9]

In other words, youth was defined in terms of public recognition and success; being "young" meant being relatively unknown to the market, to the art consumer. Youth described a position as much as an age.

¶ Another reason "younger" artists received so much attention during the 50s is the perceived acceleration of time—with regard to both the course of a career and change in the world of art in general. The following passage from Thomas Hess's "Great Expectations" is typical:

"Any attempt to define current professional usage of terms indicating the passage of time in modern art indicates how drastically the tempo of this change has accelerated..."[10]

¶ For many, this distinction blurred further during the 60s. Lawrence Alloway inveighed against the confusion between new and novel, blaming it on the institutional demands of the artworld:

"Whereas, formerly, the new in art existed in an aggressive and dynamic relation to an established, fixed style, revolution is no longer its only justification. Revolutions, and what look like revolutions, still occur, but paced now by publication and exhibition."[2]

¶ Often critics linked art still more explicitly to the rhythms of advertising and consumer culture. William Seitz stated this quite clearly:

"New manifestations now appear with such regularity and rapidity that the professional or collector who wants to remain in style must switch quickly....As in automobiles and dishwashers, it would appear, obsolescence is built into new forms."[3]

¶ Who would provide these new products? Not the old artists. Jackson Pollock and Franz Kline were both soundly rebuffed in their attempts to change styles, to depart even mildly from the kind of work the artworld had come to expect of them. Rather, critics and dealers (and collectors) began to look to the "next" generation. In 1954, Art in America began its "New Talent" exhibitions and accompanying special issues; in 1958, ArtNews began a feature in the reviews section entitled "New Names this Month."[4]

Young

"To 'make one's name' means making one's mark, achieving recognition (in both senses) of one's difference from other producers, especially the most consecrated of them... To introduce difference is to produce time."[5]—Pierre Bourdieu

One form that America's "newness" took was a metaphorical characterization of the American artist—and even American art—as young (and as such, the very embodiment of newness).[6] The artworld's sense of the new was affected not only by the larger mid-century consumer culture, but also by the "new" youth culture that sprang up in World War II America: the term "teenager" was first used in 1941. For French critics, as well as for the conservative American artworld, this emphasis on youth carried negative connotations of the callow, unruly child; however, many Americans understandably saw it as a (re)birth of art. Perhaps the most famous instance of this is, again, in Rosenberg's essay. Rosenberg acknowledges the Abstract Expressionists' typically mid-career breakthroughs and changes in style, yet casts their metaphoric artistic age as young:

New

In the late 50s, several important factors defined the newly emergent American artworld, each of which seemed to follow from the other:

the establishment of Abstract Expressionism as a definable style with the capacity to regenerate itself; the emergence of younger artists who represented the continuity of the style; the academicization of Abstract Expressionism, as the style quickly appeared to become formulaic; the death of the avant-garde, to the extent that it was identified with Abstract Expressionism; and the boom in the market for American art.

¶ What happens when the "new art" becomes the old art? And why does it happen so quickly? The five factors listed above in sequence generated each other rapidly, although not inevitably. During the 50s, it was probably the economic potential of the art, as well as the expansion of art schools, that sped "new American painting" along this course, from defining the style and developing a new generation of followers to the academicization that signaled both the end of the avant-garde and success in the marketplace. This last result—success in the marketplace—is made possible by an identifiable product in good supply, one that seems new and familiar (and perhaps status-providing) all at once.

¶ Harold Rosenberg epitomized one critical reaction to the situation of the late 50s, making a distinction between the new as high modernism and the novel as the exploitation of that modernism in mass culture. In "The American Action Painters," Rosenberg defined authentic newness (the art of the present moment—the "Art of the Modern") against the "NEW," which appeared in the form of the mass consumption of "Modern Art." In a "revolution of taste," art is addressed to the masses in the form of design:

"Through Modern Art the expanding caste of professional enlighteners of the masses—designers, architects, decorators, fashion people, exhibition directors—informs the populace that a supreme Value has emerged in our time, the Value of the NEW, and that there are persons and things that embody that Value."[1]

¶ Rosenberg's complaint, similar to those made forty years earlier about the popularization of Cubism, was lodged against the market ("profit-making enterprises") and the use of art to propagate middle-class culture by converting it into superficial newness, the novelty that is the mainstay of capitalist business systems, whether it's to appear as shoes with a new line, or drawing with a new line.

Young Americans

In the past few months, I have heard two similar stories from the East and West coasts.

At Yale, where graduating painters customarily pick names out of a hat to decide the rosters of their M.F.A. shows, some students have recently expressed interest in "curating" their own exhibitions, matching themselves not with other painting students, but with the best students in the sculpture and photography departments.

Insisting on his right to present himself in the most flattering, professional light, a student protested to a skeptical teacher: "But Thelma Golden's coming!" Across the country at UCLA, there are students who won't listen to the advice or critique of older faculty members, whose careers they feel don't carry sufficient weight. One student in particular apparently rebutted a professor's negative evaluation of a work by saying:

"Mike Ovitz already came by and bought it."

¶ Although they come from reliable sources, these stories have an apocryphal sound to them. They seem to illustrate almost too neatly certain current ideas about the declining authenticity of art schools and, beyond that, of the entire artworld. The apotheosis of the art school, the inflated market, rampant careerism, and youth culture are all commonplace targets of complaint today. These complaints have a history.

BY KATY SIEGEL

Keiko Sato, *Untitled*, 2000. Glass and sand. Dimensions variable. Installation at South London Gallery, London, 2000

Street space run by Tamara Chodzko and Thomas Dane, where Hirst made the important early installation piece *In & Out of Love* using live butterflies, or the Milch Gallery where Lawren Mabel organized the remarkable first and last London showing of work by the late Hamad Butt, a seminal early attempt to make an effective link between the languages of art and science. The Shop on Bethnal Green Road, run by Tracey Emin and Sarah Lucas, marketed "bad-girl" artifacts—the first systematic attempt to reflect upon the increasing commodification of the London scene—and the betting-shop-turned-art-gallery City Racing mounted occasional exhibitions with many of the new generation of artists, including Mark Wallinger, Sarah Lucas, and Sam Taylor Wood.

¶ During the eleven years of Thatcherism a seismic shift had occurred in the character and operation of the London art scene. In a way though, it had come full circle. Once a slightly sleepy, even rather comfortable place for artists to live and work, now it was much more commercially active and professionally competitive. However, what had started off as a radical, artist-centered initiative set to bypass both the gallery system and the orthodoxies of the middle-class cultural establishment, by the mid-90s had drifted into a new kind of commercially focused, commodity-oriented conservatism. For the most part, the new generation of British artists had succumbed entirely to the heady blandishments of the galleries and surrendered themselves to the institutions of the state, to be used jingoistically in the promotion of the economically revitalized new Britain.

¶ In this respect, it is interesting to compare developments in British art during the second half of the 90s with the direction art was taking on mainland Europe. While continental European artists were exploring ways of dissolving the art object by adopting informal installation strategies and the use of new media (I am thinking of artists like Suchan Kinoshita, Keiko Sato, Eran Schaerf, and Joelle Teurlinckx), British art remained wedded to the object and to its treatment as the furniture of spectacle with a few notable exceptions—Steve McQueen, for example, or the Wilson twins. This was perhaps the most noteworthy characteristic of the "Sensation" exhibition held at the Royal Academy in London in 1997. While European artists were becoming more and more preoccupied with developing "positional" critical thought in clear opposition to the idea of the work of art as saleable object or commodity, British artists seemed to have given themselves over almost entirely to the gallery system and embraced the mythology of freedom that goes hand-in-hand with the ideology of the open market. This is not to say that the British art scene of today is without critical dimension, just that it has been temporarily drowned out by the clamor of artworld successes. Indeed, the critical issue remains the same:

a continuous undercurrent in British art since the time of John Ruskin and William Morris that is about cultural ownership, art's humanizing mission and its ultimate intelligibility.

¶ By the late 80s monetary economics, coupled with the natural course of industrial change, had produced a severe contraction of Britain's traditional manufacturing base. Large tracts of land where industry had once ruled supreme were in urgent need of regeneration, and all sorts of new quango-style organizations were put in place to help facilitate this process. In London a vast area to the east of the city, north and south of the river Thames, known as Docklands had been laid waste, as had tracts further east and on the margins of north and south London, too. Many of these sites were in the hands of development agencies or tied to local planning initiatives through public/private partnerships of different kinds. Not surprisingly the agents were looking for short-term "lets," anything that would help them bridge the income gap before full-scale development could begin.

¶ Artists and artist organizations moved in to create studio complexes, followed by temporary exhibition spaces aimed at escaping the usual processes of institutional scrutiny. In the event, the new breed of property entrepreneur proved more prepared for risk-taking cultural ventures than the old-style arts establishment. Docklands became a place for artists to live, work, and show their wares. The first major initiative of this kind to capture the public imagination was Damien Hirst's ground-breaking, three-part exhibition "Freeze," held in a disused tally-warehouse in Surrey Docks over the summer of 1988. Featuring work by three generations of Goldsmiths students including Angela Bulloch, Mat Collishaw, Ian Davenport, Angus Fairhurst, Damien Hirst, Gary Hume, Sarah Lucas, Simon Patterson, and Fiona Rae, it attracted widespread critical attention both in Britain and abroad. Hirst, who was only in his second year at Goldsmiths, had achieved a breakthrough in the exhibiting options available to young artists, one that would be imitated many times over in the course of the next five or six years. Notable examples from 1990 include "Modern Medicine," a joint curatorial venture between Hirst, Billee Sellman, and Carl Freedman at Building One, which introduced the work of Abigail Lane to the art-going public; Sellman and Freedman's "Gambler," which included Hirst's first large-scale vitrine piece, *A Thousand Years*; Michael Landy's vast, thematic, solo show, "Market"; and Sarah Lucas and Henry Bond's "East Country Yard Show."

¶ As the property-market roller-coaster rumbled on into the 90s, so the round of exhibition-making continued. Warehouse shows that sought to imitate those at Saatchi Gallery or Kunsthalle-style showing conditions became almost routine. A symbiotic relationship was established between the property market as the alternative art scene and its exhibitions became part of the selling and letting strategies of estate agents. Although commerce had effectively closed down many of the spaces that the young artists of the 80s had worked so hard to open up, suddenly, a more conventional type of gallery space began to look like an attractive proposition again. Many of them were run by artists—mostly on a short-term basis—without the trappings of art-dealing attached: the Woodstock

¶ Most critical commentators on the Goldsmiths artists describe the work as a collision between Duchamp and Minimalism. Naïve though this description is, it is not entirely erroneous. Two of the earliest shows at the Saatchi Gallery—a group exhibition of American art including a major showing of Minimalism that inaugurated the gallery in the autumn of 1985 and one year later, "New York Art Now," were of great importance to successive years of Goldsmiths students graduating between 1986 and 1990. Indeed, they exemplify two of the main concerns shaping attitudes at Goldsmiths at that time: the desire to be formally lucid and materially direct, and the intention to deal with the emerging complexities of contemporary life in an open-handed way.

Firsthand experience of major works by Donald Judd, Brice Marden, and Richard Serra, previously accessible only through magazines and catalogues, taught them something about a way of "thinking" and "making," while the Neo-Geo artists Ashley Bickerton, Robert Gober, and Jeff Koons—as well as fueling their desire to be sharp and stylish—demonstrated a way of referencing the world without representing it. The bar-room chat of the time held "expressiveness" to be absolutely out and the "dumbshow"—work that refused to disclose—absolutely in.

If there is a distinctive flavor to the Goldsmiths brand of irony, then, it would seem to subsist in the pretense that as long as works of art look thoroughly at home in the current "commodity-scape," they can simply lie doggo and that's enough. Gary Hume's door paintings and Damien Hirst's spots, some of which were made at Goldsmiths College as early as 1987, seem to exemplify this approach. It is of course a pose, a rather disingenuous form of self-stereotyping—a façade of ironic chic. Beneath the smart outward show and the assumed rhetorical ease, this so-called Goldsmiths style, which by now has come to represent a much broader strand of British contemporary art, is focused in reality on the question of "values." This is its Duchampian aspect. Skeptical towards both the market and the institutions of cultural attribution, at its toughest—and here it is appropriate to cite the work of artists like Tracey Emin, Sarah Lucas, Bob and Roberta Smith, Mark Wallinger, and Gillian Wearing—it is steeped in the spiritual ennui that attends all radical forms of doubt. Furthermore, to choose to live the conflict—artworld as comfortable "habitus" versus artworld as a "grand folly"—rather than simply coming down on the side of the status quo in the British context ties the debate inevitably to the question of social class.

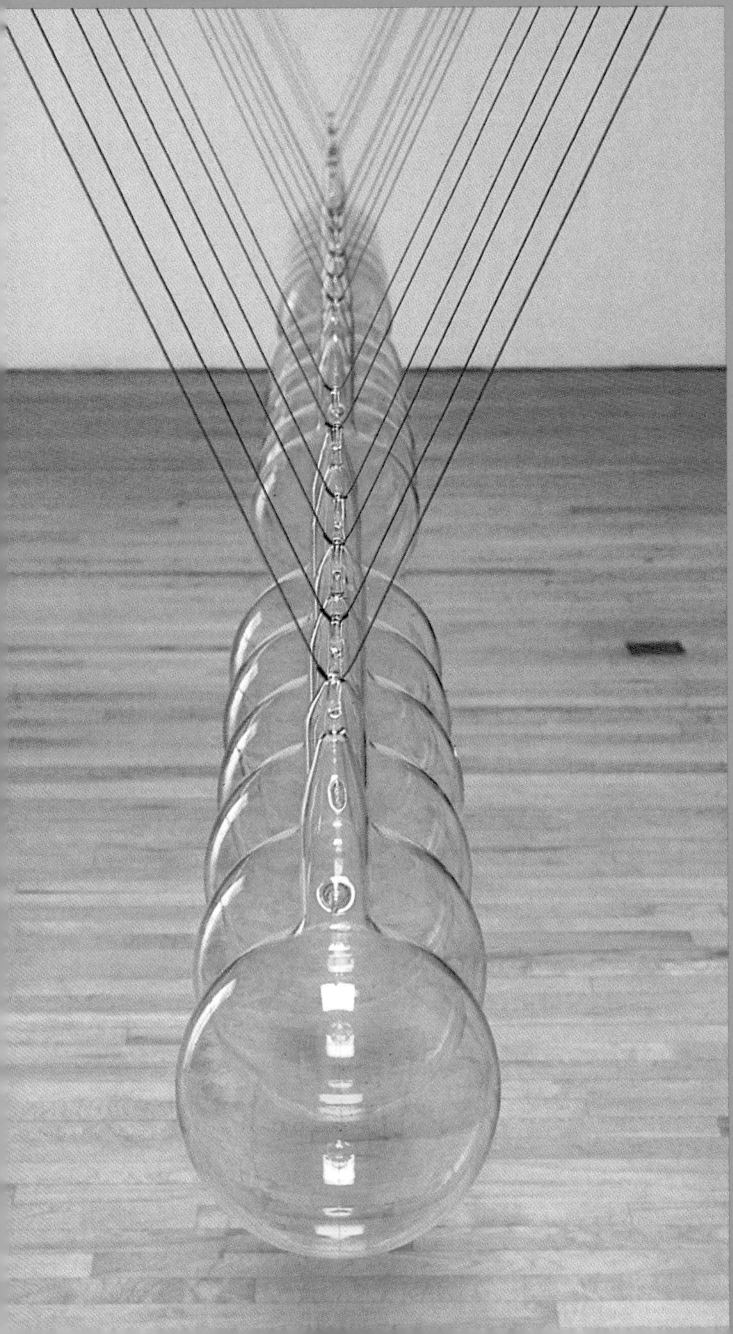

¶ Since the Second World War, British art has tended to draw its energy from popular culture, while its values have continued to be shaped by an older order: the patrician connoisseurship of the educated middle class whose members have traditionally filled the ranks of the civil service and occupied key positions in the mainstream cultural institutions and quangos (Quasi-Autonomous Non-Governmental Organizations) put in place to control them. In this respect, the formation of cultural values has mostly been a case of like minds agreeing with like according to a shared agenda of interests. This natural consensus remained unchallenged until 1979 when Margaret Thatcher came to power. Part of the objective of the Thatcherite counter-revolution—she puts it very concisely in her political memoirs—was to remove the "deadening hand" of the liberal, middle-class consensus from affairs of the state. In Thatcher-speak this meant professionalizing its administrative functions by importing sound business methods and expertise into every level of public life. Accordingly, the arts saw the advent of a new breed of administrator. The "arms-length" principle, in place since the 30s, was comprehensively breached by a whole series of politically motivated appointments, and the existing, privileged executive class was replaced by one in which business interests were at least as important as cultural ones.

Hamad Butt, *Familiars Part 3: Cradle* (detail), 1992
Chlorine, glass, steel, wire, and white paint
Installation at Tate Gallery, London, 1995

¶ **From the inter-war period on, private galleries had clustered together on and around Bond Street, the most expensive and exclusive commercially rated shopping area in London's West End.**

With the notable exceptions of Nicholas Logsdail's Lisson Gallery on Bell Street; Nigel Greenwood Inc. near Sloane Square; and Matt's Gallery, a pioneering, studio-style showing space in the East End run by the artist and teacher Robin Klasnick, this was still the case at the beginning of the 80s. But as the decade got under way, chiefly because of economic pressure, the gallery scene began to disperse. New galleries were opened by a new generation of gallerists and dealers. Situated in less predictable, sometimes quite obscure parts of the capital, most of these were focused around what was already being referred to as new art: "new" having by this time superseded "contemporary" in the lexicon of the fashion-conscious cultural set. New British art also needed an informed audience and a committed group of collectors. Both were there for the building as the recovery gathered pace. New British art also needed to find its place in the international art scene—and not simply along the old transatlantic axis that had served previous generations of postwar British artists so well.

¶ Like the global economic landscape, the landscape of the global art market was undergoing rapid change. New York was losing its dominance. The European revival was underway in Germany and Italy. Many of the new breed of London gallerists—Karsten Schubert, Victoria Miro, Mario Fletcher, Nicola Jacobs, Maureen Paley at Interim Art, and Robin Klasnick at Matt's—had considerable international experience and were ideally placed to assist in this process of contextualization. Others, like Anthony Reynolds, Laure Genillard, Nigel Greenwood, and Richard Salmon, concentrated more on the task of securing a place in the market for the emerging generation of British artists. Younger collectors of new art had started to emerge in growing numbers where few had existed before. A new moneyed class had begun to show itself—one that was mostly involved in the increasingly successful service sector of the British economy.

Margaret Thatcher's policy of deregulation had spawned a new type of nouveau riche—lifestyle junkies determined to be at the cutting edge. And cutting-edge art was an important part of their social currency both at home and at work. Advertising and public-relations agencies, television and graphic-design studios, fashion houses, and new designer stores led the way, establishing a different approach to the working environment in which up-to-the-minute works of art were an important part of the "image-building" array.

¶ Fashionable tendencies depend on leaders of fashion, and Charles and Doris Saatchi were tailor-made for the task. He was rich, successful, socially active, and culturally engaged. As one half of the advertising partnership Saatchi and Saatchi whose slogan "Britain Isn't Working" brought Margaret Thatcher to power, Charles was also politically tuned in. Doris Saatchi, by contrast, was an artworld insider, an art historian with a passion for collecting contemporary art. During the late 70s and the first half of the 80s, working together and out of the public eye they built a truly extraordinary collection, staggering in its scale and quality. It was made visible only in 1985 when they opened a gallery on Boundary Road. The British art public had seen nothing like it. America, it seemed, had come to Britain. And while there were detractors—dark murmurings of American imperialism—the enthusiasm of the young was unconfined. As founding members of the Friends of New Art, influential international collectors, and owners of an important, semi-public gallery space in the capital, the Saatchis were uniquely placed to influence public institutions and public taste. They set about doing both. Indeed, their activities were instrumental in feeding the desire for change. But it would be misleading to suggest that there was some grand purpose behind their activities, beyond personal ambition and the public display of a shared enthusiasm for new art.

Nevertheless, their early curatorial activities at the Boundary Road gallery conspired with other factors in the development of what became known as the "Goldsmiths style."

¶ **Most serious dealers and gallerists, especially those** who work at the cutting edge of the international art market, seem gifted—like gamblers everywhere—with an unreasonable degree of raw optimism. Buying and selling contemporary works of art inevitably involves taking risks; even when the cold wind of recession is blowing at its most chill, rather than simply battening down the hatches, their first instinctive response tends to be a commercially aggressive one. Instead of retreating, they redouble their efforts to make sales, search for new markets, and, perhaps most important of all, look for new artists with distinctive new products to promote. This was very much the prevailing atmosphere in the London of the early 80s. The dealing fraternity was out and about visiting studios, making mixed exhibitions, giving opportunities to young up-and-coming artists to make their mark. The first, tentative signs of economic recovery seemed to set into motion a process of transformation that, over time, was to bring about the complete restructuring of the London artworld. Driven by a consensus on the need for change, which at the time seemed almost to have arisen subliminally, people began to behave differently towards artists, towards each other, and towards the larger artworld outside.

Damien Hirst, *A Thousand Years*, 1990. Steel, glass, rubber, flies, maggots, MDF, insect-o-cutor, cow's head, sugar, water, and bolts. 84 x 168 x 84 inches

¶ Enthusiastic observers of the London art scene have tended to attribute its revival to the activities of particular institutions, key individuals, or the advent of certain important regular events: the founding of the Tate Gallery's Friends of New Art in 1976, Patrons of New Art in 1982, the start of the Turner Prize in 1984, the collecting activities of Charles and Doris Saatchi in the 80s and the opening of the Saatchi Gallery in 1985, or Damien Hirst's "Freeze" exhibition in 1988. All of these and many more besides were clearly of great moment and served to influence the subsequent pattern of events in important ways. But, as is so often the case, the truth is more complex than that. It is clear, for instance, that by the mid-80s there were a lot of people in the London artworld who were seeking to make a more contemporary response to the changes that were occurring in the practice of artists and in the global art market. New money had replaced old as the engine of cultural capital.

The exclusivity of the collecting habit had begun to break down, and this in turn was transforming even the geography of the London gallery scene.

¶ By the early 80s forces were already at work that would change the London art scene dramatically within a decade. While it is undoubtedly true that the commercial gallery system tends to shrink as a recession takes hold, it is also true that the art market is often one of the earliest strands of the economy to respond positively to signs of an economic upturn. Optimism and pessimism can also sometimes appear to coexist, and this was very much the case in the London artworld of the early 80s. Sales of high profile, blue-chip contemporary artists were becalmed while another space in the market was beginning to open up.

¶ Periods of economic depression can hold within them the seeds of change and offer the opportunity to build something new. In the case of fine-art sales (as with all commodity markets), a subtle shift in the economic climate can precipitate a change in the prevailing mood of consumers. Margaret Thatcher's monetarist experiment suffered its darkest hour in the winter of 1980-81. By January, "good-weather" adherents of the monetarist cause, including some cabinet ministers, had begun to abandon ship; and in February, the conservative *Times* newspaper, in an attempt to change the direction of the government's economic policy, carried the headline "Wrong, Wrong, Wrong."

But Margaret Thatcher stuck to her guns and the budget of 1981 was again solidly moneterist in its drift, though at the behest of her closest economic advisor, Sir Alan Walters—and against the advice of the Treasury—it included measures designed to allow the monetary base of the domestic economy to grow more quickly. The seeds of economic recovery had been sown. By the close of the year the first green shoots of an economic upturn were beginning to show through, all but buried beneath the debris of a disastrously inadequate social policy. Just two short years later, in 1983, Margaret Thatcher was able to announce to the House of Commons that public finances had improved to the point that she was able to fund the 1982 Falklands campaign out of the government's contingency reserve, with no extra taxation and no adverse effects on the financial markets.

Michael Landy, *Market*, 1990. Installation at Building One, London, 1990

Beyond this, as she states in her memoirs, society is a useless "abstraction." On the surface, there is nothing particularly reprehensible about such a notion, if it were not for the fact that Thatcherism worked with a version of the individual that was obsolete except in the conservative clubs of small-town, rural Britain. Exemplary of what she describes as "Victorian virtues," they were to be hard-working family-builders, self-disciplined and self-reliant, with a strong sense of civic pride and responsibility. Even if they happened to be poor, they had to be on the right side of the moral divide between the "deserving" poor and the "undeserving."

¶ This Thatcherite "individual" was also relatively uncultured. During her eleven years as prime minister, there was no cabinet portfolio for the arts or for culture. And in almost nine hundred pages of political memoirs, she devotes only four to arts policy, a retrospective apologia for her stand against increasing state subsidies to the arts. In passing she defines the arts as "unplanned, unpredictable, eccentrically individual" and, in their effect, "serving only the vested interests of the arts lobby." Artists, in short, were beyond the proper scope and reach of the responsible state. "No artist has a right to live off his work," she writes, "independent of market forces." Again it was the very opposite construction of the role of the artist to that envisaged by the Goldsmiths model, which started from a belief in the absolute necessity for a mixed economy in the arts. As true individuals—inventive, free-acting, non-conforming, critically responsible members of a lived, continuously evolving culture—artists would come in every shape and size, and would involve themselves in many different forms of practice, some of which would find no very comfortable or appropriate niche in the commercial art market.

Abigail Lane, Prop I, 1990. Painted MDF, photograph on aluminum. 24 x 48 x 48 inches

¶ Though the objective behind the Goldsmiths model was simple, by starting with the very basic question of what should be taught to an ambitious art student in the last quarter of the twentieth century, it came to threaten many of the most cherished and long-standing beliefs of British art education. The traditional, craftbased divisions between painting, sculpture, and print were dismantled and replaced by an integrated, idea-led model that embraced all of the new forms of practice on equal terms. Compulsory drawing was abandoned. Classes and short-course teaching were stopped and a tutorial system installed, which for the first time embraced art theory as an integral part of practice. It amounted to a radical review of the idea of "studentship" itself. In a comparatively short space of time the residual pedagogy of the old academies and the institutionalized authority of the teacher had been replaced by something approaching a community of artists talking and working together.

¶ In the event, Goldsmiths' program produced strongly committed young artists of radical disposition who were also self-confident and articulate, well able to hold their own in any arena of critical debate. Even so, they were shunned by the main post-graduate centers because they were said to be "too formed," "too clever," or, most damning of all, "too professional." As late as the mid-80s, the barely ghosted figure of the nineteenth-century grand amateur still stalked the corridors of British art schools. The annual exhibition of Goldsmiths student work had become a notable event on the London arts calendar, attended by dealers, critics, and collectors, and yet there was still nowhere else in the so-called higher levels of art education for Goldsmiths graduates to go. By now it is a matter of history that at a certain moment—sometime during the first half of the 80s—they stopped trying to go anywhere and opted instead for the direct leap into the world of professional practice.

Goldsmiths, alone amongst British art schools,

existed in a funding limbo between local authority financing and direct grants from the government with neither institution prepared to take full responsibility. Having no single, all-powerful funding authority tugging at its purse strings meant that, while it was in no position to ignore this process of regulation, it was at least able to invent its own solutions to the problems that it caused. This state of uncertainty continued into the late 80s and it generated a spirit of independence which, in concert with the reforms set in motion by the occupation of 1969, contributed to the transformation of Goldsmiths into the most significant center of fine-art education in Britain.

¶ This freedom to determine its own course of action was of considerable importance to the subsequent development of the fine-art department. Seen in the context of the rest of British higher education, from the late 60s through the 80s Goldsmiths was an entirely unique institution. The form of teaching that is now referred to as the Goldsmiths model was intended to achieve one very simple objective: in line with student demands, it was to make the educational experience for young artists correspond more closely to the conditions prevailing in the professional world outside. However, to call it simple is not to disguise the more problematic, even contradictory political dimension of the project; the fact that, although it sprang from an entirely different ideological perspective—that of the principled, libertarian left—the underlying objective found an extraordinary (and, some have argued, more than fortuitous) echo in the individualistic brand of conservatism espoused by Thatcherism. Such arguments, though, are deeply misleading.

Mat Collishaw, *Untitled (crucifixion)*, 1990
Slide projection
Dimensions variable

¶ Expecting to obtain the cabinet portfolio for education in Margaret Thatcher's first government, Sir Keith Joseph, Margaret Thatcher's ideological mentor, coined the phrase "education for working life" prior to the election victory of 1979. It subsequently became almost a political *cri de coeur* for New Conservatism. Under Thatcher education was to be made responsible and purposeful; all New Conservative citizens were to be equipped to live a useful life.

The difference between the education philosophies of Goldsmiths and the ruling conservative government, then, is crystal clear. Goldsmiths' objective was, in the deepest sense, educational. It was intended to release and radicalize the creative potential of young artists. Joseph's philosophy was aimed at achieving conformity. Young people were to be taught how to occupy prefigured, idealized roles as full participants in the commercial and social construction of a new middle class. They were individuals only insofar as they were able to contribute a necessary component within an essentially asocial, conservative utopia. As a disciple of the American theologian and social scientist Michael Novak, Margaret Thatcher hated the very idea of society except as a "concrete" entity, a "structure of responsible individuals."

¶ The worldwide campus uprisings and occupations of 1968–69 occurring in the States in places like Ann Arbor, Berkeley, and Madison, and on mainland Europe at the Universities of Paris, Milan, Rome, and Turin—found their sharpest point of focus, not surprisingly, in Britain at the LSE (London School of Economics). More curiously, the most intense secondary points of confrontation occurred at art schools, with prolonged student disturbances and occupations occurring at Hornsey College of Art on the northern fringe of greater London and at the opposite end of the city at Goldsmiths. Despite the distance between these two institutions, subsequent analysis has shown that the two groups of student leaders were in close communication with each other and presented their respective colleges with a common agenda for reform: a set of quite reasonable demands for improvements in both the substance and delivery of their courses, and fairly standard requests for greater participation in the decision-making processes governing student life. Mixed in with these was an array of highly contentious proposals—including the purging of named members of staff with largely imaginary "fascistic" tendencies, and a call for collegiate declarations of solidarity with a number of global revolutionary movements headed by such fashionable figures as Ho Chi Minh, Fidel Castro, and Mao Tse-tung.

Mark Wallinger, Fountain, 1992. Hose pipe, water, and gallery. Dimensions variable

¶ Thus far, whenever Goldsmiths' story has been told it is hardly ever mentioned that, but for astute handling by the academic leadership of the college, what local history now calls the "Hornsey Affair" might easily have ended up as the "Hornsey/Goldsmiths Affair." The reactions of the two institutions were strikingly different. Prompted by their public-sector paymasters, Hornsey opted for a policy of confrontation and resistance. By contrast, Goldsmiths, which enjoyed greater scope for independent action, straightaway entered into negotiations with its students, applying at the same time a strategy of "controlled inertia." The intention was to be as constructive as possible, but also to slow down events so as not to be forced into conceding too much too quickly. Predictably, the Hornsey troubles were brought to an end more decisively, but with a great deal of damage to the social and academic fabric of the institution, while the gradualist approach adopted at Goldsmiths allowed the argument to rumble on into the early 70s, but with certain very positive outcomes for the future of the college.

¶ The 70s saw increased regulation of the British art education system. Edicts from the government were delivered on an almost weekly basis which, taken together, spelled a potentially very damaging restructuring of the whole provision. Although Goldsmiths' real estate was owned by the University of London, it was not funded by the Court of the University or by the University Grants Commission. It cherished a longstanding ambition to become a school of the university, and it taught University of London degrees across a wide spectrum of subjects, but its application for school status had been blocked for political reasons on successive occasions.

Donald Judd, *Untitled*, 1981. Plywood. 138 3/8 x 927 5/8 x 45 3/8 inches. Installation at The Saatchi Gallery, London, 1985

¶ For the most self-aware of the schools—those in metropolitan centers in particular—this change towards a more professional attitude had, in any case, already started to gather pace from the beginning of the 70s. Force of circumstance now meant that this process was greatly accelerated. Exceptionally, at Goldsmiths College, tucked away in one of the poorest districts of south-east London, the change had already been achieved by the middle of the 70s.

Whenever the revival of the British art scene is talked about it is invariably linked with the rise of the Department of Fine Art at Goldsmiths College. And if you list the names of young artists who came to prominence in the 80s and early 90s, you would observe that a substantial number were taught there. The reasons why this particular school was able to be so prominent by the end of the 80s, during a time of steadily increasing political and economic control, are very complex.

The presence of a very high-quality staff comprising young, professionally committed artists, all working on part-time contracts, was one very important factor. Perhaps it was even the most important. But there were other reasons, too. The recent history of the place—the Marxist/Leninist- and Maoist-inspired occupations of the late 60s—had made it ripe for reform. And the anomalous position of Goldsmiths College within the higher education sector meant that reform was possible.

¶ But Thatcherism is not so easy to define in strictly social terms. Arising out of an almost theological dispute over economic method, it mixed moral imperatives with practical economics. It may be most easily defined as a hard-line, Milton Friedman-like monetary experiment designed to energize the British economy by deregulating and liberalizing the market; its main concern is for "honest" money. There were shades of moral rearmament about it, too. As a realpolitik it required a dramatic change in the economic culture: in the public and the private sectors of industry; in the banking and finance houses; and in the minds of trade unionists and of the public at large. Margaret Thatcher referred to this process of reform in almost messianic terms, as "a crusade for national regeneration" intended to halt "the drift into state socialism." In this respect the Thatcherite "counter revolution" was designed from the outset to reach far beyond the boundaries of routine economic policy.

¶ Analysis of Margaret Thatcher's speeches from her first period as prime minister also reveals a highly ambivalent social dimension, expressed very often in carefully crafted sound bites concerning "ending the dependency culture" and "rolling back the nanny state." Thatcherism was intent upon teaching the British people how to be tough and self-reliant. It was a high-risk strategy, and it was clear that Thatcher and her colleagues fully accepted there would be casualties along the way.

By the summer of 1980, there had already been a record number of bankruptcies, and by 1982 the national unemployment figure had risen to

3.25 million.

Informed opinion had always held that if unemployment in Britain reached beyond the two million mark there would be serious civil unrest, and indeed the period between 1981 and 1985 saw a marked escalation in incidents of urban disorder. Some of them—occurring in such major cities as Bristol, Manchester, London, Birmingham, and Liverpool—involved full-scale rioting with a disturbing racial dimension. For the first time since the 30s, Britain was witnessing the formation (and, some have argued, the deliberate construction) of an urban underclass.

¶ Given the crusading objectives of this first Thatcher government—its intention to reenergize and renew not just the economy, but the British way of life—it seems highly paradoxical that it reserved some of its most destructive and socially divisive policies for the state education system.

As unemployment was allowed to grow, the education budget was allowed to wither under inflationary pressure until its share of the gross national product had fallen by seven percent. Universities and polytechnics, as well as schools and departments of art and design—the higher education sector—were hardest hit. Class sizes were forced up and research budgets were cut. Top academics began to quit their posts. Brilliant young scholars began looking to make their futures elsewhere. By the mid-80s, the "brain-drain," as the press had christened it, had reached frightening proportions. This period of imposed financial stringency had a tremendous impact on the art education system. Apart from the immediate, very obvious consequences—the loss of human and material resources— it raised vital long-term questions of a deeper, philosophical kind, in particular the issue of whether the art school's primary function was to produce artists or whether it was just another limb of the general education provision. In the past, wiser minds quite rightly had thought it a question that was best not asked. Now, in the colder economic climate, it emerged center stage.

¶ Predictably, in the asking, it changed altogether the liberal, vocational ethos of these historic institutions, as well as the career intentions of their graduates. The British art-school system had grown out of the utopian ethos of nineteenth-century political thinkers such as Arthur Bradshaw, William Morris, Robert Owen, and John Ruskin. They shared the same ideological roots as the WEA (Workers Education Movement) and had always shown an open door to anyone who could demonstrate even the smallest amounts of creative ability, regardless of their social class or academic qualifications. During the inter- and postwar periods, art schools had come to function as an escape route for the educationally disaffected, providing an important opportunity for thousands of young people who for one reason or another had been unable to prosper in, or benefit from, the experience of mainstream schooling. Now this open door was gradually being forced shut by a series of government-inspired measures linking recruitment to academic qualifications by means of fiscal inducements; the art schools became more and more the domain of the educated middle class. Having been stripped of their principled alternative educational function, and with the teaching profession contracting at every level, the schools were forced to professionalize their educational objectives. There was nowhere else or graduating art students to go except into the outside world as practitioners.

The Economics of Culture: The Revival of British Art in the 80s

The link between the art market and prevailing economic conditions requires little explanation. It can be put very simply: When an economy is booming and producing a surplus for spending at the luxury-goods end of the market, cultural purchasing power is also greatly increased.

We need look to only one set of statistics to support this view. Almost always in times of economic depression, private galleries close down; conversely, when the economy is on an upward path, new galleries open up. However, the well-being of the art market is not simply an economic matter. There is also a political, even ideological, dimension governing its performance, particularly in countries like Britain where the institutions of cultural patronage and the great majority of public museums are funded either directly or indirectly by the government. When the main purchasing power lies firmly in the hands of state-funded institutions, and when there is virtually no long-standing tradition of private patronage—no collecting class, in other words—then the ideology of the government of the day tends to impact very directly on the effective role of private galleries and the workings of the art market in general.

¶ In Britain too, the power of the government to influence the shape and behavior of the art scene has been greatly enhanced by the historic strength of the art school system. A de facto system of patronage as well as a form of education, the art schools were still the most important means of direct support to artists by the beginning of the 80s. In the absence of an indigenous collecting culture, they were virtually the only means by which artists could live and support their practice. This state of affairs was to change dramatically as Thatcherite monetary conservatism, inaugurated by the squeeze on public finances in the budget of 1979, gathered pace during the 80s. In the ten years that followed the art schools lost their power of patronage and with it their independence.

¶ By the end of the decade, along with the rest of Britain's cultural institutions, the art schools had been made subject to the new cult of public accountability. Margaret Thatcher's first term as prime minister began in May 1979. There followed three consecutive periods of office, ending in the autumn of 1990. The young British artists who came to prominence during the late 80s and early 90s, including Damien Hirst, Gary Hume, Chris Ofili, Sarah Lucas, and Rachel Whiteread (all of whom are represented in "Public Offerings"), were schooled, trained, and achieved early recognition as artists under Thatcherism. For this reason, as well as attracting such titles as the Brit-Pack and the YBAs (Young British Artists) from the tabloid press, more serious newspapers have sometimes cast them as part of a wider generational grouping, Thatcher's Children. As Thatcherism's products they acquire a more negative social gloss: Thatcher's Children, by definition, are self-seeking and lack any sense of collective social purpose.

BY JON THOMPSON

¶ As at Goldsmiths College, there are no lecture courses or master classes at the HfbK. Students are free to visit classes held by many instructors (including not only Walther, but also Bernhard Blume, Werner Büttner, and Bogomir Ecker) as long as the number of participants does not exceed the class limit. Apart from Bock, Jankowski, and Meese, the painter Daniel Richter, who studied under Büttner, also numbers among the better-known young graduates from the HfbK Hamburg. Parts of Richter's life story are often emphasized in the reception of his work, such as his time as a squatter and his involvement in the club scene for which he designed flyers. Again, subculture and alternative environments become the breeding ground for artistic production.

¶ Among the recurring accusations against Germany's art academies by many students (and from the outside, as well) are the lack of theory in the curriculum and overrating the traditional student/master relationship. In this context it should be mentioned that the Kunstakademie Düsseldorf still uses the title Meisterschüler (student in a master's class) for the rank that some students can achieve during their final years at the academy. The often-lamented absence of a broad and current theoretical discourse at the academies is especially paradoxical considering the origin and history of the academy as an institution. The term itself can be traced back to the sanctuary of the Heros Akademos where Plato met with his students. But very little of the origins in philosophical teaching can be found in today's German academies. On the contrary, the emphasis they place on craftsmanship clearly contradicts the original concept of the academy. Greek scholars who had come to Italy to negotiate a unification of the Greek and Roman Church revived the term in Italy during the fifteenth century; by the beginning of the sixteenth century, it was used to distinguish artists from those in the craftsmen's guilds.[10] From today's point of view, these free, informal gatherings were about an interdisciplinary exchange of ideas that could involve such different subjects as religion, philosophy, and the (natural) sciences—that is, they correspond exactly to the activities practiced in Germany's subcultural and alternative environments.

¶ Despite the critiques of it as an institution, the German academy has its advantages and offers a kind of freedom. As a governmental and socially recognized educational institution, it not only makes available the necessary work spaces and technical equipment, but also insures students and affords financial assistance for their education. Apart from these practical motivators, the primary reason that young artists enter the formal academy is the opportunity it provides for serious discussion of their work. They expect, then, not only freedom of artistic production, but also a level for critique and reflection. An academy cannot offer more than that because, as Andrea Fraser asserts in the quotation at the beginning of this essay, art can neither be learned nor taught.

Translated by Rosanne Altstatt

Notes

1. Andrea Fraser, in Stephan Dillemuth, ed., Akademie (Munich: Kunstverein München, 1995), 63.
2. See Harald Fricke, "Das alte und das neue Berlin," Texte zur Kunst, no. 38 (June 2000): 50-59, and Diedrich Diederichsen, "Letter from Berlin: Stage Frights," Artforum 36, no. 8 (April 1998): 49-52, 132, 135.
3. See my article "Letter from Cologne: Fair Wars," Artforum 35, no. 3 (November 1996): 31-33.
4. Bettina Funcke, Berlin Biennale Kurzführer (Berlin: Berlin Biennale, 1998), 99.
5. See Gunnar Reski, "Bewohnte Kunst," Texte zur Kunst, no. 29 (March 1998): 65-67.
6. On the history of the Städelschule, see Hubert Salden, ed., Die Städelschule Frankfurt am Main von 1817 bis 1995 (Mainz, Germany: Verlag Hermann Schmidt, 1995).
7. On the galleries and their programs, as well as the general situation of the art scene in mid-90s Cologne, see Sarah McFadden, "Report from Cologne: Changing of the Guard," Art in America 83, no. 2 (February 1995): 61-67.
8. See Hans-Christian Dany, Ulrich Dörrie, and Bettina Sefkow, eds., dagegen dabei: Texte, Gespräche und Dokumente zu Strategien der Selbstorganisation seit 1969 (Hamburg: Edition Michael Kellner, 1998).
9. Isabelle Graw, "Interview," Kanal (November/December 1991): 27.
10. On the origin and history of the academy, see Nikolaus Pevsner, Academies of Art, Past and Present (1940; reprint New York: Da Capo Press, 1973).

¶ In Berlin, Daniel Pflumm has also created a subcultural space with his club Elektro Full Customer Satisfaction. During its operation from 1992 to 1994 in a former store in eastern Berlin,

it was a place where the city's art and music worlds met.

As a founding member of the Elektro Music Department, Pflumm, along with Klaus Kotai and Gabriele Loschelder, has also operated on the cutting edge of music and art by producing records and CDs, as well as videos and T-shirts under the label since 1994.

¶ Like Pflumm's earlier club, the Golden Pudel Club in Hamburg functions as a place where the city's young music and art scenes meet. This venue, which is primarily known for music, also has a small exhibition space called Nomadenoase, which is used by the Akademie Isotrop to show their own work or that of artists invited from other cities. Founded in 1996, the Akademie Isotrop is a group of about twenty artists, musicians, and writers who practice a kind of academic operation that is beyond given institutional structures. Dissatisfied with the structures of conventional academies, they see their work in the collective as a possible expansion and alternative model to what normal art-school education has to offer.

Akademie Isotrop installation in "Kunstmarkt & Avantgarde" exhibition, Galerie Nomadenoase, Golden Pudel Club, Hamburg, 1999

¶ Artists such as Jonathan Meese, Markus Selg, and Stefan Thater are part of Akademie Isotrop, as are theorists and communicators such as Roberto Ohrt. Among the collective's activities are lectures, performances by members and invited guests, participation in both group and solo exhibitions as a group, as well as the operation of Nomadenoase. In addition, they publish the magazine *Isotrop*. Apart from their work as a group, some of them also perform as solo artists, the best known being Jonathan Meese, who links ancient myths from different cultures to historically laden material and pop culture in his performances and scattered installations. Meese studied together with John Bock and Christian Jankowski under Franz Erhard Walther at the Hochschule für bildende Kunst (HfbK/University of Fine Arts) in Hamburg. Today, they number among the most renowned German artists of their generation, and it is striking that the artistic production of all three has a performance base that seems to be more than a little influenced by Walther.

John Bock, *LiquiditatsAuraAromaPortfolio*, 1998
Installation at Berlin Biennale, 1998

Alternative Environments, Subculture, and Music

At the end of the 80s and beginning of the 90s official institutions like museums and art schools were not as important to the development of many young producers of art in Germany as self-organized groups and activities like the leftist media groups Minimal Club in Munich and BüroBert in Dusseldorf, and the alternative space Friesenwall 120 in Cologne.

Fanzines such as ANYP in Munich and Dank and Neid in Hamburg fulfilled a similar function; they were the meeting places and mouthpieces for an alternative to the dominant art (market) system.[8] The operators of Friesenwall 120, Stephan Dillemuth and Josef Strau, also belonged to the close circle around Texte zur Kunst (TzK). At the beginning of the 90s editors Isabelle Graw and Stefan Germer began TzK as a forum for the debate that October had already partly initiated in the United States. Cultural studies, feminism, and questions of identity as well as contextual and structural analysis are still the essential theoretical underpinnings of the journal's approach to current cultural production. Content as well as personnel joined TzK and the various alternative attempts to clearly separate a politicized youth culture from the ruling establishment. Many of the journal's writers were active in the Wohlfahrtsausschüsse, an association of leftist cultural producers established at the beginning of the 90s in many German cities, as well as in the organization of Messe 2ok, a counter-art fair held in Cologne. The close community of artists, writers, theorists, and other intellectuals living in Cologne at the time was described by Graw a year after TzK was founded: "in Cologne there was a particular context, galleries, a center for reflection and exchange like Friesenwall and a magazine like Spex (Diedrich Diederichsen's magazine of music culture and theory). In this context, we are all quite close, we discuss everything, including the magazine's content."[9]

Friesenwall 120, Cologne

The social sphere and one's interactions with like-minded colleagues are also ongoing factors in the work and performance of artists Kai Althoff and Cosima von Bonin, both of whom live in Cologne and have been supported by TzK since the beginning of their careers. In cooperative actions by Althoff and von Bonin at the Künstlerhaus Stuttgart (1995), for instance, or the Museum Abteiberg in Mönchengladbach (1996), group behavior and the machinery of exclusion play just as great a role as the very private, seemingly fictive stories made up by the artists. Althoff and von Bonin work within the context of the music scene, and the link between artistic and musical production characterizes their practice. Althoff is a member of the group Workshop while von Bonin often organizes events to which she also invites musicians. The close link between these arenas is not just characteristic of Cologne.

Cosima von Bonin and Kai Althoff, performance during the "Heetz, Nowak, Rehberger" exhibition, Städtisches Museum Abteiberg, Mönchengladbach, 1996

The Rhineland

Cologne's art scene is expecting a great deal from König's move. As in Berlin, the galleries have contributed more to the strengthening of young art than has its school—in this case the Kunsthochschule für Medien Köln (Academy of Media Arts, Cologne), which was founded in 1990. There are two generations of galleries in Cologne. The older spaces (including Gmurzynska, Karsten Greve, Orangerie-Reinz, Der Spiegel, and Michael Werner) have been active for several decades and have done much to give Cologne its reputation as Germany's city of art. Emerging in the 80s, the second generation (including Daniel Buchholz, Luis Campaña, Gisela Capitain, Jablonka, Johnen & Schöttle, Christian Nagel, and Monika Sprüth) not only represents the ideas and artists of that decade, but also continues to introduce younger artists.[7] Cologne has yet to nurture a cadre of very young but internationally relevant galleries to match those in Berlin. In the meantime, the Academy of Media Arts represents Cologne's ambition to become Germany's center for film and media. Accordingly, one can attend specialized seminars on television, film, and media design in addition to seminars and workshops on media art, the academy's visual-art program. Many media-arts graduates are successful in the film industry or work for advertising firms and e-companies. Until now, however, none of the young artists educated in the program have been particularly successful in breaking into the realm of international contemporary art.

¶ The Kunstakademie Düsseldorf plays a more important role. From the mid-70s through the mid-80s artists such as Andreas Gursky, Thomas Ruff, and Thomas Struth studied there under Bernd and Hilla Becher. The academy's students thus later achieved fame as members of the Becher School. Demand also studied in Dusseldorf, albeit some years later, and then at Goldsmiths College in London. His large-format photographic works might seem associated with the Bechers' at first glance; their backgrounds, however, are completely different. Demand's interest in sculptural work is more the result of his study under Dusseldorf professor Fritz Schwegler. At the beginning of his career Demand exhibited the models he made of thin, colored cardboard. It was not until later that he began taking photographs of them and presenting the images as the actual works.

¶ Compared to the spectacular events of the 60s that put the Kunstakademie Düsseldorf in the public eye—the actions by Joseph Beuys and his students like Jörg Immendorff and Blinky Palermo—at the end of the 80s and the beginning of the 90s it was relatively quiet there. The academy's director, Markus Lüpertz, dominated the atmosphere with his conservative, even retrogressive discourse on painting, which produced few relevant possibilities for younger artists. But a new and lively energy has emerged at Dusseldorf as a result of the recent appointments of Trockel and Herold as professors.

¶ While Berlin's young art scene has developed increasing strength over the past ten years, until now the Hochschule der Künste has played only a minor role in influencing the development of new art in the city. Berlin's magnetism does, however, insure that the number of applicants to the HdK from Germany and abroad has dramatically risen in the last few years. Founded in 1975 by the fusion of the Staatlichen Hochschule für Musik und Darstellende Kunst (State Academy of Music and the Dramatic Arts) and the Staatlichen Hochschule für bildende Künste (State Academy of Fine Arts), it is the largest art school in Germany with an enrollment of over 4,300 students, and one of the largest in Europe. There are a variety of reasons for the HdK's relatively minor influence on young German art. Germany's federalist system distributes art schools and academies across the entire country. Braunschweig, Frankfurt, Hamburg, Karlsruhe, Leipzig, Munich, and Stuttgart all have art schools. While these cities may not be as exciting as Berlin, good professors and distinctive teaching motivate students to study elsewhere than in Germany's largest city.

¶ In contrast to Berlin's cultural appeal and its link to young art, HdK's conservative faculty, with professors such as Georg Baselitz, is oriented toward traditional painting. The average professor's age is between fifty-five and sixty-five. The overwhelming majority of the faculty are men and—with the exceptions of Dieter Appelt, Baselitz, Lothar Baumgarten, and, among the few female professors, Rebecca Horn and Katharina Sieverding—few have international reputations. With continued pressure to cut costs, vacant posts often go unfilled, which exacerbates the development of an aging faculty. What momentum there is for change comes from the so-called "free classes," where student committees invite outside artists and other intellectuals as guest professors for a specific period of time.

¶ The Free Classes at HdK are not unique, however; Germany's other art schools also appoint guest lecturers. The Städelschule Frankfurt, under the direction of Kasper König, is a case in point. Among the artists who have taught there under the chancellor's invitation are Andrea Fraser, Herold, Isa Genzken, Dan Graham, Martin Kippenberger, and Matt Mullican.[6] König directed the Städelschule and the affiliated Portikus, an exhibition hall in the center of Frankfurt where he exhibited internationally renowned artists from the winter of 1987 through the fall of 2000. König not only appointed many new professors to the Städelschule, he also introduced structural reforms that abolished the course system in favor of studies with a single professor. His successes are evident not only in the good reputation the Städelschule enjoys with professors such as Thomas Bayrle, Peter Kubelka, and Christa Näher, but also in that some of today's most successful young German artists such as Matti Braun, Stefan Kern, and Tobias Rehberger studied there. König also initiated the Institute for New Media at the Städelschule, which ended up being his only apparent failure. Since November 2000 König has served as the director of the Museum Ludwig, Cologne. Last year Daniel Birnbaum was elected his successor at Städelschule, and will most certainly bring new interests as a representative of a much younger generation. His work as the director of the International Artist Studio Program in Sweden (IASPIS) and as correspondent for Artforum makes him no less distinctive and internationally connected as König.

¶ The biennial was ill-fated. Proof can be found not only in the quarrels that motivated biennial co-curators Hans-Ulrich Obrist and Nancy Spector to officially distance themselves from the event, but also in the delay of its sequel. The second edition of the Berlin Biennial should have taken place in 2000 but has been postponed for a year—for financial reasons, according to officials. Another no less controversial initiative is the Hoffmann Collection in Berlin-Mitte's Gipshöfen. The city allocated the Hoffmann couple a large building complex on the condition that they make their comprehensive private collection of contemporary art available to the viewing public.[5] Every Saturday visitors with advance reservations may put on felt overshoes and tour the Hoffmann's private apartment, furnished with their art.

¶ Apart from these half-private undertakings the city itself has endeavored to become the capital of young art. These range from the Hamburger Bahnhof, the National Gallery's branch for contemporary art, to the National Gallery Prize for Promoting Young Artists recently established by the Friends of the National Gallery. The prize is clearly, even embarrassingly, patterned after London's Turner Prize. Like the London prize, four young artists are nominated and presented in an exhibition, and the winner is announced during a gala dinner. The similarity suggests the ambitions of Berlin's cultural promoters and taken together these projects testify to the effort with which Berlin is pursuing big-city culture. The goal is to become comparable to other metropolises like London and Paris. Again and again, the current mood in Berlin is compared to that of the roaring 20s, when bohemians from all of Europe frequented the city. Even if the comparison seems somewhat exaggerated, it is certainly true that many international artists chose Berlin as their temporary home after the fall of the Berlin Wall. The DAAD artist programs and the Künstlerhaus Bethanien's studio stipends (both well established in the city) contributed more than a little to this. Above and beyond that, *Texte zur Kunst*, a magazine founded in 1990 in Cologne, moved to Berlin in 1999. This can be seen as further proof of the city's increasing importance in the German discourse on art.

A Diversity of Academies versus Centralism

The focus on the new capital city is remarkable inasmuch as it stands diametrically opposed to the history of the Federal Republic. Before Berlin was chosen as the capital in 1991, postwar German cultural policy was defined by federalist principles. Even though cultural policy is still in the hands of individual states, the former national Minister of Cultural Affairs, Michael Naumann, has increasingly challenged their autonomy by, for instance, financially favoring larger, historical cultural institutions in Berlin over smaller ones he considers less important. Since Berlin's Hochschule der Künste (HdK/University of the Arts) is not on the list of Naumann's prestigious institutions, it has not profited—at least not financially—from the city's status as the capital.

Thomas Demand
Still from *Tunnel*, 1999
35-mm film

However Thomas Demand's contribution skirted the subject of Berlin; he exhibited several photos and his first film, *Tunnel* (1999), which was produced for London's Tate Gallery as part of his DG Bank stipend. Perhaps the fact that he lives in Berlin (but only part time—he also lives in London) was enough reason for his selection. In contrast, Manfred Pernice's work was interpreted in the Berlin Biennial's short guide as a reflection on the exhibition site itself: "First he [Pernice] takes a fragment of the base of Vladimir Tatlin's model for a tower for the Third International from 1919–20, in order to use it as part of his own giant model, which will be shown on the very spot in the Academy building where Albert Speer showed his 'Führer,' the model of the great North-South Axis, in particular the Great Hall."[4] Most of Pernice's installation works are related to their respective exhibition situations in form, and often in content. *Sardinien* (1996), the work included in "Public Offerings," makes its relation to the art-fair site for which it was originally made absolutely clear; the sculpture's dimensions were determined by—and very nearly match—those of his gallery's booth at the 1996 Art Forum Berlin. Pernice's piece for the Berlin Biennial refers not only to the exhibition site's historical past, but also to present-day Berlin. Although formally his five-meter-high circular wooden tower clearly recalls Chicago's famous 60s high-rise Marina City, it can certainly be seen as a commentary on the many high-rises now being built in Berlin.

The sculpture was initially entitled **Tatlin Tower** during the Berlin Biennial, but Pernice later renamed it **Haupt/Centraldose** (Main or Central Can). The new title emphasizes the link between the work's formal aspects and his can objects, and at the same time makes an ironic wordplay on the exhibition's site, the Hauptstadt, or the capital city of Berlin.

Manfred Pernice
Haupt/Centraldose, 1998
Wood
212 1/2 x 80 3/4 x 80 3/4 inches

¶ It is the younger artists for whom Berlin is the place of promise.

The galleries founded in Berlin during the early to mid-90s—Arndt & Partner, Mehdi Chouakri, Contemporary Fine Arts, Klosterfelde, NEU, neugerriemschneider, and Schipper + Krome, to name only a few of the most ambitious—have motivated their own young artists to live in Berlin, in turn attracting many other artists of the same or a younger generation. One illustration of this international community forming around Berlin's new galleries for support, interaction, and protection: Designed for the first anniversary exhibition of the gallery neugerriemschneider, Tobias Rehberger's *One* (1995) featured nine different vases, each one representing an artist who exhibited at the gallery that year, and emphasized the social and artistic solidarity of the gallery's artists (among the artists were Sharon Lockhart, Jorge Pardo, and Rirkrit Tiravanija, artists also included in "Public Offerings").

Tobias Rehberger, One, 1995
Installation at neugerriemschneider, Berlin, 1995

¶ Although the process of establishing Berlin as the center for young art began a few years after the merger of the two German states, the city has been regarded as an art center for only a relatively short period, perhaps three or four years. Curators like Klaus Biesenbach understood how to use the city's energized atmosphere and the resulting private and public partnerships for their own projects. With the support of the Stiftung Deutsche Klassenlotterie Berlin (German Lottery Foundation, Berlin) and funds for the protection of historical monuments, Biesenbach transformed an old margarine factory in Berlin-Mitte into Kunst-Werke (Art Works), a site for internationally competitive studios and exhibitions.

¶ The Berlin Biennial that Biesenbach initiated at the end of 1998—again financed by the German Lottery Foundation, Berlin, and the Ministry of the Interior's capital city cultural funds—might also be interpreted as a promotional event for strengthening contemporary art in Berlin. The biennial was fully focused on the city: only artists from Germany and abroad who had already spent a considerable amount of time in Berlin on stipends or by their own initiatives were invited, and organizers sought to choose works that dealt explicitly with Berlin.

¶ These selections reflect the link between schools and urban centers. The art schools function not only as educational institutions but also as points in a greater social network. But above and beyond the art schools, of course, these large cities offer cultural and, more importantly, subcultural attractions that can be decisive factors in choosing a place to live and study—and for supporting an artworld.

¶ With its new exhibition spaces and events, reunified Berlin has attempted to position itself as Germany's single cultural center, but a number of factors—from Germany's federal system of higher education and its support of art schools nationwide to the continuing strength of the community of artists and intellectuals in Cologne—have checked Berlin's ascendance. Consequentially and perhaps counter to the thesis of "Public Offerings," I will argue that it is not the art schools, whether in Berlin or Frankfurt or Dusseldorf, that have been the most important factor in creating new art and a new context for it, but rather the involvement of young artists and writers in the music and club scenes and in alternative politics across Germany.

Mythos Berlin

Berlin's cultural climate has changed markedly since 1989. Much attention was paid early on to the city's artistic underground, to the squats and studios in Berlin's Mitte district, but the greatest impetus for its transformation has come from overhead, from the city's changed political, social, and economic situation.[2] The large building projects that mark Berlin's skyline have provided not only an atmosphere of new beginnings, but also—thanks to a clause guaranteeing that a certain percentage of a new building's total construction budget is spent on art—direct financial stimulation of the city's art market. Over the last few years a number of young, internationally recognized galleries have opened in Berlin, and many Germans see the city's upswing as a threat to the cultural supremacy that the Rhineland held during the postwar years.

Since 1996 the city has had its own art fair, Art Forum Berlin. Unlike Cologne's Art Fair, the first worldwide art market,[3] the Berlin fair has specialized in young art of the past ten years. The Rhineland (which includes Cologne and Dusseldorf as well as the old administrative capital of West Germany, Bonn) is still the stronghold of established collectors and many successful artists such as Georg Herold, Sigmar Polke, Gerhard Richter, and Rosemarie Trockel, who continue to live and work in Cologne. With the exception of Polke, all now teach at the Kunstakademie Düsseldorf.

Art Academies and Alternative Environments

"Art academies have the contradictory function of providing vocational training in a profession whose character as a profession must be denied in order for it to be reproduced."[1]

The situation of German art has changed astonishingly in the last decade. Before the difficult "reunification" of 1989 there were a number of different yet relatively equal art centers—a pluralism that is reflected in the representation of German artists here in "Public Offerings." Although Thomas Demand and Manfred Pernice, like many other younger German artists, have lived in Berlin for quite some time now, their education took place elsewhere: Dusseldorf and London for Demand, and Braunschweig as well as Berlin for Pernice. This seems worth noting, given that the other nations represented in "Public Offerings" have a much greater concentration of artistic activity in one or, at most, two cultural centers. In Great Britain, two of London's art schools—Goldsmiths and the Royal College of Art—generated the momentum for the new art scene that emerged at the end of the 80s. The Japanese artists in the exhibition are almost exclusively graduates of the Tokyo University of Music and Art. In the United States many successful young American artists, after completing their education, continue to live in Los Angeles (University of California at Los Angeles, Art Center College of Design, and California Institute of the Arts), as well as in New York (where the Whitney's Independent Study Program and, further afield, Yale University and the Rhode Island School of Design have emerged as important feeder schools).

BY YILMAZ DZIEWIOR

1. "Against Nature: Japanese Art in the Eighties" was first installed at the San Francisco Museum of Modern Art between 15 June and 6 August of 1989, and traveled to six other American venues; its curators were Kathy Halbreich, Thomas Sokolowski, Shinji Komoto, and Fumio Nanjo.
2. Lynn Gumpert, "A Distant Mirror," Art News 89, no. 3 (March 1990): 132-37; and Alexandra Monroe, "Wandering Position," Flash Art 25, no. 163 (March/April 1992): 71-74.
3. Eiji Otsuka, Shojo minzoku gaku (The folklore of girls) (Tokyo: Kōbunsha bunko, 1987), 20-21.
4. Akira Asada, Kōzō to chikara: kōzōshugi o koete (Structure and power: beyond structuralism) (Tokyo: Keisō shobō, 1984), 20-21.
5. See Shigeo Chiba, Gendai bijutsu itsudatsu-shi (The history of Japanese contemporary art as deviation) (Tokyo: Shōbunsha, 1986), 81-82; as documented by Chiba's acclaimed book, Japanese avant-garde movements from 50s Gutai to 70s Mono-ha were characterized by their opposition to judging art by standards of formal autonomy. During the late 70s and the early 80s, Greenberg's and Michael Fried's theories of formalist painting were belatedly imported by the scholar and critic Teruo Fujieda; Fujieda's claim to orthodoxy was reinforced by the exhibitions of contemporary Japanese painting he curated: "Kaiga no mondai" (Problems of painting) at Seibu (Sezon) Museum of Art and "Kenjō to kōsei" (Emotion and composition) at Yokohama Citizen's Gallery. Fujieda's authority was challenged by the scholar and critic Toshiaki Minemura, whose theory of painting based on the aesthetic of Mono-ha, the Japanese counterpart to Minimalism and Land Art, was supported by his 1977 exhibition "Kaiga no yutakasa" (Beyond the planes), also at Yokohama Citizen's Gallery. Though polemical rivals, Fujieda and Minemura together dominated the discursive field of Japanese gendai bijutsu through their writing in Bijutsu Techō magazine and their affiliation with the Sezon Museum of Art throughout 80s.
6. Tomio Koyama, interview with the author, 2 August 2000.
7. Min Nishihara, letter in reply to my questions, posed 12 through 18 August 2000; the account of her meeting with Hasegawa, Kurosawa, Murakami, Ozawa, and Sone in this essay is based on her responses.
8. Dedicated to the interventionist idea of public art and inspired by the 60s Japanese avant-garde group Hi Red Center, Masato Nakamura organized two public events in Ginza and Shinjuku in 1993 and 1994, involving young contemporary artists and critics including Iwai, Kurosawa, Murakami, Nishihara, Ozawa, and Sone, among others. Entitled respectively "Ginbrart" and "Shinjuku Boys' Art," these events are documented in Hideki Nakazawa's informative article, "Tokyo chokusetsu hyōgen shōshi" (A brief history of direct expression by Tokyo artists), Bijutsu Techō 52, no. 791 (August 2000): 90-97; refusing to conform to predicated patterns of avant-garde, Murakami parted ways with Nakamura after "Shinjuku Boys' Art."
9. Keizaburo Mizuno, et al., Tokyo geijutsu daigaku hyakunen shi (The history of Tokyo University of Music and Art commemorating its hundredth anniversary), vol. 3 of Tokyo bijutsu gakkohen (The book of Tokyo bijutsu gakko) (Tokyo: Ghosei, 1987), 959-84.
10. "Murakami Takashi intabyū" (Interview with Takashi Murakami), Ur, no. 9 (October 1994): 89.
11. "Nihonga no jubaku" (A Curse of nihonga), Nikkei Art (January 1994): 17; and "Takashi Murakami," Gekkan Bijutsu, no. 217 (October 1993): 180-83.
12. Midori Matsui, "Towards a Definition of Tokyo Pop: The Classical Transgressions of Takashi Murakami," in Takashi Murakami: The Meaning of the Nonsense of the Meaning (Annandale-on-Hudson, New York: Center for Curatorial Studies, 1999), 22-23.
13. From Takashi Murakami's letters in reply to my questions in August 2000. My reconstruction of Murakami's activities at TUMA and his Röntgen involvement, including a minute account of Sea Breeze, is based on his documents.
14. Noi Sawaragi, "Murakami Takashi no hon-yaku ni yotte hakuraino Simulation art to dento no Nihonga wa hyori ittaino monoto naru" (Takashi Murakami bringing Simulationist art and Nihonga together), Esquire Japan (August 1994): 124.
15. Yusuke Minami, RP by TM, brochure accompanying Takashi Murakami's exhibition "Sansei no hantai nanoda" at Hosomi Gallery, December 1991.
16. From my interview with Noi Sawaragi on 7 August 2000.
17. Noi Sawaragi, Simulationism: House Music and Appropriationist Art (Tokyo: Yosensha, 1991), 27-28.
18. Sawaragi, Simulationism, 54.
19. "Röntgen geijutsu kenkyusho" (Röntgen Kunst Institute), Rhutsu Service Shinbun, no. 144, 24 January 1992, n.p.
20. From my interview with Tsutomu Ikeuchi on 1 August 2000.
21. "Nani o surunoka rentogen geijutsu kenkyusho" (What are you up to, Röntgen Kunst Institute?), Takarajima, no. 246 (24 April 1992): 15.
22. The name Neo Pop or New Pop was given by Bijutsu Techō editor Kiyoshi Kusumi and temporarily adopted by Sawaragi. For a discussion of the development of his idea of Tokyo's New Pop, see Matsui, "Towards a Definition of Tokyo Pop," 20-29.
23. Taro Chiezo showed his moving sculpture made of little girls' dresses pitched over engines for toy cars at Shiraishi Contemporary Art in April 1992; Kodai Nakahara presented appropriationist sculptures incorporating the figure of popular anime character Nadia and lego blocks at Satani Gallery, Ginza, in January 1992; Minako Nishiyama showed her Nice Little Girl's Wonderful Dressing Up Room, a sculpture that combined the function of a peep show and the cute appearance of a paper dollhouse at a group show at Art Tower Mito in March 1992; Yukinori Yanagi, internationally acclaimed for his World Flag Ant Farm (1990), showed Banzai Corner, an installation of desktop figures of Japanese sci-fi movie hero Ultraman arranged in the shape of Hinomaru, the Japanese flag, at the Hillside Gallery booth at Nippon International Contemporary Art Fair '92; Kenji Yanobe had a solo exhibition presenting his anti-nuclear survival machines shaped like sci-fi monsters at Kirin Plaza, Osaka, in February 1992. Their works are discussed in Noi Sawaragi's "Rorripoppu—sono saishogen no inochi" (Lollipop: its smallest life), Bijutsu Techō 44, no. 651 (March 1992): 86-98. The works of Yanagi, Murakami, and Chiezo are discussed in Alexandra Monroe's Flash Art article, "Wandering Position," 72-74.
24. Sawaragi, "Lollipop," 86-98.
25. Sawaragi, "Dangerously Cute," Flash Art 25, no. 163 (March/April 1992): 75-76.
26. "Sabukaruche riariti no aridokoro o megutte" (Thinking about where the reality of subculture lies), Brutus (15 March 1992): 268.
27. Murakami's written proposals to Hosomi Gallery, dated 28 and 30 October 1991, are now preserved in the archive at Röntgen Kunstraum, Tokyo.
28. Sawaragi, "Bijutsu to iu anomari: yokogaki no nihon gendai bijutsu" (Anomaly called bijutsu: Japanese contemporary art written from left to right), in Anomaly (Tokyo: Röntgen Kunst Institute and Autobahn, 1992), n.p.
29. Sawaragi, Anomaly, n.p.
30. Ibid.
31. Takashi Murakami, "Post-Hobby Art in Japan: A Conversation with Kenji Yanobe and Kodai Nakahara," Bijutsu Techō 44, no. 651 (March 1992): 76.
32. See Keiko Sonoda, "Anomaly," Taiyō, no. 377 (November 1992), n.p.; Peter Bellars, "Beware: Artists at Play—Madcap Inventors," Asahi Evening News, 17 October 1992, 9I; Lorna Ryan, "Exhibition Definitely an 'Anomaly,'" The Japan Times, 11 October 1992, 12; and Hideto Akasaka, "Anomaly," Shukan Asahi (9 October 1992): n.p.
33. In his interview with Mitsunobu Nakamura, Murakami states that "a work of art can be produced only through a very complex thinking," as "the intense speed of his thinking keeps overriding his initial understanding of things"; Murakami also expresses his deep distrust of "the art made according to a parochial explanation," and defies the misunderstanding of himself as a strategic artist. See "Senryakuteki hyogenjin Murakami Takashi" (Takashi Murakami: a strategic artist), City Road (September 1993): 39, 41.
34. Hideto Akasaka commended Ozawa's Jizoing as an example of a new photographic expression that freshly transmitted the artist's fragile corporeality and the sense of transit from everyday space to an estranging one; see "Fo(u)rtunes," Asahi Camera (April 1993): 98.
35. The details of Tsuyoshi Ozawa's Jizoing trips are documented in his article, "Jizo konryu" (Building Jizo) in Radium Egg, no. 2 (Tokyo: Röntgen Kunst Institute and Autobahn, 1992): 16-20.
36. From my interview with Tsuyoshi Ozawa on 19 August 2000.
37. Yutaka Sone, "New Landscape, New Emotion: Intabyū," Bijutsu Techō 49, no. 738 (April 1997): 117.
38. In his interview in Bijutsu Techō, Sone states that his work is determined neither by object nor idea: "I must be in equal distance from the autonomous force of a thing in itself, the power of an idea, and the landscape in which the idea disintegrates." In Bijutsu Techō 49, no. 741 (April 1997): 122.
39. From my interview with Shin Kurosawa on 18 August 2000.
40. The tendency was most typically represented by the roundtable discussion between Teruo Fujieda, Kunio Motoe, and Akira Tatehata, in "Kaiga no tenkai: 80 nendai no chihei" (Openings of painting: The horizon of the 80s), Bijutsu Techō 43, no. 646 (October 1991): 95-111. Murakami and Sawaragi criticized the painters featured in this special issue for "deliberately ignoring the gap between the international standards and the foreclosed narrative of the small Japanese selves" by "expressing their private sentiments through their wall-paper paintings," in "Rude Rude Rude," a discussion by Noi Sawaragi, Takashi Murakami, Tsutomu Ikeuchi, and Hiroshi Nakajima, Radium Egg, no. 1 (Tokyo: Röntgen Kunst Institute and Autobahn, 1991): 24-29.
41. Sawaragi, Nihon, gendai, bijutsu (Japanese, contemporary, art) (Tokyo: Shinchosha, 1998), 12.
42. Asada's call was issued in the introduction to his bestseller, Kōzō to chikara (Structure and power), an introductory survey of the ideas of Deleuze and Guattari; Sawaragi's formulations of Simulationism and Anomaly are deeply embedded in the context of postmodern debate as exchanged between Asada and the philosopher Kojin Karatani since 1984, concerning the merits and demerits of the deconstructionist analysis of contemporary Japanese culture. For a rudimentary discussion of New Pop's position in this discursive field, see Matsui, "(De)Constructing Whether There Is No Structure?: The Debate over Postmodernism in the 1980s in Japan and the Formation of the New Critical Trend in Visual Art," in Literary Intercrossings: East Asia and the West, eds. Mabel Lee and A. D. Syrokomla-Stefanowska (Honolulu: University of Hawaii Press, 1998), 80-90.
43. For Murakami's earliest statements on the significance of anime and Nobuo Tsuji's interpretation of Japanese art in terms of eccentric style or mannerism, see "Fax Letter from Takashi Murakami to Midori Matsui," in Takashi Murakami, the catalogue accompanying "Which Is Tomorrow?—Fall in Love," his solo exhibition at SCAI the Bathhouse, 17 June–16 July 1994, 48-51; as well as Murakami, "A Theory of Super Flat Japanese Art," in Super Flat (Tokyo: Madra Publishing, 2000), 8-25.
44. I discuss the pictorial transcription of "adolescent" sensibility, defined by Julia Kristeva as "an open psychic structure," achieved in Nara's and Peyton's paintings in my essay, "New Openings in Japanese Painting: Three Faces of Minority," in Painting at the Edge of the World, ed. Douglas Fogle (New York: D.A.P., 2000).

¶ In contrast to Murakami's critical positioning of Tokyo art, the art of Ozawa, Sone, and Nara carries the nuances of a public sphere beyond the Japanese vernacular. Ozawa's use of the marginalized items of Japanese everyday life as a vehicle for conceptual performance, infusing the protected interior of the gallery with the fresh air of the outside, and Sone's evocation, through a twist of common sense of the inseparable relation between freedom of imagination and physical limitation, associated them with the new conceptual art that has emerged globally since 1995. They have since taken part in such international exhibitions as "Nutopi," "Skulpturen Projekte at Münster," and "Cities on the Move."

¶ The discussion of Nara as the guiding spirit of Japanese art after 1995 cannot be contained in the scope of this paper. Nonetheless, he anticipates the characteristics shared by important Japanese artists of a younger generation—Tam Ochiai, Michihiro Shimabuku, Hiroshi Sugito—whose early living and study abroad articulated its aesthetic sensibility as hybrid from the beginning. Nara's painting, evoking at once various vernacular styles of Western painting including Neue Sachlichkeit, very early Lucien Freud, and Yasuo Kuniyoshi, also shares its strange representation of time and space with the drawing of Japanese illustrator Takeshi Motai, whose work poetically transcribed the hybrid character of Japanese urban culture during the 30s. **The adolescent fluctuation between adult and child and male and female in Nara's paintings also finds a counterpart in Elizabeth Peyton's portraits of androgynous youth which, like Nara's, gained public attention after 1995.**[44]

¶ These repercussions ensure the significance of the new Japanese art discussed here, as well as its potential. It is quite remarkable that these artists and their friends were able to construct a context in which their works could have public significance, intellectual relevance, and popular appeal by playing against the negative conditions of their schools and exploiting the uncultivated potential of their native culture. It is still unclear how the rich areas of expression opened by these artists **—critical simulation of Japanese popular culture, lyrical conceptualism, and intensely personal figurative painting—** will extend their influence into the next century. But their revolutionary role in the problematic history of Japanese contemporary art will remain unchallenged.

IV. Departures: A Conclusion

In his acclaimed book *Nihon, gendai, bijutsu* (Japanese, contemporary, art), Noi Sawaragi described Japanese contemporary art as "a closed circle" and "a bad place."[41]

The expressions refer to the lack of historical continuity and international appeal of Japanese contemporary art, owing to the absence of a conversation between generations and of a critical language and discursive field in which such a conversation might be carried out. In short, the expressions refer to the absence of a public space in the field of Japanese contemporary art. While Sawaragi's book records the failures of various Japanese avant-gardes, his activities have been dedicated to creating a public field in contemporary art in which the works of his contemporaries, however disproportionate they might appear to a textbook understanding of "contemporary art," can be appreciated and discussed intelligently. I believe that every actor in the new scene discussed here was dedicated to the task.

¶ Murakami and Sawaragi were pathfinders of this scene. Their consistent efforts to speak critically on the significance of New Pop in relation to Japanese high culture won it intellectual respectability, and distinguished it from a mere nostalgic reconstruction of Japanese Boy culture or a simple act of Bad Boy iconoclasm. While Sawaragi's adaptation of postmodern theoretical categories to Japanese art brilliantly answered Akira Asada's call to the younger generation to apply their eclectic theory to contemporary phenomena, Murakami's deconstructive referencing of nihonga and otaku cultures demonstrated a smart way to reflect on the ambiguity of domestic culture without depending on academic jargon.[42] Although they seem to have gone separate ways since "Anomaly," their paths keep crossing as they articulate the significance of Japanese Pop. Since 1994, Murakami has been elaborating his idea of Superflat, an aesthetic that connects the stylistic eccentricities of traditional Japanese painting and sculpture and Japanese anime and otaku figures as an alternative to the impoverished conventions of Japanese contemporary art.[43] His claim that a dynamic beauty can be found in the marginalized fields of Japanese premodern and postmodern expression was given a larger context by the exhibition "Ground Zero," curated by Sawaragi for the Art Tower Mito in 1999, in which the works of Murakami, Yanobe, and other New Pop artists were juxtaposed with those by Japanese Pop artists of the 50s and 60s, and with Tohl Narita's kaijyu figures. "Ground Zero" argued for an alternative artistic tradition relevant to the Japanese public imagination.

Yoshitomo Nara installation in "In The Deepest Puddle" exhibition, SCAI the Bathhouse, Tokyo, 1995

6. The End of a Party and the Beginning of a New Period: Enter Yoshitomo Nara

The tides were steadily turning between 1993 and 1995. With the successive openings of new galleries that concentrated on nurturing and marketing individual artists—Wako Works of Art, SCAI the Bathhouse, Ota Fine Arts—the idea of marrying subculture and contemporary art was becoming irrelevant. Postmodern cultural critique was giving way to a reevaluation of personal emotions and the reconstitution of a conceptual attitude out of corporeal and quotidian experience. As Sone's and Ozawa's conceptual art was gradually winning audience approval and critical attention, "In the Deepest Puddle," Yoshitomo Nara's first solo exhibition at SCAI the Bathhouse in the spring of 1995, had a harrowing effect on those members of Tokyo's emerging artworld who were growing weary of the facile irony and ostentatious theatricality of installations made by New Pop's epigones. Nara's poignant portraits of children viscerally evoked an ambiguity of innocence and evil. During the summer of 1995, he was invited to install his sculpture *Cup Kids* (1995) at Gunma Municipal Museum of Art, and his painting was featured in the August issue of *Bijutsu Techō* as a central feature of a phenomenon it called *kairaku kaiga*, or painting for pleasure. Nara's rapid rise in the Japanese artworld (leading to a figurative-painting boom between 1995 and 1998) was a delayed response to his neo-expressionist training at Aichi University of Music and Art (AUMA) and the Dusseldorf Academy of Art in Germany during the early 90s.

The productivity of AUMA's talented graduates—the painters Takanobu Kobayashi, Nara, Nobuhiko Nukata, and Hiroshi Sugito—was realized only after the turbulent opening of a new artistic arena by New Pop and personal conceptual art which contested the moribund formalism of derivative abstract painting considered mainstream as late as 1991.[40] Having played a significant role, Röntgen closed in December 1995 following its final exhibition, "Anomaly 2," which literally carried the idea of Pop beyond the reach of contemporary art, as the impact of a noise musician and an underground cartoonist overwhelmed the work of the two other artists included.

Yoshitomo Nara
In the Deepest Puddle II, 1995
Acrylic on canvas
47 x 43 inches

¶ There is a natural affinity between Nishihara's and Sone's conceptual attitudes.

In my view, Nishihara's translation of "Bari tune" revealed another aspect of "anomaly" in Japanese culture, as it presented the positive results of an imperfect translation and perversion of technology. It also captures the function of artistic *différance*: the ability of art to transform rules of representation by making its deviation from standards a source of new discovery. Frustrating the riders' wish to be functional, *Her 19th Foot* also endlessly provokes their desire to ride, making them gratuitously expend their energy, which nonetheless provides intense pleasure.

The process reveals art's self-referentiality. The use of frustration, delay, and distance to stimulate the imagination was an important characteristic of all of Sone's early work,

including *Artificial Lawn Performance* (1994), *Night Bus* (1995), and *World Championship for Knitting* (1995). The tension between creation and frustration is most intense in *Night Bus*, a work in which Sone sent his friends on trips throughout Southeast Asia and California with instructions to shoot videos from the windows of night buses while he remained in Tokyo, waiting to edit the results. The concrete object or video documentation consists of traces of the artist's original vision and the supplementation of his absence in the filmed scene.[38] This process of metonymical reference was embodied in "Departures," Nishihara's second exhibition for Röntgen. Sone's *World Championship for Knitting*, a woolen hanging bearing the image of a tournament chart, asked its audience to imagine powerful images of unknown cities evoked solely by their names, and to trace the flight of imagination encouraged by the arbitrary links between them, as in Proust's *Remembrance of Things Past*. It was shown with a kindred video, *Eyeglasses for seeing Invisible Section* (1995), which recorded Sone playing soccer by himself in a field covered with artificial grass, wearing a mask made of artificial grass that was intended to cover the parts of his face that lay beyond his own field of vision.

¶ Sone's quick rise on the local and international art scene also owes much to Shin Kurosawa. The first curator to realize Sone's ideas through his ability to secure funding to produce *Her 19th Foot* for the Mito workshop, Kurosawa continued his vigorous promotional campaign by bringing the work to the Nippon International Contemporary Art Fair, producing video documentation of it and attracting the attention of Lars Nittve, the curator of "Nutopi," an international group show of young contemporary artists exploring the relation between art and life.[39] In the spring of 1995, Kurosawa also staged Ozawa's *Consultation Art University* (1993) in a workshop at the Art Tower Mito. The two-month session transformed Ozawa's painting through discussions with its participants under the supervision of various lecturers, artists who were also friends of Ozawa. The significance of Ozawa and Sone as intellectually challenging and refreshingly lyrical conceptual artists was confirmed by the enormous success of the Mito Workshops.

¶ Nishihara's concept for the exhibition "Bari tune" excellently summarized the artists' sensibility. Referring to the expression used by amateur racers who tune up their domestic automobiles in order to race on local public roads, the term embodies the eccentric transformation of technology through private obsessions, producing effects that violate standards of normal functioning, and are as exciting as they are dangerous. The exhibition title was a pun on this idea, while indicating the extremely private nature of the artists' conceptualism. In the exhibition, the idea was best illustrated by Nakanowatari, whose work reflected his deep involvement in biker culture. But the artist who best exemplified this idea, Yutaka Sone, was to meet Nishihara soon, through his brilliant debut sculpture and performance piece, *Her 19th Foot* (1993).

5. Yutaka Sone: A Conceptual Traveler

Appearing on the Tokyo art scene out of blue, Yutaka Sone had also undergone a long period of soul-searching. A graduate of the architecture department of TUMA, Sone early on gave up the idea of becoming a professional architect, disillusioned by the commercialism supporting the late-80s postmodern architecture boom. Having spent his student days traveling and accumulating plans for "ideal architecture," Sone decided to become an artist in order to realize these plans after visiting MOCA's Temporary Contemporary in Los Angeles. After the failure of his exhibition-proposal presentations to various American museums, Sone contacted Shin Kurosawa in the Art Tower Mito's education department, who decided to present *Her 19th Foot* in the department's 1993 public workshop.

Yutaka Sone installation in "Departures" exhibition, Röntgen Kunst Institute, Tokyo, 1998

¶ Nineteen bicycles converted into unicycles and chained together, *Her 19th Foot* is a standing enigma. Min Nishihara maintains that it has been misinterpreted as a vehicle for benevolent communication. At the workshop she saw "an endless hell of discommunication" amplified by the perverse structure of Sone's infernal machine: nineteen riders constantly falling over one another, dragged down by each other's weight. Sone explained to her that the work embodied "the seduction of form," playing on the gap between the expectation raised by the familiarity of the bicycle and the impossibility of overcoming its physical contingencies. Their conversation about *Her 19th Foot* brought Nishihara and Sone into intellectual partnership; their collaboration in performance and video documentation continued from their public performance in the group event "Shinjuku Boys' Art" in 1994 through Sone's video installation *Magic Stick* in 1998.

Tsuyoshi Ozawa
Twilight Jizoing, 1987–99
Performance at "Fo(u)rtunes" exhibition
Röntgen Kunst Institute, Tokyo, 1993

Even though Ozawa had a close relationship with Murakami and had helped to set up his "Anomaly" performance, their differences were obvious. In contrast to Murakami's simulation of *anime* and plastic models—products of Japanese mainstream popular culture—Ozawa referenced the underground subcultures of the 70s: the comic magazine *Garo*, the experimental theater of Juro Kara, mondo-Pop records, and hand-written free papers. Ozawa's attachment to local details disappearing in modern urbanization led to a series of conceptual projects, the most remarkable of which was *Jizoing*.

¶ Since 1989, Ozawa had been traveling in Japanese cities and throughout rural and often conflict-torn districts of Asia, leaving traces of his visit in effigies of *jizo*, a Japanese road deity. He documented his metaphorical act of "building *jizo*" in photographs. During Ozawa's physically demanding, low-budget trips, *jizo*, initially carried as a small sculpture, became more and more metonymical, reduced to a drawing or even a shadow on the earth. This fragility and mutability fit the time-bound project, suggesting that its significance did not lie in a material object, but in the act of visiting the place and knowing its particularity. Photographs were shown in sequence, indicating the continuity of his journey, which included China's Tiananmen Square, Moscow, Iran, Nepal, and the border between North and South Korea. Despite the obvious political associations, Ozawa's pictures offered only the ominous tranquility of landscapes steeped in the blue-gray mist of Asian twilight.[35] The obscurity, sometimes even absence, of the *jizo* effigy within the pictures indicated the artist's modesty—the partial renunciation of his autonomy—and his willingness to accept the accidental.

¶ Ozawa's modest gesture at the opening party of Murakami's exhibition at Hosomi in 1991, sheepishly handing out his calling card stamped with a tiny Buddha-like symbol, led to an exhibition of *Jizoing* photos there in the fall of 1992. But it was his installation in "Fo(u)rtunes" that brought him critical and public attention. Conceived as a prop for showing his photos effectively in the spacious loft, a stack of futons, one on top of another over a supporting structure, created a small hill. The view invoked the audience's memories of playing among heaps of futons drying in the sun. Climbing the stack to see the *Jizoing* photos hung high up on the wall, the audience's inhibitions about emotionally responding to contemporary art evaporated. The effect was fresh after New Pop's aggressive polemic and loud materialism. The installation was inspired by a scene from the comic *Yoshibo no hanzai* (The crime of boy Yoshi) by Yoshiharu Tsuge, the main cartoonist for *Garo* magazine, which had a special significance for the Maoist rebels of the late 60s.[36]

The combination of the *Jizoing* photos, the performative aspect of the installation, and the nostalgic references to Tsuge's comic and Japanese childhood amplified the evocative power of residual materials to touch the audience's cultural unconscious.

On the night of the opening, the trailer, its shutters closed on both sides, was dragged into the gallery, greeted by the ritual dancing of a naked hula hooper on a high pedestal.

As an aria from Mozart's *Magic Flute* was sung by two opera singers, male and female, the shutters were slowly raised to reveal the sixteen-eyed idol. When lit, the 16,000-watt/1,600-volt floodlights emitted an intense light and heat that prohibited the audience from approaching it. Condensing the climactic episode of a Japanese animation, the scene of a rocket launch, into a visual and tactile transcription of its ecstasy, *Sea Breeze* fulfilled Murakami's wish to "make a transcendent artwork." An overwhelming material presence at once seducing and frustrating vision, the structure surpassed any single explanation, embodying the contradiction and mystery of a pure work of art.[31]

¶ Despite the excited media reception, "Anomaly" marked the beginning of a schism. Many reviewers enthusiastically responded to the exhibition as a cultural event representing the sensibility of Japan's television generation, but failed to evaluate individual works as artistic expressions.[32] The "Anomaly" artists were also a looser group than the one presented by Sawaragi in his "Lollipop" essay. The discord among them was obvious from the beginning: Nakahara, who was interested in the conceptual displacement of sculpture, regarded *otaku* culture mainly as a stylistic resource; Yanobe was a craftsman realizing his childhood sci-fi fantasies by building gigantic Godzilla cars and survival suits for himself and his dog which were reflective of his obsession with the atomic apocalypse. Murakami, a dedicated *anime* fan, treated *otaku* culture as a coherent structure and language. In the exhibition, Nakahara's grim irony fell lame against the pure fetishism of Yanobe, and confirmed Murakami's fear about his fundamental indifference to the rigorous formal aesthetic of *otaku*.

¶ While the dangerous trap of political correctness always threatened the hip cynicism of New Pop, Murakami's works have expressed his resistance to this one-dimensional discursivity. Stepping out of the zone of deconstructive cultural critique with *Sea Breeze*, Murakami was heading for the construction of an aesthetic that did not conform to any ideological clichés.[33] The ideas outlined in his 1993 doctoral dissertation,

"The Meaning of the Nonsense of Meaning,"

were to guide Murakami through the next few years to the conception of his faux *anime* character DOB in 1994, and the inception of *Project Ko^2* (1994–2000), a series of collaborations with professional *otaku* sculptors.

4. Tsuyoshi Ozawa:

The Return of Memory and Emotion

Min Nishihara's exhibition "Fo(u)rtunes," held from January to May 1993, inaugurated Röntgen's second phase. The poetic tone of the exhibition and the preoccupation of its four artists with a personal sense of the body indicated the emergence of an artistic sensibility radically different from that of New Pop.[34] Four of the artists—Makoto Aida, Yasutaka Nakanowatari, Nobuhira Narumi, and Tsuyoshi Ozawa—were graduates of TUMA's oil painting department. Born between 1965 and 1969, they also grew up in the midst of Japan's economic boom, but had different responses to it than those of the New Pop artists. Many of the New Pop artists—Taro Chiezo, Murakami, and Minako Nishiyama in particular—demonstrated a strong public concern in their criticisms of the closed field of Japanese art, and stressed the cultural contradictions exemplified by the conflation of power and cuteness, often armed with the polemical edge of postmodernist or feminist discourse. In contrast, Ozawa and the other artists included in "Fo(u)rtunes" turned their attention to personal, local, or underground aspects of Japanese culture.

Emerging in the early 80s as a subculture of the anime generation, it had developed into a substantial branch of Japanese popular culture by the early 90s, with an enormous market surrounding professional makers of "figure" and a critical language of its own. In his essay in the exhibition catalogue, Sawaragi explained the otaku as "anomaly." Growing up on native soil, "fragmented and disproportionate" as a result of imperfectly translated American culture, "Japanese Pop (poppu) abnormally proliferated through electric products... kaijyu, plastic models, manga, anime, computer games."[29] This "monstrous development," he argued, defined a new arena of imagination. Like "the otaku network belonging neither to the purely Japanese nor the Western culture, but spreading all over the world," anomaly in the guise of New Pop signified the freedom to go beyond the closed field of Japanese art.[30]

¶ The opening night saw a riot; an audience of over four hundred packed in to see the "artistic monstrosities."

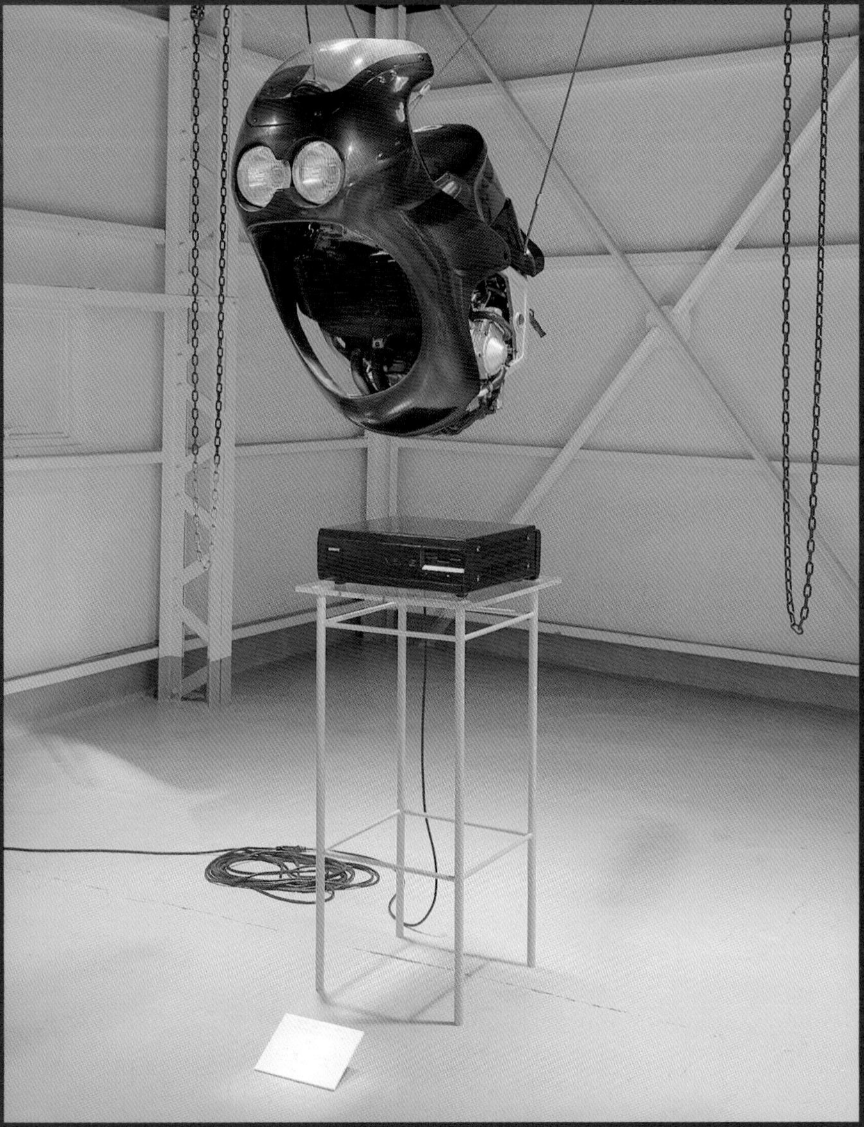

Nakahara commissioned an iron isolation tank, a sphere three meters in diameter filled with water that recalled New Age relaxation chambers. Yanobe made a mobile nuclear shelter that he alone could operate. Gabin Ito best embodied Sawaragi's theory, presenting a series of objects expressing abnormal transformation, hybridization, and implosion, including a Frankenstein monster made of dried noodles, a computer without a screen, and a procrustean motorcycle as a shell enveloping the engine. Murakami presented Sea Breeze (1992), the work that represents him in "Public Offerings."

¶ Sea Breeze was Murakami's first sculptural masterpiece. In it his formal training and his attachment to Japanese anime conjoined without irony, achieving plastic beauty. A gigantic, round steel wheel adorned on each side with eight stadium floodlights was contained in a trailer painted a fluorescent greenish yellow on one side and a brilliant red on the other.

Gabin Ito
I cannot remember what I wish to forget. (PURE MOTORCYCLE), 1992
Motorcycle and winch
33½ x 23½ x 63 inches (not including hanging system)

¶ Murakami's other project at Hosomi was an installation of school bags—remade in the skins of cobras, harp seals, whales, ostriches, crocodiles, hippos, and sharks—called **Randosel Project** (1991). One of its aims was to expose the arbitrariness of the International Commission on Whaling and its 1986 worldwide moratorium on whaling by including prohibited whale skin along with other, unregulated animal hides. (Murakami obtained his whale skin from an old fishing village; a found object, it antedates the treaty that established the whaling commission, which was signed in Washington D.C. just after the end of World War II.) Murakami commissioned the bags from Cosmo Tenchido Company, the exclusive manufacturer of **randosels** for the prestigious school attended by imperial heirs, in order to make a sinister link between imperialism, militarism, and education. Initially a bag borne by a soldier, the **randosels** came to be used by Japanese elementary school children in the early twentieth century. By presenting the **randosel** as a precious object, Murakami emphasized its symbolic power—the way its military history was displaced by connotations of innocence—

and conjured up the process by which children are integrated into the hierarchical system presided over by the symbolic authority of the emperor.

¶ In his proposal, Murakami stated that the installation intended to clarify the boundaries surrounding Japanese art and power.[27] One is the boundary between conceptual art and craft. By commissioning the randosels from Cosmo Tenchido, he emphasized that artistic meaning consisted in his analysis of cultural symbols, not in their formal reconstruction. Another boundary he worked was between daily norms and activities and the extreme situations of militarism, imperialism, and the ecology movement's claims of crisis. While the pretty appearance of the randosels exposed the uncanny working of ideology through pleasant form, the simulation of the arbitrarily set boundaries between commercial products and ecologically protected animals revealed that the norms of good and evil are determined politically to serve the interests of involved groups. Finally, Murakami was attempting to criticize the ambiguity of nihonga as an artistic institution. Its domestic influence was largely supported by its connection with the imperial family, as nihonga paintings were periodically dedicated as official gifts. By simulating the consecrating process of gift-giving through a performance that evoked a Shinto ceremony, and then desecrating it in another performance by installing the randosels on the wall as art objects, assisted by two race-car queens and buoyed up by noise music, Murakami exorcized nihonga through the secular activity of art.

3. "Anomaly": Climax and Discord

The exhibition "Anomaly," which ran from September through November 1992, won New Pop and Röntgen Kunst Institute wide recognition as significant cultural phenomena. Curated by Sawaragi, the show featured four artists, Murakami, Kodai Nakahara, Kenji Yanobe, and Gabin Ito, an editor and designer of computer graphics. Their idea of anomaly, taken from molecular physics, refers to a "phenomenon that causes a contradiction in an orderly structure in spite of the fact that it constitutes a necessary part of it."[28] In the context of the exhibition, the word referred to the art of the otaku generation. Otaku, which is now popping up in English vocabulary, is the Japanese name for the culture of adult fans of manga, anime, and plastic models of anime characters called "figure."

Takashi Murakami, *Randosel Project* (detail), 1991
Cobra skin, seal skin, whale skin, ostrich skin, caiman skin, hippo skin, and shark skin
12 x 9 x 8 inches each

¶ Coinciding with a feature on Japanese art in the March/April issue of *Flash Art*, the March issue of *Bijutsu Techō* also focused on New Pop; Sawaragi finally had the opportunity to apply his idea of Simulationism to a generation of Japanese artists. In his essay "Lollipop: Its Smallest Life," he discussed the double-edged irony of the Simulationism of Jeff Koons and Laurie Simmons, whose deliberate infantilism and saccharine cuteness castrated the inherent machismo of Abstract Expressionism and Pop while exposing their own nihilism. He pointed out that an intense version of the same effect existed in Japanese culture, where cute characters frequently concealed and enhanced state power (the police, for example, or Emperor Hirohito). Simulating that insidious relation between power and cuteness, Sawaragi argued, New Pop deconstructed it, projecting its critical consciousness through the inherent malice of its pretty works.[24]

¶ "Dangerously Cute," Sawaragi's interview with Fumio Nanjo, is a companion piece to "Lollipop." This discussion of the way in which *nihonga* functions as a model for all other genres in Japanese art, effective but confined within the national culture, is a product of his extended conversation with Murakami.[25] Murakami's own exhibitions during this period perfectly complement Sawaragi's theory. His show at Hosomi Gallery, entitled "Sansei no Hantai nanoda" (When I say yes I mean no) featured Fujio Akatsuka's radically nonsensical comic character Bakabon and his father as its presiding spirits, commenting on the absurd infantilism at the core of Japanese patriarchy.[26] Commissioning an illustrator to draw them even cuter than the original, then copying the figures onto resin plates to be signed, framed, and placed in an ornamental box—simulating a work of *nihonga* as an official item of dedication to the Emperor—Murakami insinuated the relation between insipid cuteness and formal authority, between *nihonga* and the Japanese imperial system.

III. Anomaly Years: The Rise and Fall of Röntgen Culture

1. Inauguration of the Pleasure Palace: Röntgen Kunst Institute

Tsutomu Ikeuchi, heir to a wealthy dealer of tea-ceremony utensils, started Röntgen Kunst Institute to "promot[e] a genuinely original contemporary art and creat[e] a market for it."[19] Having studied theater at college, Ikeuchi was fond of cyberpunk fiction and possessed his own unique aesthetic. The gallery space was designed as a theatrical arena separated from quotidian concerns. The whitewashed building, which resembled a spaceship looming over the banal shops in a former warehouse district, was strange enough. Entering the gallery through its automatic door, one encountered a white column blocking the way and a mesh floor exuding electric light. Behind the column was another doorway leading to a receptionist's box and catalogue stand. Everyone coming to see an exhibition passed through this area, installed as a substitute for the *yoritsuki*, the small waiting area for guests attached to a tea house.[20] The gallery, whose outlandish name reflected Ikeuchi's ambition **"to see through the essence of the world by the X-ray of artistic creation,"** was introduced as a stimulating alternative space by urban information and women's fashion magazines.[21] Its DJ-assisted opening parties emulated the fervid atmosphere of club Gold—a prestigious club whose attractions themselves emulated performance art—attracting several hundred people at a time. It was an ambition of Sawaragi, Murakami, Ikeuchi, and Co. to make Röntgen the heart of their Cultural Remix Plan, bringing together art and subculture, Japanese Neo-Geo and Cyber-Techno aesthetics. Out of their banquets and recreational trips came Röntgen's various enterprises: one-night exhibitions, the publication of the magazine *Radium Egg*, and plans for the group show "Anomaly."

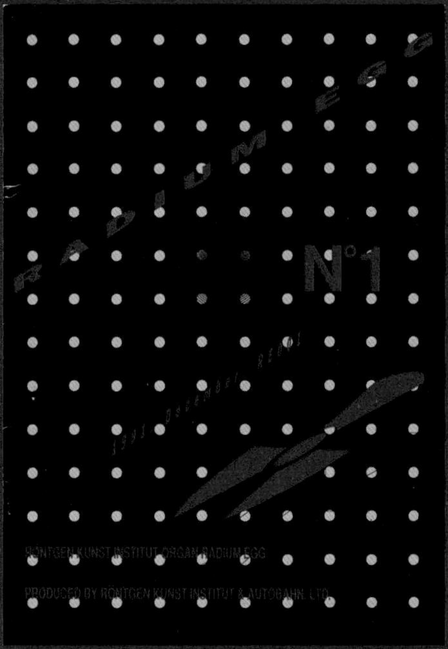

Cover, *Radium Egg*, 1991

2. Takashi Murakami: The Thinking Pop Artist

The year 1992 saw an explosive breakthrough of New—or Neo—Pop.[22]

In addition to Murakami's solo exhibitions at Hosomi Gallery in December 1991, and at Röntgen in January 1992, the artists (all born during the late 50s to mid-60s) now associated with the movement—Taro Chiezo, Kodai Nakahara, Minako Nishiyama, Yukinori Yanagi, and Kenji Yanobe—had their first solo exhibitions in Tokyo and Osaka between January and March.[23] All of them incorporated icons of Japanese *anime* and plastic-model culture in their sculpture, reflecting critically on the ambiguous relation between Japanese political power and popular culture. In March, the Nippon International Contemporary Art Fair (NICAF) organized by Masami Shiraishi, former director of the Toko Museum, featured these artists, along with a symposium on new art that included New Academic scholars Akira Asada and Shin-ichi Nakazawa.

Kodai Nakahara
Unknown, 1992
Aluminum, camera, wire release
35½ x 47 x 47 inches

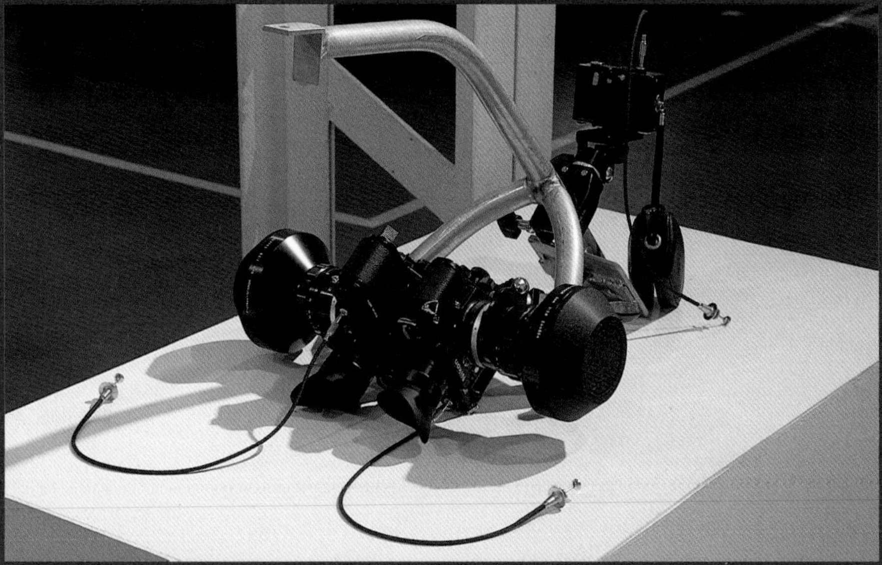

¶ Encountering Neo-Geo in the catalogue of the 1987 Whitney Biennial, Sawaragi was immediately attracted to its **"shallow and superficial style oozing out a Pop aura";** its use of "ribbons, stripes and Day-Glo paint conveyed the temperature similar to that of punk."[16] He voraciously read the materials on Neo-Geo sent from *Bijutsu Techō*'s New York correspondents. Fully aware of the American postmodern critical current established by Hal Foster, Craig Owens, and Douglas Crimp, Sawaragi avoided its minutiae. Fragments of information were filtered through his sensibility, sampled like House Music, cut up and recombined to level out the difference between important and marginal pieces of information, and between artist and anonymous sampler-cum-plagiarist. His essays published in *Bijutsu Techō* between 1988 and 1990 define his idea of Simulation as an aesthetic that is not conditioned by particular systems of representation attached to historical periods, nor by the values of a specific cultural community.

"Simulationism," he wrote, "breaks down the referential ground of cultural community embodied by the period style... leveling out the significance of all the ideological beliefs concerning matter, memory, self, Anti-Art or painterly language."[17]

¶ Sawaragi advanced Sampling, Cut Up, and Remix—the three methods of his Simulationism—as strategies to combat what he saw as the inherent essentialism of the Japanese avant-garde. He targeted Shuzo Takiguchi's Surrealism, Jun Miyakawa's Anti-Art, and Genpei Akasegawa's Theory of Eccentric Phenomenon, in which applications of quotation, collage, and parody belied belief in the ontological unity of the integrated subject and the intuitively affirmed essence of things. In contrast, Sawaragi's image of the ideal Japanese artist was a "schizophrenic who can perpetually reproduce the condition of the present culture in which every detail exists apart from its category as mere material for new mixture, in his healthy ability to forget past and future."[18]

¶ Looking back on the time, Sawaragi remarks that his own Simulationism was a "remix" of ideas. His idea of Sampling was inspired by the early 80s revival of William Burroughs among science-fiction writers and New Wave musicians. The appropriation of Burrough's "cut up" technique by the London and Brussels New Wave influenced Japanese creators of his generation, most notably the noise musician Yamantaka Eye and the punk poet and novelist Koh Machida. Sawaragi confesses that while Burroughs's novels were unfathomable to him, he found the writer's fragmented expressions and method of writing stimulating. At the same time, German industrial rock, imported in the late 70s and sold in shops in Shinjuku, moved him with its raw sound and German voices, which required no knowledge of its cultural background. These aspects, repellent to orthodox rock fans, attracted him as something directly contemporary; they exemplified a cultural transformation, kidnapping rock from its dominant English context in order to reshape it as powerful native music.

¶ Translation as misinterpretation and the willful distortion of an original cultural product in order to create an "attractive monster" characterized Sawaragi's thinking in the early 90s. And Takashi Murakami responded to Sawaragi's "broadcasting" of this attitude in *Bijutsu Techō*, **"sometimes through special issues, sometimes through columns, but every month, like a radio."** While their sources were different, they shared the mission of turning marginalized Japanese subcultures into a new artistic force. Their most notable product was New Pop, or Lorita-Pop (Lollipop), based on the Japanese *otaku* culture. Their close discussion between 1990 and 1992 coalesced into the exhibition "Anomaly" at Röntgen Kunst Institute in the fall of 1992.

As he has frequently noted in interviews, Murakami did not simply dismiss **nihonga**; he felt a mixture of awe and rivalry at its hegemony. **Nihonga** was the only genre in Japanese art that had a substantial body of collectors and whose exhibitions attracted an audience of thousands.[11] He also understood why **nihonga** captured the Japanese public: it provided representations of a shared identity. Hirayama's own "Silk Road" paintings offered an imaginary picture of the home of Japanese culture, ideologically consoling a national identity bruised by the Second World War.[12] Thus Murakami stayed in the **nihonga** department as long as possible not only to acquire skills, but to formulate an alternative to **nihonga**. He received his Ph.D. in 1993.[13]

¶ Educating himself by frequenting the Institute of Contemporary Art Nagoya, the Toko Museum, and the New Museum of Contemporary Art in New York, Murakami steadily formed a knowledge of and taste for contemporary art. His first opportunity to present himself as a contemporary artist occurred in the fall of 1990 through his meeting with Noi Sawaragi, editor of **Bijutsu Techō** magazine. He impressed Sawaragi with his enthusiasm for creating a context in which young artists could freely exhibit their work by presenting a plan for a group show involving his friends from Tachikawa Preliminary Art School. Murakami also ventured an eccentric translation of Sawaragi's Simulationism by suggesting that Haim Steinbach selling his platforms at prices based on the cost of the displayed goods could be used as a conceptual model with which to satirize the values of **nihonga**, in which paintings are priced according to the kind and amount of color pigment applied to each canvas.[14]

¶ Murakami's Simulationist exercise materialized in two works displayed in his master's thesis exhibition for TUMA in March 1991. One was a series of paintings entitled **Colors**, huge canvases painted in blue, yellow, and brown Japanese pigments that offered an ironic commentary on the **nihonga** convention in which those paintings employing the most expensive and technically demanding pigment —blue—were priced most dearly.

The other installation, Polyrhythm Boat, was a boat-shaped synthetic resin structure, its floor strewn with tiny plastic model soldiers.

The latter piece, referencing the childhood nostalgia of Murakami's generation for **anime** and plastic models, ironically exposed the superficiality of urban consumer culture during the Bubble years: a time when synthetic resin was frequently applied to the interior walls of glittery cafes and clubs.

Takashi Murakami
Polyrhythm Boat, 1991
Synthetic resins, lead, panel, paint, and Tamiya plastic models
Boat: 157 1/2 x 23 1/2 x 29 1/2 inches
Block: 86 1/2 x 35 1/2 x 23 1/2 inches

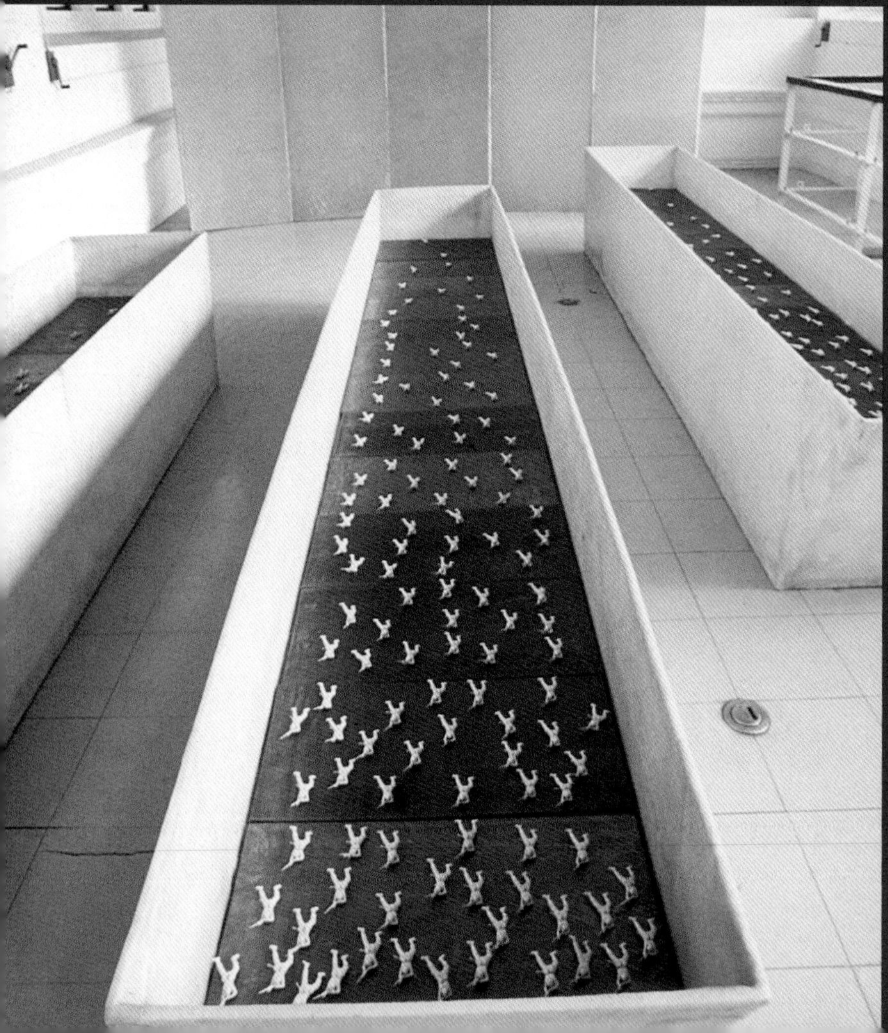

¶ Between March 1991 and Murakami's solo exhibition at Hosomi Gallery in December of that year, the artist had come to represent a stimulating new current to a circle of young curators, journalists, gallerists, and artists forming just outside the TUMA group. Almost all of the performers in Tokyo's new art scene attended Murakami's Hosomi opening: Ikeuchi, Kurosawa, Nishihara, Sawaragi, and Murakami protégé Tsuyoshi Ozawa, in addition to Toko Museum assistant coordinator Tomio Koyama and Tokyo Municipal Museum curator Yusuke Minami, who wrote the catalogue text.[15]

2. Radio Simulationist: Noi Sawaragi as Editor and Critic

Arguably the most vocal Japanese art critic of the 90s, Noi Sawaragi contributed to contemporary art first as junior editor of **Bijutsu Techō**. Between 1987 and 1990, Sawaragi filled the gap between the discursive current in American art and its Japanese counterpart. He organized ambitious special issues, including those on Neo-Geo and Simulationist feminism. In his articles and columns, he discussed the significance of such artists as Richard Prince, Jeff Koons, Peter Halley, Mike Bidlo, Haim Steinbach, Sherrie Levine, and Cindy Sherman among many others on a high critical level. Since these artists were almost totally unknown to Japanese audiences, Sawaragi's articles had an evangelical impact on those searching for a new perspective on contemporary art.

¶ This essay documents the emergence of this new art scene in Tokyo between 1991 and 1995. Although progressive artistic activity was by no means limited to this site, I will keep Röntgen Kunst Institute as the focus of my account, since its exhibitions most clearly represent two of the most important artistic attitudes developing in this milieu. I provisionally call them here New Pop and Personal Conceptualism. Represented respectively by the quartet of Ikeuchi, Koyama, Murakami, and Sawaragi on the one hand, and Kurosawa, Nishihara, Ozawa, and Sone on the other, these attitudes divided Röntgen's activities into first and second stages. Both are genuine expressions of the sensibility of the artists and critics born in the 60s, the Japanese postmodern condition. While I wish to provide an intellectual context for New Pop, which had a pronounced theoretical ambition, I will deliberately keep my account anecdotal to emphasize the heroic roles that certain individuals played in the formation of the scene. The details I am going to give will reveal a picture of an artistic community propelled by a youthful spirit, taking the negative conditions of their schools and traditional Japanese art as occasions for transformation.

II. Preparations

1. Where Were They, 1987–91?

While as late as 1989 TUMA was bureaucratically Japan's most important art school, the nation's most successful art school was Kyoto City University of Music and Art. Noboru Tsubaki, Yasumasa Morimura, and Dumb Type, all of whom were included in "Against Nature," as well as rising younger artists like Kodai Nakahara and Kenji Yanobe, graduated from and taught at Kyoto. In contrast, the most progressive studio art faculty at Tokyo University of Music and Art were steeped in nostalgia for Mono-ha, the Japanese equivalent to Minimalism and Land Art. According to Tomio Koyama, the popularity of TUMA's design department, reflecting the commercial success of recent graduates who became star illustrators on the Tokyo New Wave scene, was depressing to seriously motivated students.[6] Min Nishihara testifies to TUMA students' envy for the more liberal atmosphere enjoyed by their Kyoto counterparts.[7]

¶ Art magazines and the preliminary schools that trained candidates for TUMA frequently brought together young talent. Tatsuo Miyajima, the first TUMA artist to break through onto the international art scene, became an initial role model. Miyajima graduated from the oil painting department without painting a single picture, formulating his personal style while working as an editor for the art magazine *Atelier*. Among the editors who worked part time at *Atelier* under Miyajima were Shin Kurosawa, Min Nishihara, and Yuko Hasegawa, now a leading curator of her generation. In 1989, Hasegawa and Kurosawa became curators at the Art Tower Mito, an ambitious cultural complex that combined theater, music, and art. Nishihara's journalistic connections brought her into contact with the emerging Röntgen group. Tachikawa Preliminary Art School functioned as another social nexus for TUMA discontents. While tutoring there from 1983 to 1989, Takashi Murakami met Masato Nakamura, Tomoo Hirose, and Shigeaki Iwai, TUMA peers who instilled in him a passion for contemporary art.[8] Tsuyoshi Ozawa knew Murakami as a tutor and participated in the group's nightly discussions on contemporary art.

¶ Murakami was an unusual TUMA student in that he publicly took issue with its teaching, specifically with the *nihonga* (Japanese painting) department. The *nihonga* department was originally conceived at the turn of the century as central to TUMA by its founder Tenshin Okakura, who hoped to rescue traditional Japanese painting from neglect by amalgamating features of various regional and historical Japanese-painting traditions with those of modern Western painting.[9] By the time Murakami's enrollment some ninety years later, it had become a marginal department training students as artisans. Murakami recalls that critiques of student work consisted of long, tedious discussions about pigments; Professor Ikuo Hirayama, a painter of national popularity, maintained that intellectual discussion of art was irrelevant to mature craftsmanship.[10]

¶ **While the euphoria was not given representation until the late 80s through the architectural transformation of Tokyo supported by Bubble money, the influx of imported goods and information since the late 70s allowed young urban dwellers to choose information freely.** The fragmented nature of knowledge frequently forced them to piece together sundry materials to form a new whole in order to meet their particular demands. The idea of Remix, which Noi Sawaragi proclaimed as one of the central factors of his Simulationism, was based on his experience as a young consumer. At the same time, Japanese New Wave culture of the early to mid-80s, staged by advertisement and entertainment agencies, made graphic designers fashionable; the Annual Graphic Award, sponsored by Parco Department Store, had considerable prestige among young art school students. **But the new consumerism also compromised the promise of Tokyo as an unprecedented cultural capital;** it was in part the frustration with this failure that motivated the main players of the Röntgen group to create their own artistic scene, using the lessons of Tokyo's postmodern market.

¶ As Alexandra Monroe pointed out in *Flash Art*, up to the late 80s the Japanese contemporary art scene, or *gendai bijutsu*, lacked a structure comparable to the American artworld with its system of gallery practice and critical evaluation supporting artists. Its critical activities did not have a center or a common field. Despite critic Shigeo Chiba's assumption that Japanese art preserved its avant-garde spirit through a continuous defiance of formalism, throughout the 80s theorists of painting and sculpture arbitrarily built on a domestically construed Greenbergian formalism and Minimalism, claiming their orthodoxy against domestic conceptualism as well as an imported brand of New Painting.[5]

¶ TUMA remained aloof from both Japanese postmodernism and domestic avant-gardism. The only national conservatory, it commanded an incomparable authority and influence over the domains of government-assisted art events, awards, and grants. Founded in 1887 as *Tokyo Bijutsu Gakko* and directly managed by the Japanese Ministry of Culture and Education, TUMA had played a central role in the modernization of Japanese art during the turn of the last century. However, interviews with Koyama, Kurosawa, Murakami, Nishihara, and Ozawa suggest that their education at TUMA gave them little to work with. They found the program antiquated and irrelevant, their professors authoritarian and concerned merely with technical training. They were frustrated during their school years, meeting and forming together as a group only after graduation or in workplaces outside university.

¶ Still, TUMA played an active role in shaping these artists and creating their art scene, if only in a negative and indirect manner. Because its program was so ineffective, artists had to be self-reliant, seeking out their own histories of contemporary art and their own answers to the question of why they make art. The lack of critical criteria or direction in Japanese contemporary art intensified their sense of crisis, but Tokyo in 1989 did provide some resources. For a new aesthetic, they turned to its subculture—since childhood their most powerful and relevant domain. The postmodern *pasticheur*'s skill allowed them to amalgamate its fragments, reintegrating the lowly materials of *manga* and *anime* and the banal activities of the street into works of art.

Overlooked is the fact that between 1989 and 1992, an even fresher artistic attitude was emerging in Tokyo that would mark a sharp break with the technophilic sensibility of "Against Nature." Although it shared a lot with the "new art with a political edge" discussed in Monroe's article, this wave comprising artists, critics, curators, and gallerists born during the early 60s was characterized by its subcultural activities and by the complex use of Japanese Pop icons as a way to define a generational spirit.

¶ Sometimes called the Röntgen Group

after the gallery that showcased their work, these younger artists radically transformed the manners of artistic production and presentation, as well as the critical and journalistic language of contemporary art and the relation between the artist and the audience in Tokyo's artworld. Boasting four-meter-high ceilings and one-hundred-ninety square meters of floor space, Röntgen Kunst Institute, directed by Tsutomu Ikeuchi, was exceptional for a Japanese gallery. And unlike most Japanese galleries, its contract covered the entire production, exhibition, and advertising cost for the artist. From Röntgen's showcase emerged Takashi Murakami, Tsuyoshi Ozawa, Yutaka Sone, and Kenji Yanobe, artists who extended their activities overseas during the latter half of the 90s. Critics Noi Sawaragi and Min Nishihara provided an intellectual framework for this new art. Sawaragi's ideas around Simulationism, an aesthetic characterized by its lack of attachment to historical styles and specific cultural communities, introduced a stimulating way to think of contemporary art in a broader cultural context, and to evaluate the works of his contemporaries as vanguard expressions. Between 1993 and 1995, curator Shin Kurosawa of Art Tower Mito organized exceptionally successful workshops with Yanobe, Sone, and Ozawa, paving the way for exhibitions by younger Japanese artists in public museums. After 1994 Tomio Koyama, who had played an important advisory role in this scene, extended the spirit of the new art as director of the progressive SCAI the Bathhouse as well as his own gallery, pushing Murakami and Yoshitomo Nara onto the international stage.

¶ Although there were already the excellent examples of the Toko Museum of Contemporary Art, Heinecken Village, and the Institute of Contemporary Art Nagoya in the mid to late 80s, it is remarkable that in the years immediately following the bust of the "Bubble" economy (as the inflationary boom period between 1987 and 1990 is called) and against the grain of Japanese artistic practice, an entirely new artistic scene was instituted by people in their late twenties. The particular relation of this generation to Japanese consumer culture, to the city of Tokyo, and to the Tokyo Geijutsu Daigaku (Tokyo University of Music and Art, or TUMA)—from which Koyama, Kurosawa, Murakami, Nishihara, Ozawa, and Sone all graduated—encouraged the production of major work and helped to create a significant art scene.

Röntgen Kunst Institute, Tokyo

¶ Growing up surrounded by an abundance of goods, the artists and critics of this generation have an ambivalent relationship to Japanese consumerism. As children many if not all were absorbed by manga (Japanese narrative comics) and kaijyu (monsters from television sci-fi flicks), cultures that clearly influenced their aesthetic. Their adolescence and early adulthood corresponded with the entry of Japanese society into "the consumer stage from the productionist stage, with the majority of the nation engaged in consumerism."[3]

Tokyo was constructed by the media as a postmodern capital that superficially responded to the rising popularity of Japanese techno music and domestic designer brands.

The euphoria about the emerging cultural mix was given a high theoretical note by an intellectual trend called New Academism, represented by Akira Asada's best-seller Kōzō to chikara: kōzōshugi o koete (Structure and Power: Beyond Structuralism), in which he urged young college students newly equipped with poststructuralist theories "not to stay in a narrow autonomy of self but open up in all directions," and "to roam in the jungle of knowledge and taste every good and evil."[4]

Conversation Days: New Japanese Art between 1991 and 1995

I. Introduction

During the early 90s Japanese contemporary art became international. Whereas formerly its artistic expression had been closed within a narrow academicism and its market limited to dealing fashionable foreign artists, suddenly Japan was able to produce a series of new and unusual talents. "Against Nature: Japanese Art in the Eighties" encouraged this. The exhibition, which traveled to seven American cities beginning in 1989, featured the digital generation of Japanese artists including Yasumasa Morimura and 1988 Venice Aperto sensation Tatsuo Miyajima.[1] The March 1990 issue of *Art News* and the March/April 1992 issue of *Flash Art* embodied international journalism's enthusiasm for the newly active Tokyo scene. In "A Distant Mirror," Lynn Gumpert reported for *Art News* on the radical change on Tokyo's artistic map propelled by enterprising curators and gallerists; in *Flash Art*, Alexandra Monroe hailed the critical tendencies of younger Japanese artists whose use of technology and popular icons ironically critiqued the continuing pull of nationalist militarism beneath the surface of Japanese postwar culture.[2]

BY MIDORI MATSUI

1. Bruce Hainley, "Sharon Lockhart, Laura Owens, Frances Stark," Artforum 36, no. 3 (November 1997): 119.

2. Jerry Saltz, "The Chimes of Freedom Flashing: Some Thoughts on Recent Work," Art Vision 2, no. 2 (Summer 1994): 16. For celebrations and mournings of the current absence of thematic group shows, see Susan Kandel, "Exploring Power of Three Among Friends," Los Angeles Times, 4 July 1997, F-18 ["it's (usually) a suicide mission to group of-the-moment artists under the pretext of a theme"]; Daniela Salvioni, "The Whitney Biennial: A Post 80s Event," Flash Art 30, no. 195 (Summer 1997): 114 ("Until now hyper-thematic exhibitions have remained the dominant, albeit maligned, mode of packaging...[In the current Whitney Biennial] the relation between artworks is loose and the effect is not cumulative: the exhibition is not about using art to substantiate a theory developed from without."); and Daniel Birnbaum, "Practice in Theory," Artforum 38, no. 1 (September 1999): 154 ("this year's [Venice Biennale] was quite exceptional in its lack of theoretical framework...The two-volume catalogue gave...not a hint of any general themes...There was a time when every exhibition required a commentary by one French philosopher or another, and we all got sick of that. Now that we've reached the other extreme, I kind of miss Jacques Derrida.") Also see Laura Owens's interview with curator Russell Ferguson about his exhibition "In Memory of My Feelings: Frank O'Hara and American Art," which Owens praises for its "distinct lack of metaphor," in "The Exchange of Ideas Among the Living," Cakewalk 3 (Fall 1999): 26.

3. Much to my surprise and embarrassment, the September 1991 Artforum, in which my Barney review appeared, featured as its front cover image a still from one of Barney's videos. The magazine's decision to devote the cover to an artist's first show, especially with only a short write-up of that show within its pages, affirmed to many the feeling that the commercial arm of the artworld had flexed its considerable muscle to manipulate media exposure and hype in the interest of creating a new art star.

4. Quoted in Michael Cohen, "Cityscape: Los Angeles. Part 2," Flash Art 28, no. 182 (May/June 1995): 66.

5. Hainley, "Sharon Lockhart, Laura Owens, Frances Stark," 119.

6. Quoted in Kate Bush, "Design for Life," Frieze, no. 36 (September/October 1997): 54.

7. Daniel Birnbaum, "Practice in Theory," 154. Birnbaum has also called Rhoades "perhaps the most American of contemporary American artists." See Birnbaum's introduction to "A Thousand Words: Jason Rhoades Talks About His Impala Project," Artforum 37, no. 1 (September 1998): 135.

8. "Interview with Jorge Pardo by Amanda Cruz on September 5, 1996," Jorge Pardo (Chicago: Museum of Contemporary Art; and Los Angeles: The Museum of Contemporary Art, 1997), n.p.

9. Jason Rhoades, "A Thousand Words: Jason Rhoades Talks About His Impala Project," 135.

10. Jan Tumlir, "Gentle Purpose," New Art Examiner 26, no. 8 (May 1999): 46; Roberta Smith, "Laura Owens," The New York Times, 18 April 1997, C-28; and Carmine Iannaccone, "Entertainment Complex," Frieze, no. 49 (November/December 1999): 88.

11. Bush, "Design for Life," 55; and Kate Bush, "4166 Sea View Lane," Parkett 56 (September 1999): 153.

12. Miwon Kwon, "The Return of the Real: An Interview with Hal Foster," Flash Art 29, no. 187 (March/April 1996): 63.

13. Joel Sanders, "Frames of Mind," Artforum 38, no. 3 (November 1999): 129.

14. Jack Bankowsky, "Slackers," Artforum 30, no. 3 (November 1991): 96; and "Inside-Out: A Conversation Between Lisa Phillips and Louise Neri," 1997 Biennial Exhibition (New York: Whitney Museum of American Art, 1997), 44.

15. Bankowsky, "Slackers," 100.

16. Martha Rosler, "The System of the Postmodern in the Decade of the Seventies," in The Idea of the Post-Modern: Who Is Teaching It? (Seattle: Henry Art Gallery, University of Washington, 1981), 25, 27. See also Lawrence Alloway, "Network: The Artworld Described as a System," originally published in Artforum 11, no. 1 (September 1972) and reprinted in Network: Art and the Complex Present (Ann Arbor, Mich.: UMI Research Press, 1984), 3-15. Alloway sees the Manhattan art scene of the 60s as manifesting many of the characteristics discussed here: "The 60s was," he writes, "a brilliant decade in which an exceptional number of young artists emerged, without the tentative or inhibitory starts of their predecessors" and when "the literature of art...runs copiously beyond the reviewing of exhibitions by critics as art is assimilated to the sphere of consumption."

17. Hal Foster, "The Problem of Pluralism," Art in America 70, no. 1 (January 1982): 11.

18. Rosler, "The System of the Postmodern," 27; and Hal Foster, "Re: Post," in Brian Wallis, ed., Art After Modernism: Rethinking Representation (New York: New Museum of Contemporary Art, 1984), 200.

19. Quoted in "Making Art, Making Money: 13 Artists Comment," Art in America 78, no. 7 (July 1990): 178.

20. Arthur C. Danto, "The Age of Importance Art," Art News 87, no. 4 (April 1988): 121. The view that the artworld of late clamors after ever-younger artists simply because they represent the new and the next is expressed often during the 90s, and it surely fits with the premise of my essay; it's another sign of the routinizing of the art system, in which the new and the next are given a set and repeatable date (the graduation ceremony or thesis show) and, because the values attributed to the new and the next are only market values, unanchored by any discursive or historical importance, they can be all the more easily swept aside to make room for the next new and the next next. But it should be remembered that in the 60s, when the convergence of art bureaucracies, schools, publicity, and so on was first starting to develop into a large-scale and integrated system, the increasing recognition and success bestowed upon very young artists was often thought of differently, in more optimistic and futuristic terms, as in John Coplans's remark that "the development of younger artists seems to parallel the increasing number of mathematicians who very often produce their best work before they're 30." See John Coplans, "The New Sculpture and Technology," in American Sculpture of the Sixties, ed. Maurice Tuchman (Los Angeles: Los Angeles County Museum of Art, 1967), 22.

21. Quoted in L.A. Times: 11 Los Angeles Artists (Boise, Ida.: Boise Art Museum, 1991), n.p.; and quoted in Jörn Schafaff and Barbara Steiner, "Interview with Jorge Pardo," Jorge Pardo (Ostfildern-Ruit, Germany: Hatje Cantz Verlag, 2000), 15. A good deal of the Schafaff and Steiner interview mulls over the couple of instances when Pardo has overseen the design of a catalogue devoted to his work and in which the curator's essay or other information has been printed in a color almost identical in hue or value to the background color and thereby made virtually illegible; as Pardo puts it, the text in such cases is used as "pure decoration." See Jorge Pardo (MCA/MOCA) and Jorge Pardo (Tokyo: Person's Weekend Museum, 1993).

22. Tumlir, "Gentle Purpose," 46.

23. Neville Wakefield, "Toba Khedoori," Artforum 34, no. 2 (October 1995): 94.

24. Smith, "Laura Owens," as in note 10; see also Peter Schjeldahl, "Painting Rules," Village Voice, 30 September 1997. On Pardo, see Peggy Cyphers, "New York in Review," Arts Magazine 65, no. 7 (March 1991): 94-95; and Jan Avgikos, "Jorge Pardo," Artforum 32, no. 9 (May 1994): 101.

25. Hans-Christian Dany, "Diana Thater. Kunstverein, Hamburg," Frieze, no. 35 (June/August 1997): 91.

26. Robert Pincus-Witten, "Naked Lunches," October 3 (Spring 1977): 104; and Rosalind Krauss, "Pictorial Space and the Question of Documentary," Artforum 10, no. 3 (November 1971): 68.

27. Schafaff and Steiner, "Interview with Jorge Pardo," 15.

28. Robert C. Morgan, "After the Deluge: The Return of the Inner-Directed Artist," Arts Magazine 66, no. 7 (March 1992): 50.

29. Dave Hickey, The Invisible Dragon: Four Essays on Beauty (Los Angeles: Art Issues. Press, 1993), 6.

30. Howard Singerman, Art Subjects: Making Artists in the American University (Berkeley: University of California Press, 1999), 163.

31. Thomas Crow, "Versions of the Pastoral in Some Recent American Art," in David A. Ross and Jürgen Harten, eds., The Binational: American Art of the Late Eighties (Boston: Institute of Contemporary Art and Museum of Fine Arts; and Cologne: DuMont Buchverlag, 1988), 20.

32. Ibid., 21.

33. Quoted in Dennis Cooper, "Too Cool for School," in All Ears: Cultural Criticism, Essays and Obituaries (Soft Skull Press, 1999), 52. Lewis deSoto, director of the California College of Arts and Craft's Graduate Program, has described the new art student in more business terms: "An MFA student is committed to a contract, essentially, with a series of professional consultants who are required to give honest criticism" (quoted in Reena Jana, "Exploring the Value of an MFA Education Today," Artweek 24, no. 9 (6 May 1993): 18.

34. Laura Owens, "A Thousand Words: Laura Owens Talks About Her New Work," Artforum 37, no. 10 (Summer 1999): 131.

35. Susan Kandel, "Khedoori Explores Being, Nothingness," Los Angeles Times, 26 January 1995, F-7.

36. Roman Jakobson, Language in Literature, eds. Krystyna Pomorska and Stephen Rudy (Cambridge, Mass.: Harvard University Press, 1987), 98-106.

37. Norman Bryson, Word and Image: French Painting of the Ancien Régime (Cambridge: Cambridge University Press, 1981), 22-23, 28.

38. Lockhart: "Generally I'm not interested in metaphor in any of my work" [in Bernard Joisten, "Sharon Lockhart Interview," Purple 2 (Winter 1998-99): 329]; Rhoades: "I'm just not that interested in a lot of European art where someone lays some objects down on the floor, and it's supposed to be a metaphor for something. Everything I do has some kind of function. When I build a gun, it works" [in Ralph Rugoff, "The Show of Shows," Harper's Bazaar (March 1995): 336]; and Owens: "I dislike literal metaphor and the symbolic in art...I am thinking about the person looking at the artwork" [in Rebecca Morris, "Programming Attitude: An Interview with Laura Owens," L.A. Muscle 11, no. 3 (February/March 1997): 15]; see also Owens's comments on metaphor and metonymy in "The Exchange of Ideas Among the Living" (as in note 2). Thater is again the exception here; for example, she has described her 1995 work China as "a metaphor with many layers" (quoted in Amei Wallach, "This Video Artist Runs With the Wolves," The New York Times, 4 February 1996, sec. 2: 35).

39. Timothy Martin, "Documentary Theater," in Sharon Lockhart. Teatro Amazonas (Rotterdam: NAi Publishers, 1999), 20, 102.

40. Gregory Volk, "Jorge Pardo at Friedrich Petzel," Art in America 84, no. 12 (December 1996): 93.

41. Timothy Martin, "What Cyan Said to Magenta about Yellow," in Diana Thater: China (Chicago: The Renaissance Society at the University of Chicago, 1996), 50-51.

42. Martin, "Documentary Theater," 27.

43. Tumlir, "Gentle Purpose," 46.

44. Martin, "Documentary Theater," 17. Norman Bryson would later write something very similar in response to Lockhart's work: "At a certain point the whole effort of the gaze reaches saturation and breakdown, and into the field of vision there enters, at the gaze's exhausted edges, a force we might want to think of as the randomness of the world" ["Sharon Lockhart: The Politics of Attention," Artext 70 (August/October 2000): 59].

45. Harold Rosenberg, "The American Action Painters," in The Tradition of the New (New York: Horizon Press, 1959), 29.

46. Tumlir, "Gentle Purpose," 46.

47. Jorge Pardo (MCA/MOCA), n.p.

48. Giovanni Intra, "Sharon Lockhart, Laura Owens, Frances Stark. Blum & Poe, Santa Monica," Flash Art 30, no. 197 (November/December 1997): 76; Hainley, "Sharon Lockhart, Laura Owens, Frances Stark," 120; and Kandel, "Exploring Power of Three Among Friends," 18.

49. Peter Schjeldahl, "Festivalism," The New Yorker 75, no. 17 (5 July 1999): 85.

50. Christopher Knight, "Is L.A. a world-class city?," in Last Chance for Eden (Los Angeles: Art Issues. Press, 1995), 333.

51. Dan Cameron, "Glocal Warming," Artforum 36, no. 4 (December 1997): 17.

52. This is the argument put forward by Jürgen Habermas in The Structural Transformation of the Public Sphere. An Inquiry into a Category of Bourgeois Society, trans. Thomas Bürger with assistance from Frederick Lawrence (Cambridge, Mass.: The MIT Press, 1991) and by Thomas Crow in Painters and Public Life in Eighteenth-Century Paris (New Haven, Conn., and London: Yale University Press, 1985). See also Crow's "Modernism and Mass Culture in the Visual Arts," in Modernism and Modernity: The Vancouver Conference Papers, eds. Benjamin H. D. Buchloh, Serge Guilbaut, and David Solkin (Halifax, Canada: The Press of the Nova Scotia College of Art and Design, 1983), 215-64; and "These Collectors, They Talk About Baudrillard Now," in Discussions in Contemporary Culture, ed. Hal Foster (Seattle: Bay Press, 1987), 1-8.

53. Clement Greenberg, "The Present Prospects of American Painting and Sculpture," in The Collected Essays and Criticism. Volume 2: Arrogant Purpose, 1945-1949 (Chicago: The University of Chicago Press, 1986), 170. On "The Club," see Irving Sandler, "The Club: How the Artists of the New York School Found Their First Audience—Themselves," Artforum 4, no. 1 (September 1965): 27-31.

54. Hainley, "Sharon Lockhart, Laura Owens, Frances Stark," 120.

55. Mitchell Kane, "Curator's Note," in Pressure on the Public (Northbrook, Ill.: Hirsch Farm Project, 1992), 9.

Or is it simply nostalgic to regard artworks as still having publics at all? It's been argued that what gets called "the public" first arose hand-in-hand with modern art, that its earliest cultural manifestations in the debates waged in the new coffee houses and salons of the eighteenth century, and in the art and literary criticism that also first appeared then, served as the crucible in which modern art was formed.[52]

It's also been argued that the history of modern art has been shaped to a large extent in reaction to the collapse of that public, to its transformation into markets and masses, its surrender to engineered consent and the passifying distractions of enforced leisure. Artists have in turn often been sustained by the discussions they themselves generate, coming together to form their own publics. The Lower Manhattan art scene of the 50s, with its artist-run hang-out "The Club," is an example, as are, perhaps, the do-it-yourself apartment galleries and nomadic exhibitions that so enlivened Los Angeles during the early 90s. But such organic efforts have proven able to stem the tide for only so long. "What can fifty do against a hundred and forty million?" as Clement Greenberg once sighed, although his math now seems a bit optimistic.[53]

"Most artists of any interest whatsoever," Hainley observed on the occasion of the show by Lockhart, Owens, and Stark, "only have conversations with (make work for) a few people, two or three, not many more."[54]

¶ Curator Mitchell Kane, an early supporter of some of the L.A. artists in this show, wrote in 1992, "I have always understood the public to be a nebulous ideal, very seldom spoken of in the first person, yet always standing morally tall. I cannot for the life of me recall its complexion, or even a scent."[55]

There exists in the work I've been describing a disjuncture or a kind of ellipsis between heavy and ubiquitous structure, which seems to correspond to the stature of today's artworld, and something as light, intimate, and ephemeral as "the first person" or complexion or scent. Perhaps that's where a public is currently being searched for, in the empty space measured by that ellipsis.

L.A. has become a designation used in tandem with other place names by jet-setting collectors and curators trying to organize their expanding Rolodexes. Curators especially are assuming the role once held by critics; only those curators who travel a lot can talk comprehensively about the careers of most of these artists, and are able keep up with their work as it trots the globe.

(It was four years ago, in 1997, when Dan Cameron noticed that "Artists and curators in particular became nomads...comparing notes on what and whom they saw and on how one artist's work looked up against another's...coming to terms with what Rem Koolhaas has termed the 'glocal' is the most pressing issue for curators today." [51])

The sense of the local implied by the idea of publics and by the new interest in place names—London, Los Angeles, Berlin, etc.—has for its condition the abolition of the local as such. "L.A." and "London" and "Berlin" and "New York" only gain meaning now as functions within a larger, comprehensive set, values emanating from a system.

¶ This further begs the question: who really is the public for all this exhibition-minded work, beyond something as formidable and mechanistic-sounding as "the artworld"? What kind of public today responds to and talks about art and through that process attributes a kind of value to it that's not entirely reducible to market value?

Friendship, as part of these artists' "living situation," has to remain unorganized and inarticulate to be felt as convincingly genuine; it can't be declaratively figured, made a theme or metaphor or position. And so Lockhart, Owens, and Stark tie their show together in a literal, mechanistic way by making work in four-feet-square formats, and Pardo falls back on the metonymy of a list.

¶ To perhaps qualify the rather depressing tone of what I've written here, I should probably end by saying that I have strong doubts about my own place among the public for this work. It could be argued that the role of critics in the artworld has been both routinized and demoted, and not only because the magazines we write for are perceived as "trade journals."

Hierarchies are being realigned and intensified in the newly international art circuit, and those without the time, money, and institutional backing to travel constantly—those not directly affiliated with what Peter Schjeldahl calls the "worldwide archipelago of institutions that are crazy in love with installations"—are finding it next to impossible to join the new public and experience the development of careers and bodies of work firsthand and in the flesh.[49]

Rhoades, for example, hasn't mounted a solo show in L.A. since his first in 1994; and whereas in the past calling someone like Rhoades an "L.A. artist" was a way of sweeping him to the side ("ruinous" is how Christopher Knight described the label[50]*), now "L.A. artist" integrates rather than marginalizes; it sets the artist in circulation.*

¶ The question is not whether to turn away from exhibiting and retreat back into the privations of the artist's garret. Rather, it's a question of how this newly increased public exposure of art and artists is perceived and approached. It would be easy at this point to continue the theme of this essay and claim that the public for art today is considered for the most part metonymically, as just part of the literal and quantifiable context manifested around art and the system it must work its way through, an audience being something that emerges mechanically and punctually from art-school critiques to gallery and museum openings.

This is no doubt true, but there's more. While few would go so far as to describe existing art publics as communities (or group formations or subcultures or any word connoting a shade of agency), hints have been made at the central importance of friendships among artists. For example in a 1998 catalogue devoted to his work, Pardo listed on a couple of its pages the names of friends and influences, ranging from family members to fellow artists—just their names, with no further explanation or commentary added.[47] And in 1997 Lockhart, Owens, and Stark mounted a show together based simply on their mutual friendship, "an investigation into the nature of discourse and dialogue among friends," as the press release stated.

Sharon Lockhart, *Untitled*, 1997. C-print, edition of 6. 48 x 48 inches

Perhaps what's being signaled here (and elsewhere, as in Muller's hand-painted announcements) is a desire to imagine differently the kind of frame that situates and underwrites art, to acknowledge but then draw emphasis away from the institutional and ideological toward a more flexible social framing. And yet the publicly pledged camaraderie of Lockhart, Owens, and Stark was received as "a very cryptic show" that "in no way defined friendship or simplified the intricacies of influence"—"it's pretty much impossible," one reviewer conceded, "to document something as elusive as mutual support and its correlates."[48] Here then is an indication of the quandary art now finds itself in, its existing in public but suspecting anything as explicitly formed as a public statement.

*This is the opposite of what in the 50s Harold Rosenberg conceived of as "**rôle**"—"the way the artist organizes his emotional and intellectual energy as if he were in a living situation."[45] Today, artist and artwork (and if they're successful, perhaps the viewer, too) assume roles without fully inhabiting them; in order to approximate a living situation, they must search for some "leakage" on the margins of organization and role. Roles are assumed somewhat neutrally, not to be faked, critiqued, or undermined, nor are they believed in earnestly, but just worn as a necessary starting point and in the hope that their power to define can be made incomplete and exhaustible.*

"This is what her contribution consists of," Tumlir writes of Owens, "a gesture that is partly oblivious, partly tactical, and delivered without a trace of arrogance or irony."[46] This is, moreover, what becomes of transcendence and progress when such aspirations find themselves circumscribed within an immobile and static array—a hope to at least rattle around somewhat amid the set prescriptions and temporarily break up the system's self-completion.

¶ Finally, something should be said about the public for this work, the public referred to (even if ironically) in this exhibition's title. It seems to be taken for granted today that artworks get made to be exhibited; indeed, it's one of the system's prescriptions. The traditional romantic notion of the artist's studio as a kind of isolation tank now gets exploded early on in art school, where the studio functions much as an exhibition space, invaded by a steady stream of critical onlookers–the walk-through traffic of faculty, visiting artists, and fellow students. Rather than a far-off dream, exhibiting has become a pressing fact (the grad quarters at UCLA are the new Salon of Southern California). And this in turn has had an effect on the actual physique of art-school studios; they're not as grubby as they used to be, but now tend to be clean, well-lit spaces fit for displaying finished goods. The studio used to be seen as diachronic. Toiling under neglect, the artist made work not for some waiting audience but out of previous work and towards future work.

His or her project was sustained by being conceived as a narrative succession, a kind of bildungsroman *or life story that gained value by mirroring, even internalizing, the progression of art in general.*

Today the studio is synchronic; artworks inside it get constructed not in private and historically but in public and through a seemingly static network. The studio is a place to shoot slides, get critiqued, have meetings, make contacts, and is itself coextensive with a larger artworld circuit of showing, getting noticed, being reviewed, and so on.

If there seems little in present experience that promises historical change, only an ever greater intensification and entrenchment of the current structure (here, the artworld's routine motions recall the ongoing revolutions of computerized communications that revolutionize nothing), if there's no longer much credibility in the ambition of escaping or progressing beyond, then finding cracks and moving in between will now be where and how work gets done, where and how credible meanings and ambitions will be resurrected.

As Timothy Martin has written about Diana Thater's work, and especially the way her installations invite viewers to walk in front of the video projectors and thereby partly scramble the imagery cast onto the walls, "the cinematic subject retained by Thater ceases to conform to a static model based on identities—an apparatus, an eye, a gaze, a self, a character—and is constituted and deconstituted according to a more dynamic model based on movements."[41] And Martin has found much the same strategy employed in Lockhart's photo series Shaun (1993), in which the oppressively codified and codifying framework of clinical photography is appropriated only to be set slightly ajar, made into "the tacit, though unelaborated, structure of inquiry that permits the in-between place of [Lockhart's] free and close looking."[42]

¶ For the characters within and in front of much of this work, and for the character of the work itself—that is, for both the image and its viewers, and for the work's own place within a discipline or tradition—the inescapable enactment of certain well-established roles is both acknowledged and side-stepped as much as possible, stated as a given and then momentarily deferred. "History simply comes with the territory," Tumlir has written in response to Owens's canvases.

"To take up a painterly practice in this day and age is to position oneself, more or less automatically, in relation to all the big statements ever made on the subject. This will happen regardless of what one actually chooses to do there."[43] About Shaun, Martin continues, "while the photographs draw attention to the idea of a role being played, and thus defer the individual, it is not so much the role but the individual deferred that is the subject of the photographs.

The role is merely a kind of trapping device or leaky container from which little expenditures or leakages of personhood may spill." In order to convey "individual persons without defining them," Lockhart must "make portraits that are not portraits."[44] And, it could be added, for Lockhart to convincingly convey her own individuality in her work, she must be a photographer who's not a photographer, a filmmaker who's not a filmmaker, a painter who's not a painter, a conceptual artist who's not a conceptual artist.

Diana Thater, Up to the Lintel: Bliss, 1992
Installation at Bliss House, Pasadena, California
Videotape, projectors, mylar, and existing architecture
Dimensions variable

¶ Something similar can be found in Thater's early piece Up to the Lintel: Bliss (1992), a site-specific video installation tailored to the Pasadena bungalow home that served during the late 80s and 90s as the artist-run gallery Bliss. From inside the house, Thater projected onto the windows footage she shot earlier peering in from outside the same windows. But for the initial shoot Thater added an extra visual component, arranging long planks of painted lumber up near each window so that they partially blocked the view inside. On playback, the wood resembles video color bars—or, again, the densely hued planks of John McCracken or an early Ellsworth Kelly. And yet between the color bands there remain visible little slices of domestic scenery. Once more the modernist monochrome is countered by bits of genre or still life, by the everyday and intimate—not unlike the cameo put in by Pardo's mom in his 1991 show, or the similar appearance made by Rhoades's mom in a Polaroid buried amid Swedish Erotica and Fiero Parts; and not unlike the blue lengths of plywood Pardo bent into matching chairs and footstools in Halley's, Ikeya-Seki, Encke's from 1996 ("functional monochromes," one critic called them [40]). To this list could be added Owens's mammoth paintings, with their mise-en-abyme depictions of various smallish easel pictures (including many still lifes); and Khedoori's wall-sized image fields, the grounds of which are prepared with all-over applications of melted wax (an all-overness somewhat reminiscent of Pollock) but end up incised with the tiniest of pencil lines, timid licks of paint, and (this is the leitmotif of Khedoori criticism) arrant pepperings of microscopic studio grit like pet hair. Confronting such work, the viewer must assume and then break from the proper distance, as well as the appropriate disposition and expectation, required by grand or monumental art. Scale and structure are declared outright, along with the size and layout of the particular exhibition space the work occupies, and then are let go in favor of something that feels more random, evasive, or intimate—something for which the viewer needs to search.

¶ It's hard not to see all this as responding on some level to living today inside the artworld, as attempting to be "airily honest about how things get done." It is as if this work were giving material form to the desire not to delude ourselves with the now threadbare pretensions of theory and discourse, that what we're doing is anything other than trying to open some space, to move and search a bit within "the static array," within the plottings and designations of an increasingly routinized system.

¶ Lockhart, Owens, and Rhoades have all spoken in interviews about avoiding metaphor in their work.[38] But neither they nor any of the other L.A. artists in this show end up with anything as diminutive in size as a still-life painting. Rather, the scale of their work is more suggestive of the dramatic theatrical stagings and grandeur of history painting. Or perhaps it could be argued that such work is scaled to the artworld. And this is to be taken metaphorically, at least on a certain level; their work is scaled to how the artworld is perceived now, its formidable scope and reach, its existence as a world, a whole universe, extending from the most local scenes to the increasingly unified international art circuit, circumscribing and ordering within its wide compass the most personal and most spectacularized events, and knitting together all points in between. But it's a world that mostly operates mechanically; few would claim that it's sustained by a healthy metaphysics or even shared communal values. Rather, it's linked up by more physical and arbitrary circumstances, dominated on the macro-level by the mechanisms of an international market and the elite exchange of artworld powerbrokers, and on the micro-level by the chance encounters of art school enrollment, the rote obligation of attending gallery openings, the bare necessity of living in the same low-rent districts, and the creaturely convenience of frequenting the same nearby bars and coffee shops. This too is acknowledged by the size of this work—size here functions metonymically, stretching out as if literally to map the real, contingent parameters of the artworld's infrastructure of exhibition spaces, the actual, physical conditions of reception and encounter.

Sharon Lockhart
Still from Goshogaoka, 1997
16-mm film; color/sound
63 minutes

¶ Allusions to heroic, large-scale painting are made not just on the edges of these artists' work in its considerable width and height, but can be found in its iconography as well. A good example is Lockhart's 1997 film Goshogaoka, in which the members of a Japanese high-school girls' basketball team perform drills in a gymnasium that also doubles as the school's theater. Over the entire length of the hour-long film, the camera remains immobile, its lens fixed on the stage at the opposite end of the gymnasium floor and the lush red theater curtain that nearly fills the upper half of the film's frame. Indeed, the curtain provides a spitting image of a mural-sized modernist monochrome. But it's only outside and in front of this expansive red field that the film's action occurs, in the form of girls' exercise routines; and it's even outside these routines, in the few mistakes the girls make or the shyness or pride they betray when momentarily glancing at the camera, that every commentator on Goshogaoka has focused attention. (Surprise over such small details and "cracks in the seamlessness" is a leitmotif of criticism devoted to Lockhart's work as a whole.) Here "enfolded tropes of aesthetic formality construct a backdrop of decorum and ideality that sets the non-ideal, the subtle and indecorous inflections of human detail, into the sharpest of contrasts," as Timothy Martin has written. "Purposefully ignoring the raised stage," Lockhart prefers instead an "embrace of the mundane." [39]

Indeed, the image at the base of much of the poststructuralist (or at least the Saussurian) theory taught in schools and used in criticism is of language as a system or structure (langue over parole).

But much recent theorizing has also insisted on keeping considerations of the structured and structuring activity of language on a highly abstract level. This, Crow contends, "made it possible to continue without a break the modernist preoccupation with inherently abstract processes of sign-making and sign-receiving," which in turn meant "trivializing forms of attention...associated with the buying and selling of work, the negotiation of individual careers, the novelties that might make a painting or sculpture an object of momentary interest or gossip in the art community."[32] Today the prominence afforded things like gossip, momentary interest, and the everyday real of artworld careers and negotiations has returned with the force of the repressed.

¶ Early in the 90s the reaction against language as anything other than what knits the artworld together took the overt form of anti-p.c. art, which was in large part an opposition to pedagogy and its pretensions to be anything but the seamless conduit between performing well in the crit and doing the same in the marketplace. More recently, the dominant attitude has turned from explicit hostility toward school to a more casual denial of it. "Most art schools are about teachers and students," Charles Ray has said, "UCLA is about artists working as artists."[33] Hanging out, talking shop, and making connections with faculty and visiting artists has replaced the systems and codifications of pedagogy, of syllabi and seminars. And hanging out has likewise become a paradigm for artworks. "Ultimately," remarks Owens, "you really want to make the painting that you want to be with. Not one that is constantly telling you everything it knows."[34] Not being able to say everything is perhaps made a condition of the very imagery produced by some of these artists, most noticeably in their preference for metonymic structures—in, for example, the one-thing-after-another

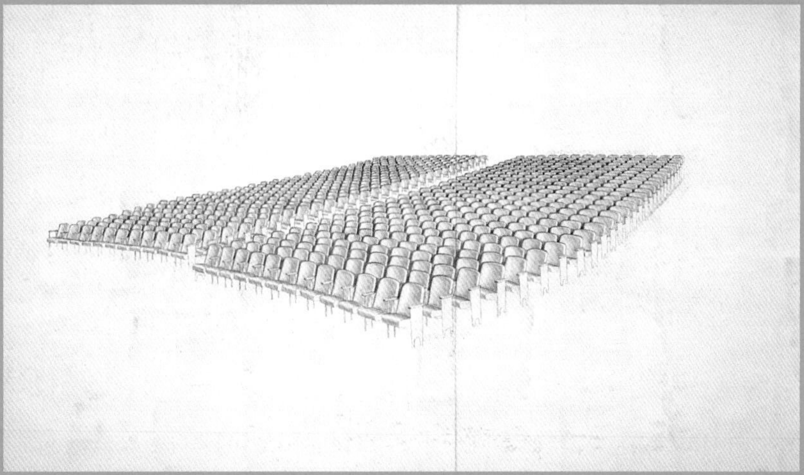

Toba Khedoori
Untitled (Seats) (detail), 1996
Oil and wax on paper
138 x 300 inches

repetition of identical units in Khedoori's drawings of windows, trains, and brick constructions (each of which "goes on and on, like something one simply forgot to stop drawing...as if they were produced by someone obsessed with details, but oblivious to the larger picture");[35] and in the rambling metonymic associations of Rhoades's Swedish Erotica and Fiero Parts (1994), which conjoin any and all objects colored yellow (toy chicks, raincoats, plastic bananas, etc.). Roman Jakobson describes the metonymic pole of language as privileging the immediate context of a message and the contiguity of its parts over metaphoric similarities that relate a message to its absent code; he also credits an overreliance on metonymy with a "defect in the 'capacity of naming'" and "a loss of metalanguage."[36] Such a reliance on metonymy—or a "primacy of syntagm, of sequences of information"—Norman Bryson finds in traditional still-life painting:

"Here an aesthetics of silence reigns, no statement is allowed to issue from the objects brought together within the frame." The result, Bryson writes, "is a mutilated language."[37]

¶ Such increased proximity between commerce and art education has been paralleled by a rise in dismissals of criticism as no different from product promotion. Pardo, for instance, has been outspoken about what he sees as the demise of effective criticism, both in his own work ("basically I want to call attention to the impotence of criticality in a work of art") and within art magazines ("I think art magazines are trade publications. They don't do anything... it is pure PR.").[21]

Owens's paintings have been described as mobilizing various strategies to block discourse; Jan Tumlir, for example, has described them as "continually reneging on the readings that they themselves initiate....she is interested neither in pushing painting forward or regressing it in any pointed manner....Here and there, a kind of self-reflexivity begins to take shape....but [this is] abandoned before any sort of explicit articulation can occur."[22] Indeed, critics themselves often applaud such evasive maneuvers; in an Artforum "Openings" piece introducing Khedoori, Neville Wakefield admired the artist's work for "standing aside from the slippery prattle of 'discourse' and the quips of gallery-opening repartee."[23] Here discourse no longer redeems art from the "immobility of prattle" but has sunk to the level of prattle itself. Along with discourse, too conspicuous a debt to conceptual art has aroused suspicion; the few early negative reviews Pardo and Owens received invariably chided their work for being "overly conceptual."[24] Thater, exceptional among the six L.A. artists in her vocal affirmation of a theoretically grounded art (she would even compile alphabetical lists of references in the manner of a back-of-the-book index to accompany each of her early shows), has had her work accused of being "trapped in a Lacanian voice 'of the father' mode."[25]

¶ This is a far cry from the 60s and early 70s, when art criticism was hailed for its "august clairvoyance" and "expansive confidence."[26] (Even Pardo points to the art magazines of that period as "actually addressing the body of knowledge that was going on at the time directly."[27]) But by the 80s all this changed. Or at least our own recent image of 80s criticism, with its heavy reliance on continental theory, has come to portray it as nothing but a strong-arm tactic for hyping art and artists. "One way of succeeding," wrote Robert C. Morgan in 1992, "was to be adopted by a writer or a magazine—preferably both...who would quote Benjamin, Adorno, and the five famous French poststructuralists, and thus to reify or legitimate one's position in the mainstream."[28] Pictured in this way, the use of theory (whether in criticism, theme shows, or the artschool critique) means appealing to a higher authority in order to advance purely private interests, an underhanded or unfair business practice. Now it's all part of the system, with only more or less honest or fair ways of working it. And so the popularity in the 90s of a writer like Dave Hickey, who promotes an idealization of "commerce" ("characteristic of all human cultures") as the model of a level playing field.[29]

¶ What criticism shares with art schools is an investment in language—language as it assigns places to art (in history, in theory) and constantly questions and reconstructs the frames around art's different media. "Speech is now a requirement for the M.F.A.," Howard Singerman argues; he then goes on to quote from the College Art Association's current statement of standards, according to which "a large part of criticism of self and others is verbal....The need for continual writing, criticism, and self-explication in the careers of most artists is self-evident."[30] But with the growing loss of belief in language and dis-course as protecting and nurturing art's "progressivity," language is more and more suspected of the opposite, as intensifying the sense of staticness and immobility, as that which captures and codifies, what "knits the art village together on all levels," as Thomas Crow recently put it. "This vocabulary," Crow continues, "has become...part of the everyday, informal processes by which artists explain their works to others and to themselves...part of the dealer's helpful explanations and the collector's proud accounts of his acquisitions."[31]

Less than a year later, Hal Foster voiced a similar concern, writing that, with the triumph of pluralism, "in lieu of the historical sequence we confront the static array."[17] Despite their deep misgivings about modernism, both Rosler and Foster called for it to be revised and reinvented in the hope of restoring "a leading idea that serves, as it were, as the engine of art production" (Rosler) and could thereby "avoid the immobility of prattle and connect to the historical chain of discourses, the progress (progressus) of discursivity" (Foster, by way of a quote pulled from Roland Barthes).[18] These were the circumstances that gave rise to postmodernist art and critique, which didn't really react against an already long moribund modernism but revived it (in order to "progress" from it) in its more direct reaction against pluralism.

¶ Similarly, now that postmodernism itself has waned, art practice today, for all its seeming disparity, doesn't simply float free of determinants and parameters but finds itself all the more penned in by them, remaining undergirded by a functionally if not theoretically coherent and homogenous system. It's perhaps an unease over the growing sense of that system's "staticness" and "immobility"—traits Foster pointed to—that has led so many artists to privilege gaps and gray areas, instances of privacy, and mobility across roles and disciplines. "An artist can't stay outside," Rosler remarked in 1990, rephrasing her warning from ten years earlier, "because there is no outside anymore."[19]

Those two arenas presumed to stand relatively outside the art market—the art school, with its supposedly solitary environment encouraging the undistracted pursuit of studies, and art writing, with its necessary critical distance—are now perceived as totally enmeshed within the web of market forces. If Arthur Danto could complain back in 1988 that "the period between art school and art market cannot be too short, for youth and novelty...connote the potential for growth—in the stock-market sense of the term," then what's become notable about the 90s (and emerges as a touchy thematic in "Public Offerings") is the presence of the school within the market.[20] Just compare the artists' exhibition histories and their graduation dates elsewhere in this book; or look again at Pardo's Jerry—the photographs that accompanied Saltz's rave in Arts are all of Barney's 1989 graduation show. Still, Barney didn't exhibit commercially while enrolled as a student unlike Jason Rhoades, who was included in two group shows at Rosamund Felsen Gallery before graduating (and then mounted two solo shows less than a year after receiving his diploma). Khedoori, a classmate of Rhoades's at UCLA, actually held her M.F.A. thesis show at the David Zwirner Gallery in New York.

¶ All this can be taken to prove that, as Miwon Kwon noted in 1996, there is a "drive in much of new site-specific work toward the 'real' world, privileging it over the art world, which is thought to be rather beside the point, detached and separate from the 'real.'"[12] Such a drive surely seems to propel much of what goes by the name of "social sculpture"—like "installation," another malleable coinage applied to "ambiguous objects that exist somewhere between architecture, built-in furniture, and sculpture."[13]

For that matter, a great deal of the art made over the last ten years can be seen to share a similar motivation; it was in fact attributed to instances of "scatter art" from the beginning of the 90s.

In an article titled "Slackers" from 1991, Jack Bankowsky wrote that "where the art of the '80s intoned 'plug in or expire,' slack art tunes out....Jeff Koons, Meyer Vaisman, Ashley Bickerton, et al. celebrated the penetration of art by the rhythms of capital, fueled by the electronic circulation of information; the slacker has a nose for the fissures in this dream of surface." Curator Lisa Phillips would later second this observation in her catalogue introduction to the 1997 Whitney Biennial, writing that today's "artists explode the seamless fictions of normalcy by revealing cracks in that seamlessness."[14]

But if much recent art has been made in reaction to the aggrandizing 80s portrayal of the artworld as an impersonal, monolithic corporate enterprise, it hasn't led to any discoveries of some other world or realm outside and beyond; it doesn't presume to intervene in or escape from the art system. Or rather, it's what typically escapes notice—what is so ordinary or minutely odd about the artworld that it usually goes without saying—that now gets foregrounded. And so Bankowsky's essay follows artist Laurie Parsons as "she worked as a gallery assistant for a month as her part in a group show."[15] That same year at Luhring Augustine Hetzler, Pardo revealed that even a powerful collector like Robert Rowan can suffer the consequences of a leaky roof.

¶ Without any compelling experimental, stylistic, or theoretical directions to advance, and in the absence of a modernist, postmodernist, or avantgardist paradigm to lend coherence to the field of practice, what's left is the field itself: the artworld.

As the ambitions of the discourse circulating through this world have waned, there emerges into view little but the circuitry itself–the system's routinized doling out of recognition through the steady turnover of shows in galleries and museums, of essays and reviews in magazines and catalogues, and the just as steady production by art schools of ever more recognition-hungry artists. "A growing systemic unity belies the diversity of styles"—this, from Martha Rosler, was written twenty years ago, but what she was responding to was a widespread pluralism much like today's.[16] She too surveyed a field abundant with spread-out and personalized artworks, often interdisciplinary and autobiographical, but it was "the increasing orderliness of the artworld" that struck her, "an increasing regularization of the art system and a rapidly advancing bureaucratization in which the arbiters of art themselves have a changed, more routinized relation to the system, which has nevertheless declined or failed to organize the actual production of art along stylistic lines....Nothing is in principle rejected, nothing is oppositional."

¶ Certainly this inclination to spread out and incorporate different media accounts for one obvious similarity between these artists' works, namely their large scale. This goes for Sharon Lockhart as well, whose work (often big) utilizes both film and photography and whose choice and treatment of subject typically recalls past traditions within painting. But largeness *per se* is seldom privileged; rather, interest is drawn toward the gaps, interstices, and gray areas that open up between the different codified roles, disciplines, and media these artists traverse.

(Pardo: "There's a poetic that I am interested in which involves the value of relationships...relationships between shows and objects and institutions."[8]) Not only is their work divided and spread across categories, but they themselves often divide their activities between artmaking, curating, collecting, designing, etc. (Rhoades: "Museum director, curator, collector, artist—none of that means anything anymore."[9]) Here pluralism can be seen as not only characterizing the spread-out field of current art practices but invading each artwork and even its maker.

¶ Along with private details and minor asides, it's these gaps, these spaces between the identified and labeled, that indicate where the real supposedly lies, where one might expect the unexpected and unmediated, the uncategorizable and non-discursive. For example, upon considering Owens's paintings, one critic found himself "hard pressed to categorize them in even the broadest terms." They have also been likened to "glib asides" and "a wisecrack...made in passing that is intended neither as criticism nor as a fully fledged joke, but as an intentional disruption in the normal flow of communication."[10] Pardo's "chameleon-like sculptures," with such titles as *Lamp that won't hang straight, I don't know what period it's from* (1993) and *My Small Kitchen, 600 sf, $600 a Month, My Friend Harry Relis, Silverlake, I Wish I'd Made This Way the 1st Time, What a Beautiful Fucking View* (1992) have been admired for how they "evade evaluation in terms of efficient functionalism, or technological innovation, or social utopianism...[nor are they] simply apprehensible as art."[11] And there's yet another way these artists can be characterized as in-between: they first appeared as major figures in the artworld too early to be "emerging" artists in the usual sense, and yet too "fully formed" to be student artists. This, too, has found its way into the iconography of L.A. art. While still enrolled at Art Center, Frances Stark participated in a 1993 group show at Regen Projects (which also included the not-yet-graduated Khedoori) by contributing a carbon-transfer drawing of her student transcript, a document riddled with gaps, with "incompletes" and missed semesters.

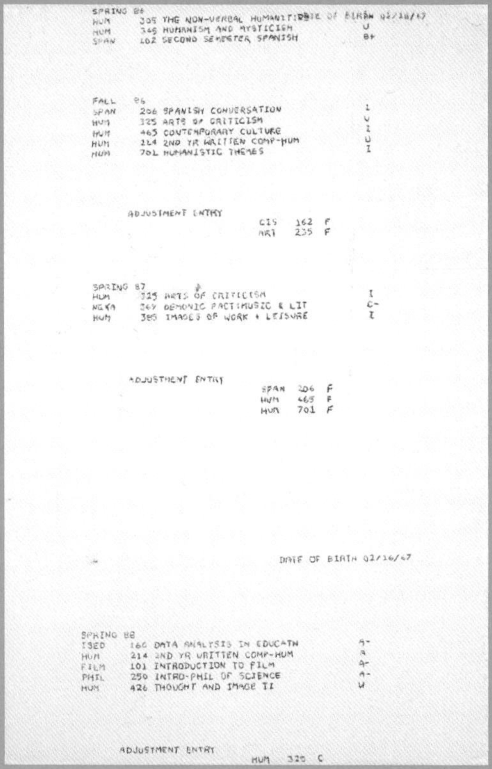

Frances Stark
Untitled (Self-Portrait /Autobiography), 1992
Carbon on paper
Diptych, 25 x 35 inches each

¶ This is an extreme case, but what now seems prescient about Pardo's show was how much it allowed itself to be flooded by the grit and ephemera of the artworld, even while it tried to reach into vicinities beyond it (or into a privacy below). Over the past decade much of what usually gets considered as having only circumstantial relevance to artmaking—career moves, connections, side jobs, fleeting liaisons, off-hand remarks, all the prosaic residue and local distractions artists and other denizens of this world might experience and chat about—has been enfolded within the art itself. The aim of much artworld activity now is to be, as Hainley writes, "airily honest about how things get done, stuff gets made, and the artworld works."[5] It's not that artists have never before paid close attention to the operations of the artworld. The difference is today's conversational and nonchalant treatment of such things as institutions, galleries, publicity, marketing, and commodification—things that art no longer makes models or examples out of but rather lives and breathes on a mundane, daily basis. (The last decade has brimmed with art—by Andrea Zittel, Angela Bulloch, Pardo, and others—that invites viewers to feel "at home" in the gallery; Pardo has commented that "I'm trying to do something radically different in a beautifully comfortable way."[6]) Familiarity has replaced the sense of revelation that once accompanied our awareness of the complex apparatus that frames and underwrites the work of art. Focus now shifts to the apparatus's fine grain, its nooks and crannies.

¶ Today's work has less to do with institutional critique than with what Hal Foster calls "the return of the real," although it's a decidedly sociological, everyday real rather than a psychoanalytic one. Nor is it an empirical real. For Pardo and most of the other L.A. artists in this exhibition, the real isn't manifested in any single, inscrutable material object, confrontational in its mute and obdurate physicality. Rather it inheres in strings of relationships, in the tenuous and intimate connections that make up an artist's scene or the ecology of his or her practice, in the interlocking and occasional slippage of components within those systems, and in their dense circulation of information (of objects, people, money, press, camaraderie, gossip).

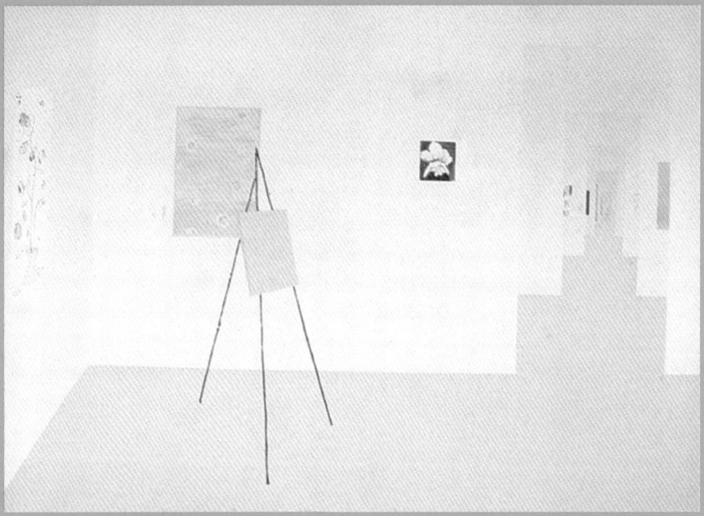

Laura Owens, *Untitled*, 1997. Acrylic on canvas. 119 3/4 x 96 inches

¶ This tendency is centrifugal rather than centripetal; it most often results not in isolated, opaque objects but in spread-out installations. Laura Owens's wall-sized canvases have often been described as existing somewhere between painting and installation; indeed, many of her works depict installations of paintings. Toba Khedoori's work is also said to blur the distinctions between painting, drawing, and installation. The ability to spread laterally is built into both Khedoori's medium and iconography: the multiple sheets of identically sized paper she staples side-to-side in each work, as well as the repeated units that often constitute her imagery—railroad cars, office windows, bricks, chain-link fencing. There's nothing limiting the ongoing lateral extension of each scroll-like paintingexcept the literal size of the wall on which it's hung. In addition, both Khedoori and Owens migrate between the pictorial orders of abstraction and figuration. Diana Thater has been credited with helping bring to prominence the hybrid genre of video installation, but her play across different media goes further: her early work using landscape imagery has routinely drawn comparison to painting and was included in the 1996 show "Painting—The Extended Field" at Magasin 3 in Sweden. As for Jason Rhoades, with his "inherently centrifugal" room-choking proliferations, he's been hailed as "the archetypal contemporary artist."[7]

¶ Most pointed of all were two pieces that dealt directly with Matthew Barney. One was *Jerry* (1991), a framed contact negative of an *Arts Magazine* article on Barney written by Jerry Saltz; the other, a collage titled *Painting for Page 24 of the J. Crew Catalogue (Spring)* (1991), featured images of Barney modeling a recent line of J. Crew menswear (Barney worked as a model during his student years at Yale in the late 80s). Bringing up the subject of Barney had an unmistakable tabloid-like timeliness.

He was hot gossip in the artworld in 1991; not only had the Saltz profile appeared exactly a month before Pardo's show went up, but Barney had just debuted his own first solo show two weeks earlier at the Stuart Regen Gallery a few miles away in West Hollywood. Indeed, it was next to impossible to appreciate Barney's show at Regen apart from the buzz about his sudden rise, about all the commercial and institutional firepower harnessed to launch him, about his two upcoming shows already planned for later that fall at Barbara Gladstone Gallery and the San Francisco Museum of Modern Art, and also about those fashion shoots he did for J. Crew. The jolt I felt walking through Pardo's show was due in part to the fact that I had just written an enthusiastic review of Barney's debut that was scheduled for publication in an upcoming issue of *Artforum*.[3] I, for one, had done my part in that review to separate out and elevate Barney's art above all the innuendo and conspiracy theories. It seemed obvious that Pardo felt the two shouldn't be separated.

¶ This wasn't the last time I'd walk into a show and find work that referenced another artist's show running concurrently: Dave Muller would start producing watercolor renderings of exhibition announcements a few years later, although these had a completely different, almost diplomatic air about them, as if they were seeking out not only the conflicts but the common ground between commercial promotion, critical engagement, and pat-on-the-back peer support. As for *Jerry*, I remember thinking it was a cheap shot, but part of my discomfort had to do with how acutely implicated it made me feel. It was a picture of art criticism after all, with a fashion catalogue as its *doppelgänger* pendant; it served as a reminder of my own complicity as a critic in a side of the artworld I usually try hard to forget. My writing has tended to inflict that forgetfulness on its readers, typically perpetuating an image of the artist as transcendent of his or her material conditions. I wrote about Barney as if, to borrow the words of his dealer Shaun Caley, "he was so good and fully formed that he launched himself."[4] In contrast, Pardo showed Barney—and himself—as very much mired in real-world contingencies; Barney's image was opened to an outside and a history, and at the same time revealed as something packaged by various commercial interests. But even saying this makes Pardo's exposé on Barney sound too well-meaning, as if it sought to render a critique and thus produce insight, to enlighten. Like *Soffit* and *Rug*, these works were too particular for that, too anecdotal to be redeeming; they had very little to say about the specific, private business they were sticking their nose into. Next to them, Jeff Koons's work looked tutorial, like teacher's aids demonstrating abstract theorems about art.

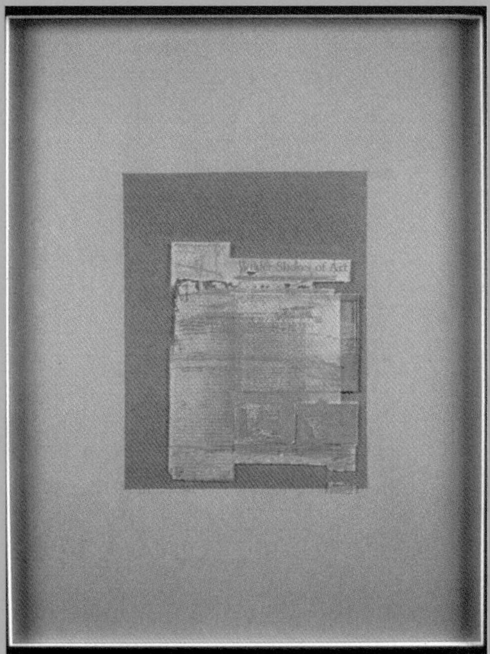

Jorge Pardo, *Jerry*, 1991
Maple, plexiglas, foamcore, house paint, chromatech, and drywall screws
27 x 21 inches

Installation of works by Jorge Pardo at Luhring Augustine Hetzler Gallery, Santa Monica, California, 1991

¶ During the summer of 1991 Jorge Pardo mounted a show at Luhring Augustine Hetzler in Santa Monica—his third solo show in the three years after his graduation from Art Center College of Design in Pasadena. Some of the works in the Santa Monica show called attention to the gallery, literally framing its everyday business operations: in Bob's Rug (1991), for example, Pardo placed the receptionist's chair and desk—contained in a squarish white cubicle—atop a slightly larger square of green carpet, so that the edges of this carpet-cum-pedestal formed a kind of outline around it. Other works in the show threatened to trespass the distinction between art and such neighboring endeavors as craft or design or architecture: there was a tastefully designed set of wood shelves conspicuously displayed by the gallery's storefront windows, and a completely inconspicuous piece attached to, and nearly indistinguishable from, the gallery's ceiling.

¶ That such work forced an awareness of the boundaries by which art's separateness negotiates with what it must be separated from didn't make it especially memorable; much more striking was the degree to which Pardo's references were specific and intimate. The show included so many peculiar or personal details as to defeat its being read discursively, its revealing generally applicable knowledge, its illuminating the function of the gallery in general, or art's contextualization or its commodification or anything else in general. What, after all, was the viewer supposed to do with the checklist, or with the various anecdotes disclosed by the helpful gallery assistants—that, for example, the rug under the receptionist's desk had belonged to L.A. collector Robert Rowan and had suffered water damage? Or that the ceiling piece was titled My Mom's Soffit (1991)?

L.A.-Based and Superstructure

Excuse me while I talk shop. It's hard not to these days, what with the artworld humming along so impressively. Business is up and complaints are few. In fact there's little discussion right now beyond reports of artworld maneuverings that feels very compelling or urgent.

Critic Bruce Hainley recently shrugged, "Who really wants premises messing up, as they too often do, the enjoyment?"[1]

Attempting any sort of high-minded summary of our far-flung artistic field, proposing any program with which to cleave the relevant from the irrelevant, assembling any set of metaphors or theoretical imperatives or aesthetic criteria, means courting disaster. On the whole, theme shows of contemporary art are unwelcome, and the only characterization of the moment widely agreed upon is that "there are no movements now, no one thing."[2] Just looking at the variety of works by the six Los Angeles artists included in "Public Offerings" would appear to prove that. All of which makes writing about these artists as a group a bit tricky; if they do share anything it's most readily apparent not in some formal or conceptual correspondence between their artworks but in the common shape of their careers. Interpreting works of art by analyzing career machinations is problematic enough, let alone doing so within the genteel protocols of an exhibition catalogue.

¶ Yet isn't this precisely the dilemma "Public Offerings" poses? The title, at least on the face of it, promises art that assumes a generous, even humble posture before a gathered audience ("audience" even seems too passive a word—publics are thought to have enough coherence to judge and act). At the same time the phrase "Public Offerings" doesn't entirely hide its origins in the world of high finance, cropped as it is from the marketplace lingo for a company's first issuance of stock ("initial public offerings" or I.P.O.s). And behind these two readings, a third way in which the title makes sense is in its suggestion that the initial, the first, the beginning—of an artist's oeuvre, of his or her career—will take place in public; it will be a public or at least a publicized event. What we're talking about are artworks and artists whose public lives start young.

¶ At any rate, this is what I take "Public Offerings" to be about, the kind of phenomenon it's referring to. At the risk of coming across as indelicate, this essay will be about the extent to which I agree that this phenomenon has become newly definitive of art made over the past ten years, with consequences for the look and make-up of the work itself. I also think I know when I first felt the buffeting of those consequences.

BY LANE RELYEA

1. Peter Wollen, "London Swings," in Who's Afraid of Red White & Blue? Attitudes to Popular & Mass Culture, Celebrity, Alternative & Critical Practice & Identity Politics in Recent British Art, ed. David Burrows (Birmingham, England: ARTicle Press, University of Central England, 1998), 22—24. See also Saskia Sassen, The Global City: New York, London, Tokyo (Princeton, N.J.: Princeton University Press, 1991).

2. John Pickard, "President's Address (April 6, 1917)," Art Bulletin 1, no. 3 (1917): 43.

3. Mercedes Matter, "What's Wrong with U.S. Art Schools?," with responses by Howard Conant and Gurdon Woods, Art News 62, no. 5 (September 1963): 40-42, 56-59; and Dan Flavin, "...On an American Artist's Education...," Artforum 6, no. 7 (March 1968): 28-32.

4. For more on these statistics, see my Art Subjects: Making Artists in the American University (Berkeley, California: University of California Press, 1999), 6.

5. "Smashing! Frieze talks to Richard Flood, curator of 'Brilliant!: New Art from London' at the Walker Art Center, Minneapolis," Frieze, no. 25 (November/December 1995): 34, 32.

6. Ralph Rugoff, "Liberal Arts," Vogue (August 1989): 328-33, 373; Dennis Cooper, "Too Cool for School," Spin (July 1997): 86-94; Andrew Hultkrans, "Surf and Turf," Artforum 36, no. 10 (Summer 1998): 106-113, 146; and Deborah Solomon, "How to Succeed in Art," The New York Times Magazine (27 June 1999): 38-41.

7. Karl Marx, "The German Ideology," in The Marx-Engels Reader, second edition, ed. Robert C. Tucker (New York: W. W. Norton, 1987), 154.

8. Ernst Kris and Otto Kurz, Legend, Myth, and Magic in the Image of the Artist: A Historical Experiment (New Haven, Connecticut: Yale University Press), 50; and Robert Pincus-Witten, "David Salle: Holiday Glassware," Arts Magazine 56, no. 8 (April 1982): 58.

9. Harold Rosenberg, "The American Action Painters," in The Tradition of the New (1960; reprint, Chicago: The University of Chicago Press, Phoenix Edition, 1982), 29-30.

10. Dore Ashton, "Young Abstract Painters: Right On!," Arts Magazine 44, no. 4 (February 1970): 31.

11. Rugoff, "Liberal Arts," 332. The pull quote appears on the preceding page.

12. Ibid.

13. Ibid., 333.

14. Hultkrans, "Surf and Turf," 110.

15. Cooper, "Too Cool for School," 92.

16. Hultkrans, "Surf and Turf," 107.

17. The bulletin is reproduced in The Collected Writings of Robert Motherwell, ed. Stephanie Terenzio (New York: Oxford University Press, 1992), 294-95.

18. Quoted in Peter Plagens, Sunshine Muse: Contemporary Art on the West Coast (New York: Praeger, 1974), 161.

19. Richard Telles, in Hultkrans, "Surf and Turf," 146.

20. Solomon, "How to Succeed," 39; and Hultkrans, "Surf and Turf," 109.

21. Solomon, "How to Succeed," 40.

22. Quoted in Albert Boime, "The Teaching Reforms of 1863 and the Origins of Modernism in France," Art Quarterly 1, n.s. (1977): 20.

23. Walter Gropius, "From the First Proclamation of the Weimar Bauhaus," in Bauhaus 1919-1928, eds. Herbert Bayer, Walter Gropius, and Ise Gropius (New York: The Museum of Modern Art, 1938), 18.

24. Quoted in Stuart Macdonald, The History and Philosophy of Art Education (New York: American Elsevier, 1970), 235.

25. For the aftermath of the reintroduction of the traditional Japanese painting craft at the Tokyo University of Music and Art, see Midori Matsui's essay, "Conversation Days," in this volume.

26. Dorr Bothwell and Marlys Mayfield, Notan: The Dark-Light Principle of Design (1968; reprint, New York: Dover Publications, 1991), back cover.

27. Both of these labels were used to describe and differentiate CalArts in its early days. See Judith Adler, Artists in Offices (New Brunswick, New Jersey: Transaction Books, 1979), 1.

28. This half-translated description is offered on the Hochschule der Künste website, at www.hdk-berlin.de/english/index.html.

29. "The Value of Theoretical Instruction in Painting" (1926), in Kandinsky: Complete Writings on Art, eds. Kenneth C. Lindsay and Peter Vergo (Boston: G. K. Hall, 1982), 703-04.

30. Ibid., 702, 703.

31. Royal Bailey Farnum, "The General and Technical Education of the Artist," in Fortieth Yearbook of the National Society for the Study of Education: Art in American Life and Education, ed. Guy Montrose Whipple (Chicago: The University of Chicago Press, 1941), 623.

32. "Exhibition of the Work of Journeymen and Apprentices in the Staatliche Bauhaus Weimar, April-May 1922," included in Bayer, Gropius, and Gropius, eds., Bauhaus 1919-1928, under the heading "Preliminary Course, Weimar," 36.

33. Gropius, "The Theory and Organization of the Bauhaus," in ibid., 26.

34. Lillian Garrett, Visual Design: A Problem-Solving Approach (New York: Reinhold, 1967), 153.

35. Graham Collier, Form, Space, and Vision: Discovering Design through Drawing (Englewood Cliffs, N.J.: Prentice Hall, 1967), 104.

36. Charles Harrison, "Educating Artists," Studio International 183, no. 944 (May 1972): 222.

37. Ibid., 223.

38. Ibid., 222.

39. Michael Rees, "Yale Sculpture: A Recent Breed of Critically Trained Artists from the Noted School of Art," Flash Art, no. 170 (May/June 1993): 65.

40. Michael Fried, "Art and Objecthood," in Minimal Art: A Critical Anthology, ed. Gregory Battcock (New York: E. P. Dutton, 1968), 134. Italics mine.

41. Patrick Heron in the Guardian, 12 October 1971, cited in Charles Madge and Barbara Weinberger, Art Students Observed (London: Faber and Faber, 1973), 268.

42. Directory of M.F.A. Programs in the Visual Arts, rev. ed. (New York: College Art Association, 1996), 6.

43. Irving Sandler, "The School of Art at Yale, 1950-1970: The Collective Reminiscences of Twenty Distinguished Alumni," Art Journal 42, no. 1 (Spring 1982): 16, 18.

44. Fried, "Art and Objecthood," 116-17.

45. Flavin, "...On an American Artist's Education...," 28, 29.

46. Charles Harrison, "Art&Language: Mapping and Filing," in The New Art, exh. cat. (London: Hayward Gallery, 1972), 14.

47. Philip Pilkington, Kevin Lole, and David Rushton, "Some Concerns in Fine-Art Education," Studio International 183, no. 937 (October 1971): 120.

48. Harrison, "Educating Artists," 224.

49. Quoted in Carol Becker, "Speakeasy," New Art Examiner 18, no. 6 (February 1991): 15.

50. Quoted in Cooper, "Too Cool for School," 94.

51. Chris Burden and Jan Butterfield, "Chris Burden: Through the Night Softly," Arts Magazine 49, no. 7 (March 1975): 68; and László Moholy-Nagy, The New Vision (1928), 4th rev. ed., and Abstract of an Artist (New York: Wittenborn, Schultz, 1947): 67.

52. Quoted in Cooper, "Too Cool for School," 94.

53. Yve-Alain Bois, Painting as Model (Cambridge, Mass.: The MIT Press, 1990), 126.

54. See his "Painting: The Task of Mourning," in Endgame: Reference and Simulation in Recent Painting and Sculpture, exh. cat. (Boston: Institute of Contemporary Art, and Cambridge, Mass.: The MIT Press, 1986), 29-49.

55. Jerry Saltz, An Ideal Syllabus: Artists, Critics and Curators Choose the Books We Need to Read (London: Frieze, 1998), 5.

56. Ibid., 41.

57. Thomas Crow, "Versions of the Pastoral in Some Recent American Art," in David A. Ross and Jürgen Harten, eds. The Binational: American Art of the Late Eighties, exh. cat. (Boston: Institute of Contemporary Art and Museum of Fine Arts; and Cologne: DuMont Bucher Verlag, 1988), 20.

58. Alison Gingeras, "Disappearing Acts: French Theory and the Artworld," in French Theory in America, eds. Sande Cohen and Sylvère Lotringer (New York: Routledge, forthcoming).

59. Patricia Bickers, "Mind the Gap: The Concept of Critical Distance in Relation to Contemporary Art in Britain," in Burrows, ed., Who's Afraid of Red, White & Blue?, 12-13, 18-19.

60. Paul de Man, The Resistance to Theory, vol. 33 of Theory and History of Literature (Minneapolis: University of Minnesota Press, 1986), 15.

61. Laura Owens, in Saltz, Ideal Syllabus, 41.

62. "Liberal Art University Experiences: David Askevold in Conversation with Paul McMahon," Studio International 183, no. 943 (April 1972): 156.

63. Allan Kaprow, "The Effect of Recent Art upon the Teaching of Art," Art Journal 23, no. 2 (Winter 1963-64): 136.

64. For a "probe of what constitutes an 'intelligible geography of public and private'" recently in the Los Angeles artworld, see Sande Cohen, "Hide Your Commodification: Art Criticism and Intellectuals in Los Angeles or Language Denied," Emergences 9, no. 2 (1999): 345-72.

65. Quoted in James E. B. Breslin, Mark Rothko: A Biography (Chicago: The University of Chicago Press, 1993), 248-49.

66. Quoted in Coosje van Bruggen, Bruce Nauman (New York: Rizzoli, 1988), 13-14.

VI.

In its spread and scale, much recent work—and indeed, much of the work included in "Public Offerings," precisely as it is successful, as it is interesting and even compelling—bears the traces of its schooling and of the place of the art market inside the school's doors.

One can, I want to argue, read the school, its community, and its architecture in the odd scale of recent work. The demand that personality be presented and made spectacular is registered and worked on in the claustrophobic-at-whatever-scale narcissism of Matthew Barney; in the life-and-death aggressivity of Damien Hirst; and in the winner-take-all spread—across the space of the studio, the group show, or the gallery—of Jason Rhoades. (Art is about turf, "somebody getting territory, this is your territory, you develop something and it's yours, it's your territory,"[65] Mark Rothko told one his students. Rhoades has taken Rothko literally.) But the space of school and the public development of identity is registered not only in excess, but in withdrawal, in the curiously domestic themes and identities that inform the work of Jorge Pardo or Sarah Lucas or Rirkrit Tiravanija. This domesticity isn't privateness, or rather it isn't the terrible aloneness of romanticism or of Rothko's turf wars. Rather, it is a space built within the artworld, as though for protection. The mirror of the aggressive marking of territory, it is the mark of the tentative nature of the professionalization of idiosyncrasy, of being an artist, or of being able to believe and make others believe that you are an artist. Things have always been traded across hallways and through studios: ideas, pictures, language, influences, music, friendship, food, sex. What seems different is that this localism—the image of the closeness of separate studios—is part of the iconography of recent work. It's there in Tiravanija's recasting of Michael Asher's opening out of the gallery in its literalness, its friendliness. It's in Pardo's desire for, or his frustrations with, My Small Kitchen, 600 sf, $600 a Month, My Friend Harry Relis, Silverlake, I Wish I'd Made This Way the 1st Time, What a Beautiful Fucking View (1992). And it's in the local and quite specifically targeted address of Sarah Lucas. If the boundaries of the studio are broken now in current school practice, it is not to enter a "post-studio" world, but to offer a "home gallery," always ready to be opened to visiting critics, curators, friends, and faculty. It is open to both school and market, and it marks that place where a particular community, a school, a set of friends, a locale, meets the cosmopolitan artworld, the place where the personal and professional cross—and, if the teaching is successful, become one and the same.

¶ The work of filling that mixed space, of installing and hosting, is part of the practice of recent work; and so too is filling time within it. The work of covering the studio in installation or in the repetitions of making eats the time and space of being an artist; it takes care of the question of what to do. With some trepidation, I'd say that this is why installation and performance are so in evidence here, are so characteristic of work made in and out of school. One way to rephrase the question "What should I be doing," of how to be an artist for oneself and others, is to ask "How is one an artist everyday outside and after what Gerhard Richter called the 'daily practice of painting.'" Phrasing it this way might at least suggest why Bruce Nauman and his filling in of the studio and time remain so important to the artists included in the show: Nauman made being out of school into a practice. "I was working very little....teaching a class one night a week, and I didn't know what to do with all that time....If you see yourself as an artist and you function in a studio and you're not a painter....if you don't start out with some canvas, you do all kinds of things—you sit in a chair or pace around. And then the question goes back to what is art? And art is what an artist does, just sitting around the in studio."[66]

Sitting around, walking around the studio, bouncing a ball, playing the violin, serving pad thai, these are the motions, the repetitions of being an artist.

To paraphrase Donald Judd's famous "a work of art need only be interesting," now, an artist need only be interesting.

¶ What does theory do outside the project of legitimation? What do all those books and all those syllabi reference or "teach"? Precisely in their proliferation those texts and any number of others provide sites for acceptance and resistance, for refusal and misreading, for the production of an idiosyncrasy that is both schooled and deeply felt. They don't unify like the modernist projects that Bois writes of, or like Harrison's project of theory: they don't do the work of metaphor, drawing up a number of practices into a single project. As Lane Relyea suggests in his contribution to this catalogue, they do the work of metonymy, connecting and extending, multiplying like Damien Hirst's title.

This is what Crow's patois and Gingeras's lingua franca suggest as well, a language that links across a surface. Legitimation now is left to the market, to being grabbed up precisely when, as UCLA's students know, "we're not all going to get grabbed." Key to Hans Hofmann's teaching, wrote Allan Kaprow, was "not so much 'modernity'...but a sense of the issues at stake which 'modernity' provokes."[63] After the issues of modernism as a lived project and the felt critique of its stakes that began during the late 60s, the relation of the individual artist to the market, and of the market to critical value, meaning, and education is much more exposed and direct. The language we use to try to explain the market's choices—either to ameliorate its arbitrariness or elide its institutionalized machinations—works to naturalize and personalize its workings, to make it about this artist alone: vision, urgency, will, ambition. But artists aren't "grabbed" naturally; they are seen and shown in relation to the interests, both personal and professional—at their best and most effective, these terms are absolutely inseparable—of curators, critics, gallerists, teachers, and other artists.

What is shared back and forth—what is the currency of this exchange—is subjectivity, self-interest, personality: the exteriorization and exaggeration of the self for another.[64]

The task of art education now, the goal of seeing someone as an artist, is to intensify and objectify personality, to specularize—that is, to make visual—sheer difference as a particular kind of artistic subjectivity.

¶ It may just be, as Paul de Man wrote in a rather different context, "that resistance to theory is in fact a resistance to reading."[60]

But certainly reading is being done, if not xeroxed and handed out then at least recommended. In response to Saltz's search, Laura Owens offered Denis Diderot's *Rameau's Nephew*, Walt Whitman's *Leaves of Grass*, Virginia Woolf's *Mrs. Dalloway*, and Jeremy Gilbert-Rolfe's *Beyond Piety*. The list, Owens makes clear, is just the "more private" syllabus that Saltz had asked for: "Creating [a] common bookshelf is like sharing your underwear anyway—gross. Choose your own books."[61] The function of these texts is not to unify, to end an isolation, but precisely to separate. A number of artists in "Public Offerings" suggested lists: Janine Antoni, Matthew Barney, Sarah Lucas, Jorge Pardo, Rirkrit Tiravanija, and Rachel Whiteread. Their authors include:

Tim Rollins and Felix Gonzalez-Torres, Mary Shelley, Gertrude Stein, Marina Warner, Sogyal Rinpoche, Heinrich von Kleist, Mark Mynsyk, Andrea Dworkin, Hélène Cixous, Norman Mailer, Gustave Flaubert, Joan Didion, Jorge Luis Borges, Franz Boas, Henriette Groenewegen-Frankfort, Leon Battista Alberti, Giorgio Vasari, Linda Nochlin, Alfred H. Barr, Jr., Penny Florence, Jeremy Gilbert-Rolfe (again), Ruth Reichl, Georges Bataille, J. G. Ballard, Rainer Maria Rilke, Vladimir Nabokov, Tony Parker, Judith Rappaport, Anthony Vidler, Richard Sennett, Robert Harbison, and Gaston Bachelard.

Eli and Edythe Broad Art Studios at California Institute of the Arts, Valencia, California
Courtesy of California Institute of the Arts

(Those of you who can connect authors and artists have already got the point—that these texts, however publicly they are offered, belong to the individual artist precisely as he or she is different, particular, idiosyncratic.) What is remarkable about the list is not only its "pluralism" but its emphasis on sensibility, on a kind of sentimental education. "Ideally, an art school should provide time for the student to become self-interested, and should provide enough thought-provoking information referring to his own sensibilities," wrote David Askevold in 1972, in and around the project of conceptualism at the Nova Scotia College of Art and Design.[62] Given the architecture of graduate school and the question around which practice is formed, all information is self-interested—it all refers to one's own sensibility and its reformation.

What then, and what of the continuous endings that Bois has also recorded?[54] What if we can no longer tell the difference between a last painting made in the practice of painting—a Ryman for example—and a last painting made about it, like the simulated deaths of 80s Neo-Geo or maybe Gary Hume's doors? For some time now, neither belief nor disbelief has been believable.

¶ One answer is that theory is over. It is a recent commonplace in art schools that theory is dead, but "theory" here is as slippery a term as "academy" was before: indeed, their slippages are much the same. Theory, particularly when it's dead—or when it is being condemned as the aesthetic kiss of death—can range from any rigorous involvement with a particular body of texts or an engagement with the politics of race or gender, to knowing what you're doing and taking Flavin's verbal responsibility for it. It means in the shorthand of its morticians both the fateful conjunction of politics and language, and a certain kind of earnest, serious work—what Deborah Solomon dismissed as "homework." Whatever the critical value of Derrida or Lacan, of Julia Kristeva or Judith Butler—however unsettling their implications are to the category of art or to the claims of expertise—the fact that they are taught and heard as lessons in classrooms makes a difference, or rather it erases certain kinds of difference. However anti-foundational they are, negative and critical, given the rooms in which they are taught, the repetitions they require, the "outcomes" they seem to promise, and, most importantly, the direction in which power flows, they are a kind of institutional "truth" on the side of a sometimes very local power—the power to speak in the critique, for example. Perhaps, as critic Jerry Saltz worried, the "art, criticism and theory [that] set out to debunk the idea of a canon ...has resulted in a canonisation of theory....[H]ow come much of what is assigned to students (at every level) is the same? Large doses of Derrida, Baudrillard and Lacan."[55] Saltz's complaint is recorded in his preface to An Ideal Syllabus, a little book published by Frieze that collects book lists from a number of artists, curators, and critics in answer to his request for a list of names that aren't Derrida, Baudrillard, and Lacan. Laura Owens sent a list along with a joke that makes clear the politics of theory in the classroom. Question: "if you have ten art students and you give them each two weeks to read 200 pages, how many pages in total would be read by class time? Answer: 200 – there is a kiss-up in every class."[56]

¶ However over it may be, theory continues to circulate like the undead: "its name is legion." In the artworld it has been characterized for a long time not by its orthodoxy but by its proliferation; it is one of the images of circulation. As art historian Thomas Crow wrote in 1988, the "patois that currently prevails in this village has been borrowed from the theories of language and the human sciences that can, broadly be called structuralist or semiotic—though the vaguely-demarcated but grander-sounding term 'post-structuralist' is favored."[57] Crow's image of the village is intended to emphasize the smallness and closeness, the intimacy of the artworld, even across a couple of continents. His "patois"—like critic and curator Alison Gingeras's recent description of theory as "the lingua franca of the artworld"—suggests a kind of mistranslation, a local and merely pragmatic appropriation: French theory in the vulgate.[58] It may be that the young British artists educated at Goldsmiths during the 80s by a faculty immersed in critical theory are now, as the critic John Roberts put it, as "indifferent to theory as armour-plating." At the same time, to borrow the argument of British critic and historian Michael Archer, "certain things have become internalized, accepted." Art historian Patricia Bickers presses Archer's case—it is she who has quoted Roberts and Archer together:

"They have no illusions, but then neither does their audience.... [N]owadays anyone can deconstruct their favourite sit-com, novel, or exhibition if they choose to, the way Victorians could parse sentences."[59]

However armor-plated he may be, Damien Hirst's current exhibition—up at Gagosian in New York as I write this essay—is entitled "Theories, Models, Methods, Approaches, Assumptions, Results and Findings." Perhaps what is important in Hirst's title is the proliferating spread of plural nouns.

¶ Theory as a practice answers what seems to me to be the formative question of recent art practice: "What should I do?" While that question may once have been posed as "What is to be done?" (in Lenin's title in relation to the demands of an objective historical future, but we could imagine it in relation to the historical demands of objective medium), its more recent manifestations have sounded like the plaint a young student at The School of the Art Institute of Chicago posed to a panel of experts—

"What kind of work should I be making anyway?"[49]

The question is repeated at UCLA; in a remark that doesn't quite separate the question of work from the question of career, one student cited in Cooper's "Too Cool for School" poses it this way: "Paul McCarthy talks a lot about making things happen for yourself. That's what he did, that's what Charley did. But fuck if I know what to do."[50] The possibilities are endless: as Chris Burden put it not long after his own graduation, art is "a free spot in society, where you can do anything" (which for Harrison is the very definition of isolation); and as Moholy-Nagy said a few decades earlier,

"Everyone is talented....any healthy man can become a musician, painter, sculptor, or architect."[51]

By now, "anything" and "everyone" no longer feel like freedom or liberation; rather, they are felt as terror. The artworld plays a kind of roulette with individuality and sensibility, and its arbitrariness is present and palpable in the L.A. articles: "my peers and I are really talented, but realistically, we're not all going to get grabbed."[52] But if art is not rendering the world or the human figure, if it's not the "skills" of drawing or of the other métiers, then how can one know what to do, where art is, or who is an artist?

V.

Perhaps I have misunderstood Harrison's point, imagining it to be not about art and society but about students who want to be artists. The role of theory I'm trying to describe is not its official role, not its "meaning," but something more like its effect. The question that the Art Institute student posed, "What kind of work should I be making?," suggests what one might call, after the theorist Jürgen Habermas, a "crisis of legitimation"; how can this activity become legitimate, how can "anything" bear the name of "art"? Or how can the name "art" still be meaningful, still necessary in the face of its freedom, in the face of "everything"?

For Yve-Alain Bois, among others, this is what modernism has been, or rather, answering this question has been modernism's project. "Modernism in the broadest sense of the term was not merely an operation of ontological reduction—Greenberg's canonical interpretation—but rather a vast enterprise of motivation, of the motivation of the arbitrary."[53] Essentialism, the search for the essence of painting that Clement Greenberg codified; historicism, the progress of that search; utopia, the dream of the last painting; and painting as a model of the social whole: these are the discourses and the strategies of motivation, beliefs that are inscribed in the work, in the choices that are brought to bear or, more often, the choices that are refused. But what to do in the face of their exhaustion, or of their "teaching." Art students have learned these lessons over and over again: the scrupulously plotted nexts, the always repeated last paintings, the easily realizable figures of utopia.

Like Michael Rees, Irving Sandler's recollection of the school of art at Yale during the 70s suggests just such a trade: "like most other graduate programs, Yale's was based on individual work done by a student in his or her private or semi-private space. The basic instruction was criticism of ongoing work by resident and visiting faculty....Work was proof of seriousness and it permitted students to enter into a verbal discourse with other serious colleagues."[43] While the school might have been "based on individual work," discourse trumps work fairly easily in Sandler's description; allowing the artist to speak is the work's purpose and outcome. At the same time, discourse secures and underwrites the work; in the critique and in the seminar it allows the work to exist by mapping it, by articulating it. This is just the threat that Fried imagined Minimalism posed to modernist painting—it "defines or locates the position" that could "be formulated in words."[44] It is also the threat that the Minimalist Dan Flavin imagined that smart young graduate students might pose to those teachers who would indoctrinate them into "professionally institutionalized technical vocational training." "As he knows, he talks," warned Flavin; he takes "overt verbal responsibility" for the work. Talking might even become the work.[45]

As Charles Harrison said early on about the formation of the Art&Language group, "The Art-Language association is characterized by the desire and ability of its members to talk to each other."[46]

¶ For those familiar with Art&Language and their critical and theoretical practice (not to mention their dripping sarcasm and their willingness to name names), this seems like an exceptionally benign and even dissembling description. Art&Language's earliest fights were to displace painting on the pedagogical level in the studios of the Coventry School of Design—and perhaps to make real the threat that Flavin's smart artist posed. Arguing in the early 70s over the implications of the Bauhaus-inspired reforms of the Coldstream Report of the early 60s, and over the dismantling of their course and their non-renewal at Coventry, Philip Pilkington, Kevin Lole, and David Rushton insisted that art theory belonged not to the "complementary studies" mandated by Coldstream, but to the practice of art itself.

"No matter what the 'finished product', Art Theory was seen as akin to Studio work and not to Complementary Studies....Art Theory was not regarded as a minor part in the work of painting or sculpture student; rather...Painting would be seen as an alternative to following the Art Theory course."[47]

Charles Harrison also wrote at the time about theory and its place—indeed its necessity—in the art school, and once again in a remarkably gentle and generous way. "The need to search for a body of theory in art—something to justify the practice, if practice it is—is an aspect of the need to end art's isolation....The pursuit of the theoria of art employs many and more instructive kinds of critique than those employed in the conventional, therapeutic, art-school search for 'meaningful' self-expression."[48] Theory and the critique it allows offer art a meaning, a use, that might end its isolation from the social or the historical. But even before that, and on a much more local level, in its "ability to justify the practice," to be more "instructive," theory can overcome the isolation of the art student that is figured by the private studio. The critique, the enlightenment or disenchantment that theory offers is both a reason and a way to practice art, an answer to that "questioning of the desire to make art." As Harrison makes clear, even if he doesn't acknowledge it, theory does more than delegitimize the discourses of historicism or self-expression, the formative discourses of the art school critique.

It is, not unlike those earlier discourses, a way of legitimating and motivating practice—by which I want to mean, not just explaining work or moving it through history and characterizing intention, but on a very particular, intimate level, a way of getting work done.

The great open expanses of general painting studios and sculpture workshops were being remade in the image of the artist:

"For those who do not frequent our art schools, let me describe the scene that is most typical: enormous working studios are invariably fragmented by small temporary partitions which define small semi-private individual work spaces, varying in size from a cubicle or cubby-hole to a decently spacious private studio. These always dissimilar working spaces have grown up in every instance around an individual student: he creates the space he needs in the style he needs it; in fact these cubicles or alcoves have the highly developed personal and idiosyncratic character of a private dwelling."[41]

It's odd to see photographs of art schools in the late 40s and 50s with their mixed economy, where individual and often abstract work takes place on easels still ranked around a model stand in the large, open areas of the general painting studio.

"CalArts: Skeptical Belief(s)" exhibition at The Renaissance Society at the University of Chicago, 1987

IV.

In newer schools the individual studios are less organic, more efficiently gridded; the divisions are built right in. What crosses the walls, what passes between studios is language. Talking is what goes on in graduate school. Even in those schools we now imagine to be "against theory," language is the medium in which works of art take place. As the College Art Association's guidelines helpfully remind us, "a large part of criticism of self and others is verbal, [thus] verbal skills must not be ignored."[42]

In the psychodrama of the critique, in seminars and visiting artists' talks, and between students in the hallways or over coffee, language is what work is traded for.

Classroom, California School of Fine Arts,
San Francisco, c. 1948
Courtesy of San Francisco Art Institute

"All of us maintain contact with each other and continue to rely upon the constant critical conversation that was so important at that time.....a way of thinking about and questioning the desire to make art."[39]

The interiority that Gropius and Farnum described seemed benevolent, at once organic and well-equipped; it offered at least in writing a way of joining the self and the world. Indeed, gridded and disciplined, the world given to vision and the vision that constructed it were a perfect match. Harrison's is clearly a more aggressive and alienated interior, but Rees's, too, in his question of desire suggests not the gridded interior of perceptual psychology but the more difficult subjectivity of psychoanalysis. Built in the exposure of the critique, this interior is precisely desiring—that is to say, wanting—at once needy and defensive, hollow and armed, like Lacan's statue man who dreams of stadiums, or maybe of private studios.

¶ If neither the figure nor the grid is a trope I can use to characterize recent art, what has taken their place might be just the space the university offers, the studios in which you do your own work, the space in which you get to be an artist, that defines you as one.

Michael Fried realized this trope early on, in and around the threat he imagined Minimalism posed to "painting," to a specific discipline that one might learn as a skill and as history. What characterized the work of Minimalism, and a great deal of work that comes after it, is the "concept of a room."[40] About the same time that Charles Harrison offered his analysis of the critique, the British painter Patrick Heron, writing on behalf of the reforms of 60s British art training—the same reforms out of which Art&Language emerged as a pedagogical experiment —and for the autonomy of the art schools, noted the emergence of a new kind of room.

The George Bridgman Life Class at the Art Students League of New York, 1940
Archives of the Art Students League of New York

Writing in 1972 in the British art magazine *Studio International*, Charles Harrison of the conceptual artists' group Art&Language touched on all of these intertwined points, including the violence of the critique: "The much-vaunted teaching system of group criticism of work and 'tough' exposure of the individual to and by the group....is one notable example of the coincidence of an 'evolutionary' approach to art with a 'group therapy' approach to art students."[36] The critique Harrison describes is an interaction, a scene intended to produce a certain kind of subjectivity alongside and as an effect of art as a historical demand—and as an effect of language. In the critique, both the student artist and the student work are, like the linguistic sign, doubly articulated, plotted both historically within a history of art and in the narrative of personal development, and across a field of positions and possibilities, likenesses and differences. The work is opened up in relation to a narrative of exploration, of what the medium or the "concern" demands and what is to be done next, and the student is pressed to make clear how the work belongs to him—how, in the last instance, it is about him.

¶ Under and through these discourses as they are focused on the student, the critique offers a teaching that is, in Harrison's words, "more psycho-therapeutic than pedagogic," and he links it as a practice specifically to the question of the artist, to making artists. "While there may be both historicity and method in teaching someone how to draw, there is little of either involved in teaching them how to be artists. It is a cliché that art students are neurotic; maybe art schools keep them that way."[37] I don't know that I want to go as far as Harrison, and I have tried to suggest some of the historical forces behind such teaching. But I do want to underline his distinction between the contents of academic training—teaching drawing as a particular, separable skill—and what turns out to be both the subject and the object of contemporary professional training: the artist. Teaching students to be artists, seeing or taking or treating them as artists, is precisely the knowledge that Charles Ray and Lari Pittman offered at UCLA, and Harrison's language makes it quite clear that being an artist is always based on the scenario of the critique, that being an artist is being an artist for another. Harrison writes of the newly graduated artist who "without finding a means to continue the therapeutic situation.... cannot even work."[38] This, too, could be said differently, more benignly, as Michael Rees does of Yale sculpture in the 80s:

The Frank Vincent DuMond Class at the Art Students League of New York, 1940
Archives of the Art Students League of New York

¶ While Kandinsky and Farnum write of what they offer their students to supplement and reorder their perceptual abilities and sense of self,

the preliminary course, both in its assignments and those discussions afterwards about problem solving, creativity, and validity, was also quite explicitly intended to take something away. At the Bauhaus, the preliminary course was, indeed, "intended to liberate the student's creative power," but unfortunately, "every new student arrives encumbered with a mass of accumulated information which he must abandon before he can achieve perception and knowledge that are really his own....The preliminary course concerns the student's whole personality."[32] The language of liberation is inviting, a language of the self as whole—but the whole personality must be disciplined and built, or rather rebuilt, as though from scratch. The teaching Walter Gropius described at the Bauhaus assumes a kind of violence; it works on the student. The course's "chief function is to liberate the individual by breaking down conventional patterns of thought."[33] The interiority of the artist has to be excavated and, I would argue, one of the primary ways it is both hollowed and modeled is out of the space between language and its objects.

When the academy posed the model and asked for a likeness, the assignment and its solution were given in the same language, or rather the same vision. In the Bauhaus and at RISD, and in studio courses throughout the twentieth century, the assignment is spoken, given in language which can never quite be copied, but only solved or understood or "spoken to" by work. Or as one design text of the 60s has it: "While the problems can be verbalized and communicated, the perceptual awareness and sensibility to visual relations that result must be developed within the individual."[34]

Not **by** the individual, a preposition that might assume both a conscious actor and a specifically acquirable skill, but **within**, a placement that renders what is learned precisely as an awareness, a sensibility.

III.

Over the preceding pages I have tried to sketch the alignment of art training with the modern university, the aspirations of its teachers to the rational and professional knowledge the university offered. I have tried to link the new art schools—their work on materials and procedures, their exploration of media and the dynamics of design, at least in their assignments—to the production of language that characterizes the university. We don't teach design fundamentals on the graduate level; we don't ask students to "make a drawing in which solid forms, rectilinear and curvilinear, move against each other and establish pressure relationships."[35] And it's not clear that the Bauhaus grid, with its roots in the schoolroom desktop and the design department drafting table, as well as in perceptual psychology, is any more present in the works in "Public Offerings" than in the easel or the academy's figure. Where the paired discourses of subjective realization and formal experimentation continue now, along with the asymptotic relationship between language and artwork, is in the group critique of student work.

¶ My purpose here is not to claim that Takashi Murakami, Chris Ofili, and Manfred Pernice remember this history, or even that they need to know it. Rather, it is to begin a history of a different kind of artistic knowledge, and an archaeology of pedagogical practices that are still in use. Kandinsky, hired at the Bauhaus to teach painting not as a studio practice but as a theory of vision and construction, understood the difference between the knowledge he offered and that of the academy. In place of what he dismissed as the "very brief scientific 'bonus'" of academic training—its scattered lessons in "anatomy, perspective, and art history"—he insisted in 1926 that any school that "aspires to recognition as a Hochschule" (that is, a university) must be able to teach objectively and scientifically "those elements that are the building blocks of art"—and to allow the student to absorb them, to acquire "the necessary inner feeling for artistic resources."[29] Kandinsky's argument for "the value of theoretical instruction in painting," is particularly interesting for where it situates the outcome of teaching, both beyond painting in a broader practice of art or vision—

"the student is led beyond the bounds of painting, albeit by means of its logical character"— and inside the psyche: "the inner, self-absorbed selection of one's means, and one's unconscious and at the same time conscious involvement with one's resources eliminate those aims that are foreign to art."[30] Kandinsky's criticism of academic training for its divisions and isolation, and for the uselessness of the knowledge it offers and the artists it makes, was repeated across Europe and the United States during the first half of the century.

¶ For Royal Bailey Farnum of the Rhode Island School of Design (RISD—Janine Antoni), writing in a flatter and more familiar language in 1941, academic training amounts merely to "dictated rendering with charcoal, pencil, crayon, and paint...supplemented by separate lectures on perspective, composition, anatomy, and possibly color, and...followed by extreme concentration in the separate fields of specialization."

This is by now a caricature of the academy: rule-bound, isolated, narrow, able to produce only copyists.

Farnum offered instead a newer approach, one more expansive, organic, and quite clearly modeled after the Bauhaus's vorlehre: A preliminary course "based upon the idea that experimental freedom at the beginning, by means of which design and technique are evolved through self-discovery...is a sounder approach to the desired objective. Discussion, guidance (rather than imposed ideas), and self-discipline lead the student to a clearer understanding of the demands of art expression."[31] What continues from Kandinsky's Bauhaus of the 20s to Farnum's RISD in the 40s is not just a critique of the academy, but the implicit insistence that an experiment with form and materials is an experiment with and a reforming of the self, the production of a certain kind of interiority.

The design program at South Kensington formed something of the Bauhaus's prehistory:

Richard Redgrave, who developed the National Course of Instruction in Practical Art there in 1853, sounded far more like the Bauhaus's Moholy-Nagy than his contemporary Ingres when he proclaimed that "each material has its own peculiar constructive qualities" and "each mode of execution has its characteristic qualities."[24] Tokyo's University of Music and Art (Takashi Murakami, Tsuyoshi Ozawa, Yutaka Sone) was founded in 1887, in no small part in reaction to the widespread adoption of Western modes of representational drawing in Japanese schools and studios; here "peculiar constructive qualities" or the "material processes of painting" might be taken locally, or rather nationally. The drive to reevaluate and revive traditional Japanese craft traditions, practices, and materials in light of new principles of design was led by Japanese art historian Tenshin Okakura and the Boston aesthetician and orientalist Ernest Fenollosa.[25] As it happens, the teachings of Fenollosa's closest artist colleague, Arthur Wesley Dow of the Columbia University Teachers College, strongly influenced the curriculum not only at the Tokyo school but at UCLA's art department (Toba Khedoori and Jason Rhoades) for more than two decades. A vocal critic of the segregation of the fine artist, which he linked directly to academic training and representational drawing, Dow was a strong advocate for the aesthetic education of every child through design fundamentals. UCLA began as the Los Angeles branch of the State Normal School, a teachers' college, and even after its designation as a university and its move to Westwood in 1929, the art department remained part of the teachers' college—the most common place for art to be taught in American colleges and universities during the first part of the century, and a placement that embodied the broad ideological naturalism that assumed and entangled the "femininity" of art and the "unspoiled creativity" of children. The university's professionalization of artists in the degree-granting art schools and departments that emerged or were founded after World War II worked to masculinize the image of art and its practitioners. The establishment of separate graduate degrees for studio art and art education made this explicit. Like the failed and incomplete academic artist, the classroom art teacher, always too local and too female, was one of the staple targets of educational reformers.

¶ The analysis of materials, the experimentation with techniques and properties, the training of vision on the industrial grid: **this teaching provides and demands a different kind of knowledge than that of the academy. It looks out not onto the visible world represented by and built for the human figure, but rather at and through the formal and material terms of representation itself—its "fundamentals," its "structure," or its "grammar," to use a set of terms that are central to twentieth-century teaching. Academic teaching could only account for the classical tradition.** Through the grid of fundamentals that modern pedagogy imagined to be the physiological order of perception—the grid through which vision already ordered the world—and the essential lesson of every work of art, it could see anything. Modern pedagogy could explain not only academic drawing and traditional Japanese brush painting, but also "a sculpture by David Smith, a Samoan tapa cloth, a Museum of Modern Art shopping bag, New England gravestone rubbings, Japanese wrapping paper, a painting by Robert Motherwell, a psychedelic poster and a carved and dyed Nigerian calabash," to borrow the claims of a 60s adaptation of Arthur Wesley Dow's *Composition*, whose lessons were first published in 1899.[26] The idea of universally applicable principles of analysis and production could also, and not coincidentally, serve the task of professionalization, of aligning the practice of art to the modern research university, where each discipline takes its place as a department or school on the basis of the coherent organization and theoretical reach of its knowledge. Even those art programs here that are not part of general universities bear the university's name and, at least rhetorically, its mandate to further knowledge and to apprehend the whole. In its early literature, CalArts (Laura Owens) fashioned itself as a "university for the arts," and, in language quite appropriate to the early 70s, an "aesthetic think tank."[27] Incorporated in 1975, the Hochschule der Künste Berlin (Manfred Pernice) is also quite specifically not an academy, certainly not the academy it was when it began in 1696 as the Prussian Academy of Fine Arts; its current literature stresses that difference, and the difference between the school and most German art schools even now. It, too, is a university of the arts, "unique in Germany in its broad disciplinary scope and in its character as a university-type *wissenschaftliche und künstlerische Hochschule*"—

a scholarly and artistic institute of higher learning.[28]

Solomon's essay isn't so local and there are differences she doesn't get: all of the art schools she visits, and even all of those she doesn't, are academies —indeed, all of "post modern art might be described as a return to the academy."[21] For her, and for many, what characterizes both postmodern art and the academy—that is, the new art school—is the combination of Bickerton's "intellectual terrorism," or at least theory-mongering, and careerism.

II.

All of this might make clear at least one of the problems with the old title, "Global Academy": for the artists represented in the exhibition and the artists who taught them, as well as for the new art schools' critics, "academy" is clearly a pejorative term. It's also, I would argue, far too easy and too slippery as a description or a criticism. Its current use doesn't help us understand the historical particularity of either seventeenth- and eighteenth-century academic training or the contemporary art school. Ralph Rugoff's quip that CalArts "offered no drawing classes (craftsmanship was considered passé)" points toward that distinction; it is both telling and wrong. Drawing the human figure and the project of representation were central to academic training; in French the word *académie* names both the institution and a drawing after the nude model. But drawing was not taught as a craft and the artists of the academy were precisely not craftsmen. As the great academician Jean-Auguste-Dominique Ingres put it, arguing against proposed reforms in 1863:

"The Ecole des Beaux-Arts, it is true,... teaches only drawing, but drawing is everything, it is the whole of art. The material processes of painting are very simple, and can be taught in eight days."[22]

The reforms that would introduce the practical workshop in painting, which Ingres dismissed along with workshops in sculpture and architecture, mistook academicians for "*chefs d'ateliers industriels*," he protested, for craftsmen, however masterful. Ingres lost: the reuniting of the artist and the craftsman through reforms such as those he stood against, as well as far more radical ones—those of the Bauhaus, for example—would characterize the new twentieth-century art school. The Bauhaus's "first proclamation" was for that unity: "Architects, sculptors, painters, we must all turn to the crafts....There is no essential difference between the artist and the craftsman."[23] Except, of course, a class difference that would continue to be enforced even after the task of representation no longer defined the difference of the artist, even after it has been replaced, first by a theorized practice on the historical matter of art—Ingres's "material processes of painting"—and then by the projection of a historicized subjectivity.

¶ All of the art schools represented in "Public Offerings" were formed or reformed after the broad late nineteenth- and early twentieth-century critique of the academy that the Bauhaus is usually singled out to represent. Picking and choosing in roughly chronological order, one could start with Chris Ofili's alma mater, the Royal College of Art in London, which was originally named the Government School of Design and then transformed into the National Art Training School at South Kensington. Perhaps the nineteenth century's most widely exported design program, it was founded in 1837 not to train fine artists—the task of the Royal Academy—but to produce designers and artists for industry and technical-drawing teachers for the schools.

Closer to home, and to the present, when CalArts opened in 1971, its first catalogue pared Motherwell's language down, announcing that "from the day he enters, the student is an artist."[18] The assumption might still recall the myth of the born artist and the well-worn idea that artists are a particular kind of being, but those models assume that identity precedes the role and the name. At CalArts and UCLA, the process more accurately approaches the inverse: being an artist means performing—and being treated—a particular way, producing oneself as an artist for those who want and expect to see you that way. Artists are neither born nor taught, but are treated and thought of as artists, perhaps until they learn to think of themselves that way, until they assume the role and performance of being an artist. This is not a fiction, let me add, or at least not any more so than modern identity. Working alone in a studio, making "work," and being responsible for its display and its interpretations, for many graduate students—indeed for most, despite the success stories—the two years in an M.F.A. program are the only time they will ever be artists or occupy that role.

¶ From one article to the next over the decade, the artists interviewed—both teachers and students—become more wary of questions and more defensive in their answers. In their responses they distance themselves not so much from the images of freedom or of anarchy (which allow them, after all, still to be artists, and make the success of their institutions seem providential), but from marketing and from their own efficiency.

What they fear most, and what comes up most often as the figure of failure, is the "academy," a word that appears in each of the articles and that, precisely in its slipperiness, does a great deal of work: "The minute it becomes an academy, it'll be over."[19] As an insult, "academy" cuts a couple of ways, both spatially across campus toward the libraries and bureaucracies of the modern university, and temporally across time toward an earlier, now discredited mode of art teaching. It stands for a variety of repetitions and ossifications—for the growing old of faculty or their careers, for the resemblance of one student's work to another's, for a putative set of rules—and always for the obvious commensurability of input and outcome: the teachability of art. In Solomon's piece Barbara Rose complains of work that looks like "homework"; Hultkrans warns of "laundry lists of theoretical tropes in lieu of objects."[20] "Academic" is invoked at some point in each of the articles in the service of local politics as well; it allows one program, newer and fresher, to supersede another. It "explains," for example, the supposed decline of CalArts under Catherine Lord (and it is currently being re-outfitted to address Mary Kelly's tenure as chair at UCLA). Made to carry the weight of language, theory, intellectual practice, and "political correctness" —quite a semantic slide—the term "academy" was a particularly important sign in the Los Angeles theory/beauty wars during the early to mid-90s, and Cooper's **Spin** essay and Hultkrans's piece in **Artforum** were explicit entries into that conflict—on the side of beauty or quirkiness or not knowing too much.

It's not certain now that term papers and research bibliographies are still being assigned, but the visiting artist and the seminar remain particularly important pedagogical practices; they define contemporary teaching. Certainly, the speed Ashton wrote of appears even more intense now: the passage more direct, the travel time much shorter. That is at least in part the contention of this exhibition: **At graduation, if not before, work and artists are expected to be fully formed, ready to hang.** Indeed the breakthrough first show—the idea on which this exhibition is predicated—might be seen as a mark of recent schooling, where the task is not to make paintings or any individual art work, but to make a show. Exhibition and display are the studio lessons of the current art school; the individual critique reworks the work, constructing both its sameness and difference, and tests its modes of display.

¶ The commentators on CalArts, UCLA, and Art Center clearly don't trust the phenomenon they are describing. At some point in each of the articles at least a certain version of the irrepressible, unteachable artist is rescued. For Solomon and perhaps for Hultkrans as well, because the schools are schools, their graduates are not in any real sense artists, or at least not yet. The L.A. art schools may be able to produce artistic careers, but the very fact that artists now come fully packaged, if not fully grown, out of art school and straight into galleries is evidence for The New York Times of the shallowness of contemporary art, its lack of culture or maturity, its aesthetic and even moral emptiness. The audiences of Vogue and Spin expect something different; what they get is youth and freedom. Schooling is not quite what is going on in Rugoff's CalArts and Cooper's UCLA, and it's because they are not schools in any conventional sense that art and artists can emerge in the spaces they provide, in the teaching they leave out. According to Rugoff's history, when CalArts opened in 1970 it "offered no drawing classes (craftsmanship was considered passé), but the course catalog included seminars in joint rolling and witchcraft."[11] The editors at Vogue seem to have understood Rugoff's attempt to rescue CalArts from being just a school; they chose this sentence of Barbara Bloom's recollection to blow-up and box as a pull quote: "For the most part, it was total anarchy. We were irreverent, drug-taking, smartass kids and we had a lot of fun."[12] They passed on the invocations of Deleuze and Baudrillard, and Ashley Bickerton's more up-to-date commentary: "Intellectual terrorism is the CalArts shtick—it's how students there prove themselves."[13] Not only students but faculty separate themselves in these essays from the work of school, and from their involvement in the task of teaching: art is, by some definitions, that which cannot be taught. "As long as I've been here," Hultkrans quotes Charles Ray, "I've never written a curriculum, never prepared for a class."[14] In Cooper's "Too Cool for School," a title that might make my point, Ray pursues the difference between UCLA and other art schools precisely aroundthe roles of teacher and student, or rather the refusal to occupy either of those roles. "Most art schools are about students and teachers. UCLA is about artists working as artists.... **The reason the kids here are getting all this early success is because they're not art students, they're young artists.** Young artists get galleries. Students study. Simple as that."[15] Brent Peterson, one of the UCLA graduate students profiled in the Artforum essay, makes it clear that the students themselves know this difference; they are taught it. "They stress production at UCLA. During orientation, Lari Pittman said, 'We don't want to think of you as students, you're just working artists who happen to be in school.'"[16]

¶ Thinking of art students as artists—or the claim to treat them as such—isn't unique to UCLA; it has been one of the defining pedagogical assumptions of contemporary professional training (and in some sense an answer to—or an elision of—the question of whether or not art can be taught). The claim has been the stated policy of a number of programs, since at least as far back as "Subjects of the Artist," an art school Robert Motherwell started with Mark Rothko, William Baziotes, and David Hare in 1948. According to Motherwell's bulletin for the school: **"Those attending classes will not be treated as 'students' in the conventional manner, but as collaborators with the artists in the investigation of the artistic process, its modern conditions, possibilities, and extreme nature, through discussions and practice."[17]**

Again, and as Deborah Solomon's title makes perfectly clear, it is not failure that is suspect but success—the quickness with which art schools, and particularly these L.A. art schools, seem to propel students into galleries, magazines, and museums. There is a very old and obviously still strongly held belief that artists, if they are real artists, cannot be taught, and certainly cannot be made in schools. In an earlier time artists were born: "Truly, he was a painter in his mother's womb," Albrecht Dürer was purported to have said of the Dutch painter Geertgen tot Sint Jans. Even as late as the 80s, Robert Pincus-Witten could write of David Salle as "a painter born."[8] In the modern period artists have far more often been formed in struggle: "Most of the artists of this vanguard found their way to their present work by being cut in two," wrote Harold Rosenberg of the Abstract Expressionists. "Their type is not a young painter but a re-born one. The man may be over forty, the painter around seven. The diagonal of a grand crisis separates him from his personal and artistic past."[9] The slow, halting formation of the modern artist is a recurring motif; the path is personal and hazardous and the outcome far from obvious. Schooling in any conventional sense always and necessarily fails, initiating a series of false starts that continues until that artist finally learns to make himself.

¶ Since the end of the 60s critics have contrasted the slow maturity of the modern artist to one accelerated by the new degree-granting art schools and the well-paved career tracks they seemed to offer. Here is Dore Ashton writing in 1970 on a group of serious young painters and the artworld they have entered:

"With a tempo that has never been paralleled, articles, exhibitions, and even books have been issued confirming the successive choices of this well-oiled commodity machine....This naturally doesn't give a student much time to be a student. He has to find his 'style' or sink."

Ashton's complaint leads directly, as do many complaints from the period, to an indictment of art schools and worse, to the spread of professional art training in the university:

"Lately even the citadels of deep knowledge—the colleges—have bowed to the times....And the universities and colleges are where the majority of young artists begin these days. Where once a painter surveyed his immediate past with some psychological distancing—there is a big difference, after all, between reading delayed issues of Cahiers d'Art from far across the sea, and picking up the latest Artforum—he is now brought up very close through ever-increasing art departments, seminars, term papers, research, bibliographies, personal appearances of the stars, and traveling exhibitions."[10]

The first M.F.A. was awarded in 1924 to one Mabel Lisle Ducasse at the University of Washington. In 1940 there were some sixty graduate-student artists enrolled at eleven institutions. By 1950-51 there were 320 M.F.A. candidates at thirty-two institutions; and a decade later there were 1,365 graduate students enrolled in seventy-two M.F.A. programs. It was only in 1960, though, that the College Art Association finally approved the M.F.A. as the single "terminal degree for graduate work in the studio area." Thirty-one new M.F.A. programs opened during the decade of the 60s; another forty-four in the 70s. During the first half of the 90s, the period this exhibition examines, more than 10,000 M.F.A.s were awarded in the United States.[4] The premise of "Public Offerings" is that this expansion, and the historically particular kind of training it represents, have had an influence on—and are visible in—the terms of artmaking in the present.

¶ A number of commentators over the past decade have taken art schools into account, using a high-profile handful of them to explain some facet of recent art and its increasingly dispersed locations. Richard Flood, the curator of the Walker Art Center's 1995 exhibition "Brilliant! New Art from London," remarked to the editors of *Frieze* that among the factors that had produced the new art scene in London,

"the art schools are pretty critical. Nowhere else is there the locus of degree-granting art schools that London has." And nowhere else did he see the same level of "entrepreneurial activity going on amongst the artists themselves," an activity he linked to a "core who were at college together staying, for the most part, in place."[5]

Nowhere else except perhaps Los Angeles where the role of the schools in shaping and networking the local artworld, and in producing entrepreneurial artists' careers, has been noted and written about since the late 70s.

¶ Most recently and controversially L.A. schools have been written about in a quartet of articles on CalArts, the University of California at Los Angeles (UCLA), and the Art Center College of Design (Art Center)—beginning in 1989 with an article in *Vogue* magazine by Ralph Rugoff entitled **"Liberal Arts,"** and spanning the 90s. Strictly speaking the four essays were not a series, but it's clear that the two earlier ones, Rugoff's *Vogue* piece on CalArts and Dennis Cooper's 1997 article on UCLA, **"Too Cool for School"** in *Spin*, became homework for Andrew Hultkrans's 1998 *Artforum* article **"Surf and Turf"** and Deborah Solomon's 1999 article for *The New York Times Magazine*, **"How to Succeed in Art."**[6] In some sense—albeit **"upside-down as in a camera obscura"**[7]—the essays characterize the decade in L.A. From *Vogue* to *The New York Times Magazine* the publications become more seriously cultural and eastern; the audience older; and the tone, not surprisingly perhaps, increasingly contemptuous.

I.

"Public Offerings" was not always this exhibition's title; early on, it was "Global Academy."

However, from the outset it was understood that there were problems with both words of the title. I hope I've begun, if only briefly, to suggest some of the discussion and difficulty that surrounds the word "global"; my primary concern over the following pages, however, is with the word "academy." The title "Global Academy" was intended to point first and most obviously to the art school. The exhibition is in part an examination and acknowledgment of the success of art schools, their presence and effects on recent art and its milieu. The exhibition's initial focus, and the model on which we imagined we could expand, was the formative role played by art schools in the new "scenes"—the new artists and dealers, new critics and collectors that seemed to characterize Los Angeles and London by the mid-80s. Certainly in those cities art schools have been visible in the past decade and a half in a way they had not been before: they have made the scene, by both arriving on it and producing it. The discourse on and about art schools, too, is different and newly visible. There is a very long tradition of decrying the failure of art schools, because they are behind the times or too swayed by them, because their graduates are ill prepared and useless: "in no other profession is there such a wo[e]ful waste of the raw material of human life as exists in certain phases of art education," lamented the president of the newly formed College Art Association in 1917.[2] The 60s saw a spate of such laments, from *Art News*' 1963 symposium, "What's Wrong with U.S. Art Schools?," to Dan Flavin's 1968 *Artforum* screed, "...On an American Artist's Education...."[3] In contrast, what is decried in recent writing is not the art school's failure but its success, the numbers of artists and careers it can now produce.

¶ The impetus for *Art News*' question and the background for Flavin's complaint was in no small part the burgeoning of American art schools and new university-based art departments in the decades after World War II. The art schools that wasted lives in 1917 were a motley collection of private drawing academies, artist colonies, teacher-training colleges, technical and vocational schools, and mail-order lessons. What the College Art Association's president was calling for was a new and rational university art education.

That's probably not quite the right metaphor since it suggests a separation between school—at least in the studio—and the market, a strict before and after. It's obvious, and it has been for a long time, that the market and its ambitions are present in the school and the studio. One of the jobs of the visiting artist is to make the path and the market clear, to embody and speak that link. It was once argued that university-based art education could protect art and its values from the marketplace—that is one of the great stories of the university and of liberal education. But it is also fully in keeping with the task of the research university, with schools that have their sights on national and international arenas of recognition in every department, to teach and to advance from the latest knowledge. It would be illiberal or unscholarly—or maybe just not worth the tuition dollar—not to teach Damien Hirst or, a little earlier, Mike Kelley.

¶ Made in school, or soon after, by artists who have for the most part stayed put in artworlds that have been structured in no small part by the schools, the work demonstrates a kind of local address and references a particular audience.

That address gives these works a double-sidedness and suggests another kind of transit, a breakthrough not only from my institution to yours, but from a particular local scene with its specific conditions and institutions, circles of friends, and discourse (and, as is particularly visible here in the work from Tokyo and London, a specific local yet exportable popular culture) to an "international artworld." That last phrase—international artworld—could use some clarification; what I want it to mean is the network of institutions, discourses, and markets that receive and circulate contemporary artistic practice, a network that is at once increasingly dispersed, even global, and ever more tightly integrated and circuited. As it turns out, the global artworld looks like and follows the globalization of information and capital.

There are still centers, "world cities" or "global cities" according to the political geography theorist and critic Peter Wollen has used to situate the address of new art from London and to argue against its Britishness.[1] The crucial site is not the nation, although it can be an exportable content, but the new cosmopolitan city, with its internationally focused banks, corporations, cultural institutions, and populations. The local sites represented in "Public Offerings" are not arbitrary or coincidental. The work is compelling and insistent; the schools that have trained its makers are among the most innovative and successful; and the local artworlds that have absorbed and circulated it are quite hot and busy. Beyond all that, above it or undergirding it, the cities themselves—Los Angeles, Tokyo, Berlin, London, and New York—are precisely where the wealth and information (and the political and cultural hegemony) necessary for work to be offered are produced, reproduced, and transmitted.

The path I want the title to suggest now, some thirteen years later, is less circuitous and usually less ironized; it is the track that runs with what seems like ever-accelerating speed from the graduate studios and seminar rooms of the art school to the museum by way of an increasingly efficient network of commercial galleries that has been remarkably successful over the decade.

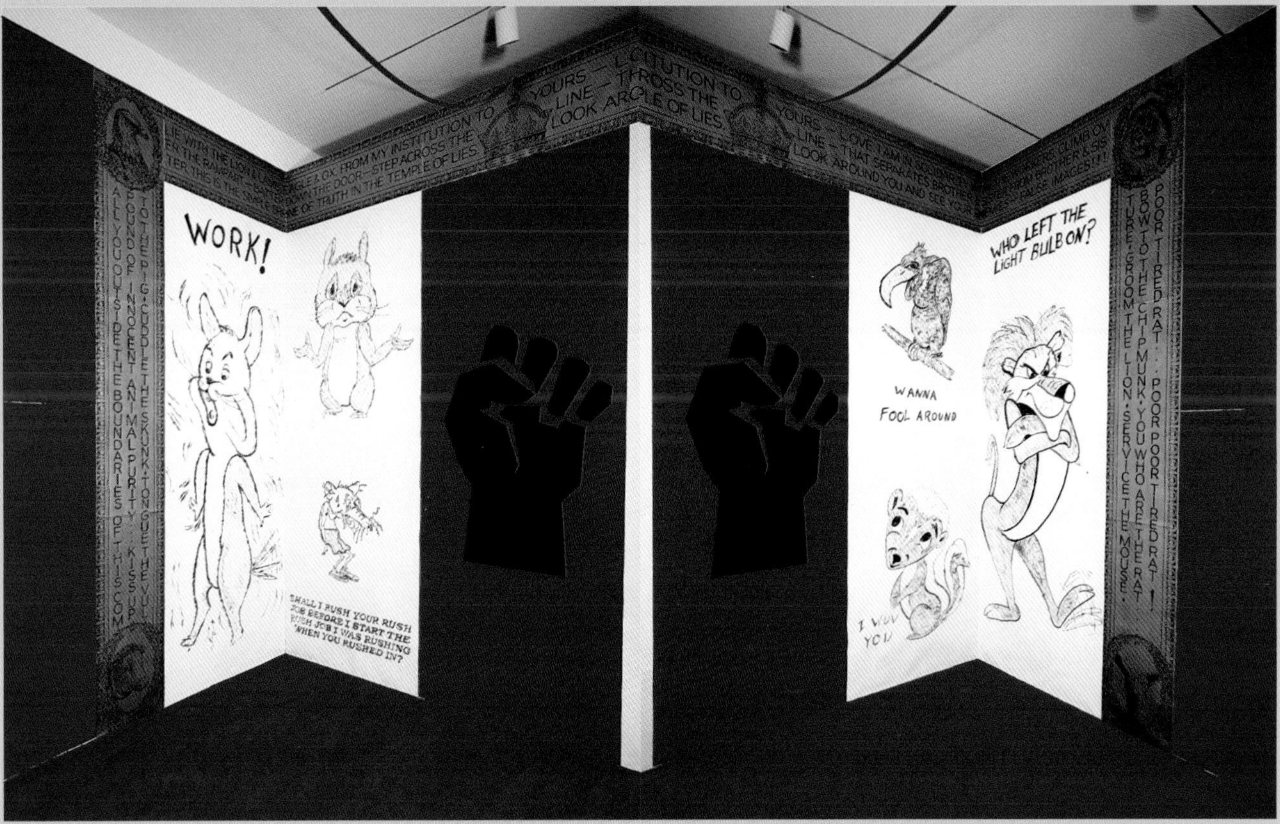

Mike Kelley
From My Institution to Yours, 1987
Acrylic on paper with carpet, ribbon, and carrot
192 x 180 x 120 inches

¶ The works that have enabled that passage for the artists included in this exhibition are what the title, "Public Offerings," is intended to name.

They were presented early in the artists' careers to an audience outside school, and they mark a transition from student work to work that stands as or feels like art. In most cases here, they mark a more fungible, more marketable breakthrough as well: the title "Public Offerings" echoes the financial world's I.P.O.s, the initial public offerings of stock, the way family- or locally owned private companies go public. The works are, for the most part, not single works or even loose groupings of single works, but installations and shows—occasionally, graduate shows or thesis exhibitions—displays that announced a kind of coming-out, the way a debutante's coming-out announced her availability, her social or sexual marketability.

Let me start with my borrowed title because in many ways it says all I want to say.

From My Institution to Yours

is the title of an installation by Mike Kelley realized in 1987 at the Los Angeles County Museum of Art (LACMA) as part of the museum's exhibition "Avant-Garde in the Eighties." A collection of drawings based on images taken from the walls and bulletin boards of the building-maintenance office at the California Institute of the Arts (CalArts)—signs and cartoons, fuzzy skunks and wily vultures—*From My Institution to Yours* took both the art school and the museum from behind or underneath (the favored positions of abjection), opening them out to the maintenance crew and the loading dock and to another aesthetic order. Or at least that was its promise: Kelley's original proposal would have led visitors from the gallery, through the offices of LACMA's professional staff and the workrooms of its craftsmen, to its loading dock—the space of the museum's blue-collar workers.

BY HOWARD SINGERMAN

CURATORIAL PROJECT DIRECTOR CIARA ENNIS

EDITORIAL ASSISTANT ELIZABETH HAMILTON
EDITOR JANE HYUN
SENIOR EDITOR LISA MARK
MANAGING EDITOR SUSAN MARTIN
GUEST EDITOR HOWARD SINGERMAN

PRINTER DR. CANTZ'SCHE DRUCKEREI, OSTFILDERN, GERMANY
DESIGNERS JONATHAN BARNBROOK, JASON BEARD, MARCUS MCCALLION
ART DIRECTION JONATHAN BARNBROOK

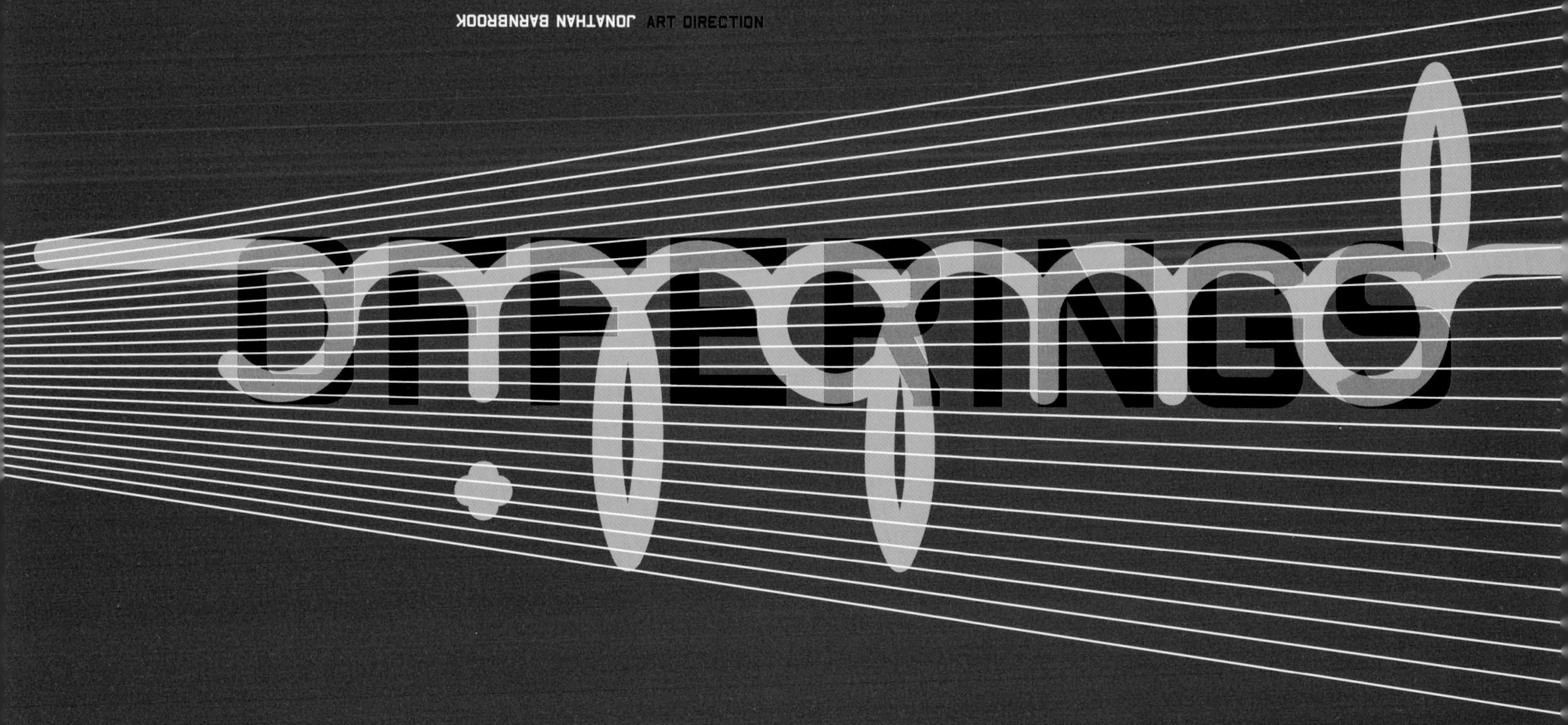

FIRST PUBLISHED IN THE UNITED STATES OF AMERICA IN PAPERBACK IN 2001 BY
THAMES & HUDSON INC., 500 FIFTH AVENUE, NEW YORK, NEW YORK 10110

FIRST PUBLISHED IN THE UNITED KINGDOM IN 2001 BY THAMES & HUDSON LTD,
181A HIGH HOLBORN, LONDON WC1V 7QX

LIBRARY OF CONGRESS CATALOG CARD NUMBER 00-109465

BRITISH LIBRARY CATALOGUING-IN-PUBLICATION DATA
A CATALOGUE RECORD FOR THIS BOOK IS AVAILABLE FROM THE BRITISH LIBRARY

ISBN: 0-500-28284-6
PRINTED AND BOUND IN GERMANY

THIS PUBLICATION ACCOMPANIES THE EXHIBITION "PUBLIC OFFERINGS," ORGANIZED BY PAUL SCHIMMEL AND PRESENTED AT THE MUSEUM OF CONTEMPORARY ART, LOS ANGELES, 1 APRIL—29 JULY 2001.

"PUBLIC OFFERINGS" IS MADE POSSIBLE IN PART BY THE SYDNEY IRMAS EXHIBITION ENDOWMENT, MARIA HUMMER AND ROBERT TUTTLE, AUDREY M. IRMAS, THE ANDY WARHOL FOUNDATION FOR THE VISUAL ARTS, THE JAPAN-UNITED STATES FRIENDSHIP COMMISSION, THE JAPAN FOUNDATION, THE BRITISH COUNCIL, BRENDA R. POTTER AND MICHAEL C. SANDLER, PASADENA ART ALLIANCE, AND NINAH AND MICHAEL LYNNE.

PROMOTIONAL SUPPORT HAS BEEN PROVIDED BY KLON-FM 88.1.

Public Offerings

ORGANIZED BY PAUL SCHIMMEL

COORDINATED BY CIARA ENNIS

EDITED BY HOWARD SINGERMAN

ESSAYS BY YILMAZ DZIEWIOR
MIDORI MATSUI
LANE RELYEA
PAUL SCHIMMEL
KATY SIEGEL
HOWARD SINGERMAN
JON THOMPSON

THE MUSEUM OF CONTEMPORARY ART, LOS ANGELES

Thames & Hudson

PUBLIC